THE MEXICAN-AMERICAN WAR EXPERIENCES

OF TWELVE CIVIL WAR GENERALS

CONFLICTING WORLDS

New Dimensions of the American Civil War

T. MICHAEL PARRISH, SERIES EDITOR

THE MEXICAN-AMERICAN WAR EXPERIENCES OF TWELVE CIVIL WAR GENERALS

EDITED BY Timothy D. Johnson

LOUISIANA STATE UNIVERSITY PRESS   BATON ROUGE

Published by Louisiana State University Press
lsupress.org

Manufactured in the United States of America
FIRST PRINTING

DESIGNER: Barbara Neely Bourgoyne
TYPEFACES: MillerText, text; Gin, display
PRINTER AND BINDER: Sheridan Books, Inc.

Maps created by Mary Lee Eggart.
All front jacket images courtesy Library of Congress.

Portions of Craig Symonds's essay first appeared, in somewhat
different form, in *Joseph E. Johnston: A Civil War Biography* (New York:
W. W. Norton, 1992), copyright © 1992 by Craig L. Symonds.

LIBRARY OF CONGRESS CATALOGING-IN-PUBLICATION DATA
Names: Johnson, Timothy D., 1957– editor.
Title: The Mexican-American War experiences of twelve Civil War generals /
    edited by Timothy D. Johnson.
Description: Baton Rouge : Louisiana State University Press, [2024] |
    Series: Conflicting worlds: new dimensions of the American Civil War |
    Includes bibliographical references and index.
Identifiers: LCCN 2024010649 (print) | LCCN 2024010650 (ebook) |
    ISBN 978-0-8071-8238-3 (cloth) | ISBN 978-0-8071-8328-1 (epub) |
    ISBN 978-0-8071-8329-8 (pdf)
Subjects: LCSH: Mexican War, 1846–1848—Influence. | United States.
    Army—Officers—Biography. | United States. Army—History—Mexican War,
    1846–1848. | Command of troops—History—19th century. | Confederate
    States of America. Army—Officers—Biography.
Classification: LCC E403 .M49 2024 (print) | LCC E403 (ebook) | DDC
    973.6/2—dc23/eng/20240405
LC record available at https://lccn.loc.gov/2024010649
LC ebook record available at https://lccn.loc.gov/2024010650

CONTENTS

FOREWORD

Anyone who studies the American Civil War comes to appreciate how strongly the conflict with Mexico resonated with Federal and Confederate officers. Most obviously, Winfield Scott's campaign from Vera Cruz to Mexico City provided lessons in turning movements and frontal assaults, in logistical problems and the option of cutting loose from lengthening lines of supply, in dealing with guerrillas and hostile civilians, in coping with disease in hot climates, and in managing the complexity of an occupation. Other operations similarly instructed U.S. soldiers about many dimensions of waging war. Although no West Pointers served as generals in Mexico, graduates of the academy held three-quarters of the line commissions at the outbreak of hostilities and also figured prominently as engineers and in the ordnance, commissary, and quartermaster departments. Service in Mexico proved a touchstone for junior officers who later led large armies in a conflict that marked the debut of West Pointers at the highest levels of military responsibility.

Scott compiled the most impressive record in Mexico and remained the ranking officer in the U.S. Army during the secession crisis. Although physically declining by 1861, the general in chief had a first-rate mind and drew on vast experience as he pondered how best to defeat the Confederacy. The example of Mexico probably guided some of his thinking in what came to be called the Anaconda Plan. The United States had blockaded Mexico's eastern ports and struck at the northern provinces of Alta California, Nuevo Mexico, Coahuila, Nuevo León, and Chihuahua. Those strategic elements removed huge chunks of territory from Mexico's control but proved insufficient to achieve victory. Scott's famous campaign of March–September 1847 directed U.S. military power into the heart of Mexico, captured the national capital, and hastened an end to the war.

Scott's recommendations about strategy against the Confederacy mirrored what had worked against Mexico. In May 1861 he proposed a "complete blockade of the Atlantic and Gulf ports" together with "a powerful movement down the Mississippi to the ocean." The latter would sheer off the Trans-Mississippi part of the Confederacy, much as U.S. operations had isolated vast expanses of northern Mexico. As an equivalent of his earlier campaign against Mexico City, Scott foresaw large-scale invasions of the Confederacy as a possible feature of Federal operational strategy. In March 1861 he advised incoming secretary of state William H. Seward that the United States might have to "conquer the seceding States by invading armies." The effort could take two or three years and "three hundred thousand disciplined" soldiers, many thousands of whom would be lost "by skirmishes, sieges, battles, and Southern fevers."

Many officers recalled their service in Mexico when addressing aspects of the Civil War. Jubal A. Early, for example, served in 1847 as a major in the First Virginia Infantry under Generals Zachary Taylor and later John E. Wool. The regiment reached Taylor's force after the Battle of Buena Vista, and thus Early saw no combat, but for two months, as noted in his memoirs, he "acted as the military governor" of Monterrey. In a jab at what he considered Union outrages against Confederate civilians in the Shenandoah Valley and other occupied areas, the Virginian observed, "It was generally conceded by officers of the army and Mexicans that better order reigned in the city during the time I commanded there, than had ever before existed, and the good conduct of my men won for them universal praise." Early further asserted that the men of the First Virginia mustered out in April 1848 with knowledge that they "had not sullied the flag of the State, which constituted the regimental colors, by disorderly conduct or acts of depredation on private property, and noncombatants."

Richard S. Ewell, a lieutenant with the 1st U.S. Dragoons in Scott's army and Early's superior for about a year in the Army of Northern Virginia, similarly drew parallels between the two wars. The route from the Gulf Coast to Mexico City had brought U.S. forces into contact with hostile civilians in many towns and cities, a phenomenon later experienced by Confederates entering Pennsylvania in the summer of 1863. While encamped near Chambersburg on June 24, Ewell, now a lieutenant general, mused: "It is like a renewal of Mexican times to enter a captured town. The people look as sour as vinegar and, I have no doubt, would gladly send us all to kingdom come if they could." He praised how his soldiers "behave in this land of plenty." Yet just as Scott's army had lived off the land when approaching Mexico City, Ewell exploited Pennsylvania's agricultural bounty in trying "to have furnished, by impressments, what it is possible to get for our men."

Service in Mexico created a sense of camaraderie among veterans that found formal expression in the Aztec Club. Established in October 1847 by officers who served in Scott's offensive from Vera Cruz to Mexico City, the organization took as its model the Society of the Cincinnati. The original 160 members included six of the subjects in this volume—P. G. T. Beauregard, Ulysses S. Grant, Joseph Hooker, Joseph E. Johnston, Robert E. Lee, and George B. McClellan. James Longstreet gained admission later as a "veteran member," while Scott, appropriately, was one of only two honorary members. Grant's certificate, dated October 13, 1849, somewhat grandly noted: "We the Constitutional Officers of the Aztec Club Hereby make known that Lieut. U. S. Grant, 4th Infty was duly elected Member of said Club in the City of Mexico, in accordance with the provisions of the Constitution and is entitled to all the privileges of such Membership." The certificate carried the signatures of John B. Grayson (president), Charles Ferguson Smith (first vice president), Robert C. Buchanan (second vice president), and Martin Luther Smith (secretary)—the first and last became Confederate generals and the second and third Union generals during the Civil War. Members of the club met at West Point in 1852 and took leading roles at reunions of the war's veterans during the late antebellum years.

Connections between military service in Mexico and later political ambitions also stood out. No one better understood this than Democratic president James K. Polk, who lamented the fact that his best generals in Mexico, Taylor and Scott, were Whigs. Taylor emerged from the war as its preeminent popular hero, with his victory against the odds at Buena Vista the conflict's most widely celebrated triumph. The fact that federal volunteers rather than regulars won that battle, together with Taylor's unassuming style and imperturbable conduct under fire, rendered "Old Rough and Ready" a strong candidate in a republic that mistrusted professional military forces and celebrated ordinary citizens. Taylor's election as president in 1848 underscored the aptness of Polk's fears. Four years later two members of the Aztec Club squared off for the presidency. Scott, whose imperious demeanor and flamboyant dress contrasted sharply with Taylor's image, lost his bid for the Executive Mansion to Franklin Pierce. Although Pierce's record as a general of volunteers in Mexico included unfortunate incidents at the Battles of Contreras and Churubusco that the Whigs tried to exploit, his home state of New Hampshire lauded his service, and Democratic campaign engravings identified their candidate as "Gen. Pierce." John Charles Frémont, whose somewhat muddled activities in California during the war with Mexico yielded both fame and notoriety, brought to four the number of Mexican War officers who ran for the presidency. The first Republican to seek that office, Frémont ran a close second to James Buchanan in the canvass of 1856.

During the Civil War, two other members of the Aztec Club summoned memories of previous links between battlefield performances and presidential politics. George B. McClellan reprised Taylor's and Scott's roles as officers whose party loyalties clashed with their president's, though his record as a commander contained no military success equal to Buena Vista or the capture of Mexico City. Democratic editors lauded "Little Mac," whose popularity among soldiers in his Army of the Potomac and elsewhere failed to translate into votes on November 8, 1864. Soundly defeated, McClellan resigned his commission immediately. Lincoln sent no personal response to his former general. "I found awaiting me the acceptance of my resignation . . . 'by order of the Presdt.,'" noted McClellan icily on November 15. "No comments are made—it is simply a formal acceptance by the Adjt. Genl."

Ulysses S. Grant attracted attention from both Democrats and Republicans as a possible presidential candidate. His victories at Vicksburg and Chattanooga in 1863 positioned him much as had Taylor's triumph at Buena Vista sixteen years earlier. Shortly after the opening of the Overland Campaign in the spring of 1864, the *New York Herald*, a Democratic-leaning sheet, called for Grant to emulate George Washington's ascension to the presidency: "We expect his election to be as unanimous as that of General Washington and as beneficial to the welfare of the republic." A few days later the *Herald* added, "Never since Washington and Jackson, has any man so nobly earned the right to be President." Lincoln initially hesitated to support Grant's promotion to lieutenant general lest it advance the prospects of an incipient political opponent. The general found ways to reassure the president that, as he wrote to his former subordinate Francis Preston Blair Jr., "Every body who knows me knows I have no political aspirations either now or for the future. . . . I hope you will show this letter to no one unless it be the President himself," added Grant, "I hate to see my name associated with politics either as an aspirant for office or as a partizan." A grateful Lincoln expressed relief after seeing evidence offered by several individuals regarding Grant's attitude. "No man knows," he remarked, "when that Presidential grub gets to gnawing at him, just how deep it will get until he has tried it; and I didn't know but what there was one gnawing at Grant."

The accomplishments of Grant and other officers who fought in Mexico lived on among cadets at West Point through the late antebellum era. Major Richard Delafield, the academy's superintendent, directed in the late 1850s that the names of Revolutionary and Mexican War battles be chiseled on rocks along Flirtation Walk. Anyone traversing that narrow path overlooking the Hudson River's western bank would pass boulders inscribed "Mexico 13, 14 Sept. 1847" (where Beauregard, Don Carlos Buell, Grant, Hooker, Thomas J. Jackson, Johnston, Lee, Longstreet, and McClellan had fought); "Palo Alto 8 May 1846" (Grant, Longstreet, and George Gordon Meade); "Resaca De La Palma 9 May 1846" (Grant, Longstreet, Meade, and George H. Thomas); and "Veracruz" (Beauregard, Grant, Jackson, Johnston, Lee, Longstreet, and McClellan). Cadets also could examine cannons captured from the Mexican army, prized as trophies from a conflict that, members of the late-antebellum West Point classes knew, had given previous academy graduates their first real test of combat as lieutenants, captains, and, in a few cases, field-grade officers. Within a few years, many subalterns who served under Taylor and Scott would command corps and armies in storied campaigns. The essays in this volume examine twelve of them, illuminating how experiences in Mexico shaped their decisions and conduct during the nation's most consequential and all-encompassing war.

GARY W. GALLAGHER

ACKNOWLEDGMENTS

The idea for this book has been in the back of my mind for a long time. Yet after spending thirty years researching and writing about the Mexican-American War, I knew it would take scholars with Civil War expertise to bring it to fruition. Therefore, I am grateful to the book's twelve contributors for agreeing to jump on board in early 2021 and for their effort in helping make this study a reality. Some of them are friends, but others I had known only by their commendable reputations from their previous work.

There are a few people who deserve to be singled out for their assistance. I have known Joe Glatthaar for many years, and he is always a wealth of wisdom when I turn to him for advice. Also, Tim Smith came to the rescue with special assistance just when it was most needed. I am especially indebted to Gary Gallagher, who offered sage guidance at every stage of this project. He suggested names of potential contributors, offered logistical and organizational advice that helped get the project off the ground, and provided helpful critiques when needed. My gratitude also goes to James Lee McDonough for his incisive reading of the introduction. I have been proud to call James my friend since 1978, when I took his Civil War course. I also thank Pete Carmichael, Chris Losson, Dwight Tays, and Paul Turner for timely aid and encouragement.

Several people at Lipscomb University deserve recognition. Marc Schwerdt and Willie Steele have provided a willing ear and helpful support. The world of technology has outpaced my ability to keep up, and so I had to lean on others to help me overcome obstacles. Longtime friends and colleagues Al Austelle, the ever-reliable IT guru, and Howard Miller, literally the smartest person I know, both bailed me out at critical moments. Lipscomb president Candice McQueen's decisive action in 2023 solved a festering impediment to my professional productivity, and I am deeply in-

debted to her. My gratitude also goes to these students who read and critiqued the introduction: Natalie Clark, Konner Gottfred, Georgia Leonard,
Maddie Parish, Parris Robertson, and Caleb Williams.

   When the manuscript for this book was nearing completion, two former
colleagues in my department, Jennie Johnson and Jerry Gaw, passed away
in the same week, and I wish to acknowledge here their decades of friendship and support. My close relationship with Jerry was especially valuable;
the void left by his passing is felt by many. When I was young, he was a
mentor, and as the years passed he shared his wisdom on a wide range of
topics professional, personal, and spiritual.

   Family support is always key to accomplishing projects like this. Jill
Burkhalter provided valuable guidance and technological expertise in this
project's early phase. As usual, Jayne, my wife of forty-five years, continues
to make it possible for me to follow my professional pursuits. Her support
is irreplaceable, though sometimes underappreciated. I am also grateful for
the inspiration and motivation provided by other Johnson family members:
Ann Claire, Pierce, Hollis, Shepherd, and Finn.

   Michael Parrish, editor of the series Conflicting Worlds: New Dimensions of the American Civil War, saw merit in this project, and I am grateful
to him for opening the door to Rand Dotson and LSU Press. I also thank
both Mike and Rand for being prompt and professional in responding to
my questions and concerns. My gratitude also goes to the peer reader, whose
valuable insights improved the finished product. The manuscript for this
book benefited greatly from copy editor Kevin Brock, who accomplished
his exacting task with competence and professionalism. Mary Lee Eggart
performed excellent and timely service in producing the maps in the book's
front matter. To Catherine Kadair, managing editor, and to everyone else
associated with the Press, I say thank you for your fine work.

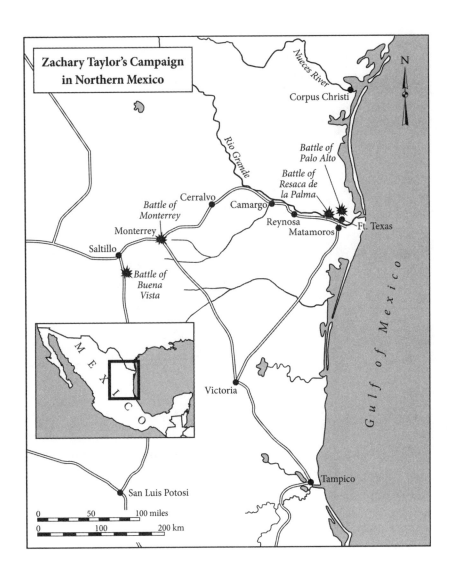

Zachary Taylor's Campaign in Northern Mexico

Nueces River

Corpus Christi

Rio Grande

Battle of Palo Alto

Battle of Resaca de la Palma

Cerralvo

Camargo

Battle of Monterrey

Reynosa

Monterrey

Matamoros

Ft. Texas

Saltillo

Battle of Buena Vista

M E X I C O

Victoria

Gulf of Mexico

Tampico

San Luis Potosi

0   50   100 miles
0   100   200 km

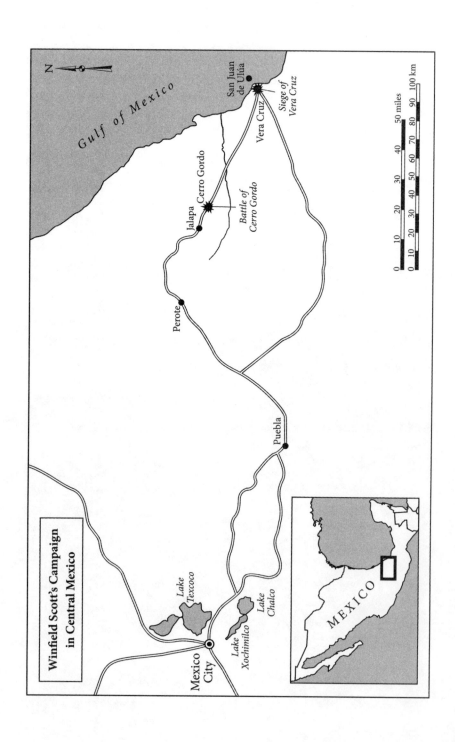

Winfield Scott's Campaign
in Central Mexico

Gulf of Mexico

San Juan
de Ulúa

Siege of
Vera Cruz

Vera Cruz

Cerro Gordo

Battle of
Cerro Gordo

Jalapa

Perote

Puebla

Lake
Texcoco

Lake
Xochimilco

Lake
Chalco

Mexico
City

MEXICO

N

50 miles

100 km

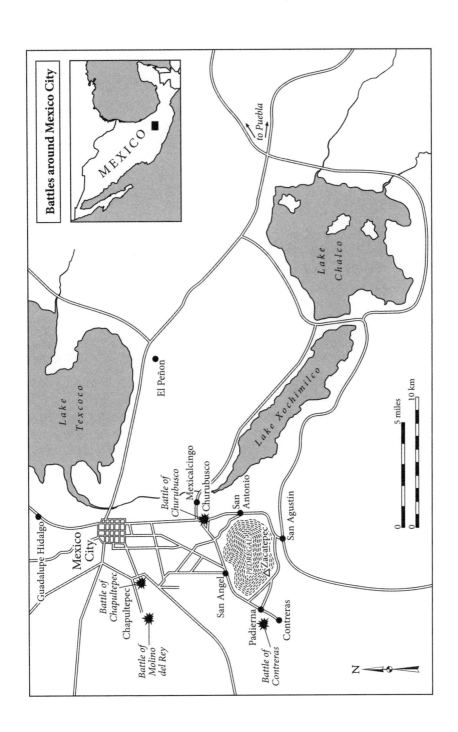

Battles around Mexico City

MEXICO

to Puebla

Lake Chalco

Lake Texcoco

Lake Xochimilco

El Peñon

Guadalupe Hidalgo

Mexico City

Battle of Chapultepec

Chapultepec

Battle of Molino del Rey

San Angel

PEDREGAL

Zacatepec

Padierna

Battle of Contreras

Contreras

Battle of Churubusco

Mexicalcingo

Churubusco

San Antonio

San Agustín

N

0 5 miles
0 10 km

THE MEXICAN-AMERICAN WAR EXPERIENCES

OF TWELVE CIVIL WAR GENERALS

INTRODUCTION

TIMOTHY D. JOHNSON

It was a warm spring afternoon, about one o'clock, when General Robert E. Lee rode into the village of Appomattox Court House. Upon reaching the designated house, he dismounted and handed the reins of his horse, Traveller, to his orderly. Ascending the steps up to the porch, the general entered the front door and turned left into the parlor before seating himself at a small table in the far corner. Removing his hat and gauntlets, Lee sat silently and, along with an aide and a Federal staff officer, awaited the arrival of his counterpart. No one knows the thoughts that ran through his mind for the half hour that he waited. Did he ponder how things might have ended more favorably if only he had made a different battlefield decision here or maybe there? Perhaps he wondered what his fate, or that of his men, would be now. Was he glad that the bloody carnage was finally ending or anguished over its failed outcome?

At 1:30 the noise of galloping horses interrupted the awkward silence inside the parlor, and soon Lieutenant General Ulysses S. Grant entered the room. Lee stood, and the two men greeted each other with a handshake. Standing side by side, they presented a stark but ironic contrast. The Confederate commander, poised and dignified, wore a clean uniform buttoned to the neck, clean boots, and a long ornamental sword. The man to whom he had come to surrender was slightly hunched, wearing mud-splattered boots and trousers as well as an unbuttoned private's blouse with only a pair of shoulder straps to indicate his rank. He carried no sword or sidearm. Lee's three-inch height advantage solidified the irony of their contrasting appearance. As Grant took a seat at a small marble-top table in the center of the room, a dozen U.S. officers entered the parlor and gathered behind

1

him. The two generals' entourages presented a second contrast, this one symbolic. Lee brought only an aide and an orderly, emblematic of a ragged and lean army that numbered scarcely 25,000 men, while Grant's host of accompanying officers symbolized over 100,000 well-fed and amply supplied Federal troops.

Grant was first to break the silence. Everyone present understood the gravity of the momentous occasion, and yet Grant's opening comment was of the war with Mexico. "I met you once before, General Lee, while we were serving in Mexico." In 1847 Grant had been a lieutenant in the 4th Infantry Regiment, and Captain Lee of Major General Winfield Scott's staff had stopped to visit at Grant's brigade headquarters. There, the two had met briefly, Grant explained. "I have always remembered your appearance, and I think I should have recognized you anywhere." At that time Captain Lee was not only a rising star in the army but also senior to Lieutenant Grant in both rank and age. The captain made a lasting impression. Now as the two men sat ten feet apart in the parlor, Lee, without meaning to insult, replied honestly, "I know I met you on that occasion, and I have often thought of it and tried to recollect how you looked, but I have never been able to recall a single feature."[1]

Their meeting at Appomattox came as the bloodiest chapter in American history drew to a close. The Civil War had brought frightful sacrifices in human and material resources and had been fought on a magnitude no one could have conceived in 1861. Despite four years of a war that had torn apart families and country, or maybe because of it, when Grant and Lee came together in that parlor, they talked about something they had in common, a shared experience. Grant was more interested in reminiscing about the earlier conflict, perhaps generously trying to deflect attention away from the unpleasant purpose of the meeting, but Lee seemed more inclined to focus on the matter at hand. Nevertheless, it was Mexico where Grant knew he would find common ground with Lee.

Indeed, the war with Mexico was common ground not just for Grant and Lee but for their peers, a time when many had learned their first lessons in combat. The two principal U.S. armies active in Mexico were Major General Zachary Taylor's, which fought four battles in northern Mexico during the first year of the war, and Major General Scott's, which fought six battles in central Mexico during the war's second year. In those two armies were 239 future Civil War generals: 137 northern and 102 southern. Moreover, eight of

Scott's staff officers rose to the rank of general in the Civil War, four on each side.[2] Many of these future leaders were West Point graduates and most were lieutenants in 1846–47, with only a handful holding captaincies or higher.

The Mexican-American War had been a defining moment in the development of their military careers. Epic battles like Monterrey, Cerro Gordo, and Chapultepec fought in a distant and exotic land taught young, budding officers many lessons while creating lasting memories. When Americans returned home, they assumed that they had just been through the greatest combat experience of their lives. Lieutenant Grant called the attack at Cerro Gordo on April 18, 1847, a "brilliant assault," while Lieutenant Thomas J. Jackson thought Scott's entire campaign was greater than "any military operations known in the history of our country." Lieutenant William M. Gardner, a future Confederate general, asserted that the army's accomplishments in Mexico would "astound the world." Even Lieutenant William T. Sherman, who was in California and had not fought in any of the battles, understood the significance of the war and spent several years coming to terms with the disappointment he felt over his missed opportunity.[3]

Veterans of Mexico believed in 1848 that their battles and campaigns might never be surpassed by the army or forgotten by the nation. Thirteen years later, as Americans divided into opposing sides, those same veterans, whether they had joined the United States or the Confederate army, were optimistic about the outcome of the coming war and the contribution they could make. But initially in 1861, Mexico remained the center of gravity in their military thought and the yardstick against which they measured success. For example, following Fort Sumter, Brigadier General P. G. T. Beauregard cited among his qualifications to lead an army his position on Scott's staff in Mexico and his participation in councils and reconnaissances leading to the capture of Mexico City. Major General George B. McClellan, in his action against Confederate forces at Rich Mountain in the summer of 1861, acknowledged that he attempted to "repeat the manoeuvre of Cerro Gordo." Also, that summer when Confederates won a minor engagement at Big Bethel, Major General John B. Magruder exaggerated the battle's significance by likening it to Scott's victories in Mexico.[4]

After 1861, the conflict in Mexico was subsumed by a war on a much grander scale, with greater complexities and more at stake. As memories of the Mexican-American War faded, they were replaced by the immediacy of a conflict that overshadowed everything that came before. In the century and a half that followed, published accounts of the Civil War dwarfed the output of histories about the war in Mexico. While historians have written about the political ramifications of the Mexican-American War and the coming of the Civil War, they have given little attention to how the battlefield experiences of the former influenced the conduct of the latter. In fact, when I began to approach Civil War historians to contribute essays to this study, one declined to participate, citing a lack of identifiable connections between the two wars. Historians, along with the general public, have just been less interested in the war with Mexico. Yet many of the key actors in the two conflicts were the same, and personal experiences in the former almost certainly would have either a negative or positive influence on behavior in the latter. Mexico was common ground for all of them—an apprenticeship if you will—and it surely taught them lessons that would inform future decision making. It was a laboratory of hands-on, experiential learning that confirmed lessons learned at West Point and gave practical skills in managing every aspect of an army in the field.

Civil War historians, especially biographers, sometimes provide a glimpse back to Mexico but seldom have conducted in-depth studies searching for connections between those two conflicts. They generally treat the war in Mexico as a brief prelude to the real event and rarely, if ever, evaluate a general's Civil War years in light of his Mexican War experience. A few, among them Grady McWhiney and Perry Jamieson, have looked at weapons and tactics and argued that much of the bloodshed of the Civil War resulted from the unfortunate combination of old tactics (Mexico) and new weapons (rifles). But Earl Hess's later rebuttal contends that the rifle had not in fact made the asserted difference on the Civil War battlefield.[5]

Other historians have gone forward in time to search for the Civil War's relevance in the twentieth century. In his 2009 study, *West Pointers and the Civil War,* however, Wayne Wei-Siang Hsieh cautions against attempts to find deeper meaning in the Civil War by comparing it to later wars. Instead, he suggests, "it would be more fruitful to look at the Mexican War, which not only occurred fifteen years before the Civil War but also shared many of the same commanders and participants." Hsieh later writes, "The experience the old army acquired in Mexico, both as individuals and as a corporate institution, could not help but have a substantial influence on the conduct of the Civil War."[6]

A few historians have written books that acknowledge a connection between the two conflicts. The title of Alfred Hoyt Bill's 1947 survey of the Mexican-American War couches its subject as a *Rehearsal for Conflict*. John C. Waugh provides a snapshot of West Point graduates in his book *The Class of 1846* (1994), which includes McClellan, Jackson, George E. Pickett, and others. Waugh chronicles the bond formed by those cadets who then went to Mexico together before fighting against each other a decade and a half later. More recently, retired U.S. Army officer Kevin Dougherty has offered brief samplings of how experiences in Mexico might have shaped the conduct of Civil War leaders in *Civil War Leadership and Mexican War Experience* (2007), but this study's brevity and its reliance on secondary sources make it merely an appetizer for something more.

One other historian who found the Mexican War's imprint on the Civil War warrants notice. In 1992 Archer Jones makes several astute observations in *Civil War Command & Strategy: The Process of Victory and Defeat*. Like Hsieh, Jones finds West Point training and the war with Mexico to be significant contributors to Civil War leadership. After thirty years of relative peace, except for guerrilla-style fighting against Native tribes, it was in Mexico where the U.S. professional army was able to test its ability against a numerous foe that fought like European armies. Jones further explains that Mexico provided tactical lessons in not only the use of artillery and cavalry but especially in the virtuosity of skillful maneuver to execute successful turning movements. He also suggests that General Lee's understanding of strategy came in part from his utilization of Mexican War examples. Of course, young army officers in 1846–47 watched both Generals Taylor and Scott for examples of how to lead troops in combat, but Jones believes that it was the latter who served as a particularly accomplished mentor.[7]

Furthermore, Jones contends, it was not just Civil War generals who benefited from the Mexican War model. Presidents Abraham Lincoln and Jefferson Davis followed James K. Polk's previous example of maintaining firm control on the conduct of the war. The strongest American commander in chief up to that point in time, the opinionated Polk had a hand in organizing the army and formulating strategy. Like him or not, Polk's leadership was decisive. Lincoln and Davis were "well aware of President Polk's management of the Mexican War," writes Jones. "Success endorsed his method and both presidents followed it."[8]

The following chapters suggest that there are worthy comparisons to be made between the two conflicts and that, in some cases, the Mexican-American War should be viewed as a form of apprenticeship for Civil War commanders. Winfield Scott is a case in point. When the opening shots thundered at Fort Sumter in Charleston harbor, the commanding general of the U.S. Army knew that the crisis had to be defused with great care. At seventy-four, he was too old and infirm to take the field, but his perceptive mind remained sharp. The previous October Scott had worried about such an episode and had written to President James Buchanan to express his concerns. He warned that if the South opted for secession, that act might also be coupled with "the seizure of some or all of the following posts: Forts Jackson and St. Philip, on the Mississippi, . . . Fort Morgan, below Mobile, . . . Forts Pickens and McRee, Pensacola Harbor, . . . Fort Pulaski, below Savannah, . . . Forts Moultrie and Sumter, Charleston Harbor, . . . and Fort Monroe, Hampton Roads." Scott was primarily concerned with their inadequate garrisons. He further urged Buchanan to use "firmness and moderation, which the country has a right to expect—*moderation* being an element of power not less than *firmness.*"[9]

Scott's admonition harkens back to his strategic thinking in Mexico. During the Mexico City Campaign, his army fought and won six major battles. Although in one, Cerro Gordo, he decimated the enemy, at no time was Scott's objective the destruction of the Mexican army. His strategy throughout the six-month campaign was one of moderation, especially when his army gained the outskirts of Mexico City. He advanced, fought a battle, then waited for a peace overture. Even after the bloody Battle of Churubusco on August 20, when his men believed they could have marched into the capital and when intelligence revealed that Mexican morale was low and desertion high, Scott agreed to a pause in the fighting in the hope that negotiations would follow.[10] His strategy was both military and political, for Scott astutely took into account the instability of the Mexican government. Thus, the general's moderate approach showed firmness and displayed military strength while also giving his opponent time to reflect on the futility of further resistance. His willingness to cease operations periodically showed his desire not only to produce a political result but also to limit bloodshed. Remembering his success in Mexico, Scott proposed these same elements to President Buchanan in late 1860—demonstrate firmness and a show of force as a way of convincing southern leaders of the futility of secession and military conflict. It was a moderate approach conceived as a way to prevent excessive bloodshed.

The following spring, with hostilities opened and a southern confederacy created, President Lincoln turned to Scott for a plan to subjugate the rebellion. His plan again contained evidence of Mexican War influences. Like his strategy of moderation fifteen years earlier, Scott devised a plan aimed at political results, not the destruction of enemy forces. He proposed a naval blockade of the South's Atlantic and Gulf coastlines, which would economically isolate the wayward states. Next, he advocated seizing the Mississippi River to divide the Confederacy and deprive it access to that important waterway. Controlling the river would effectively cut off the Trans-Mississippi theater, ensuring that it would be no more than a sideshow similar to what he had done to the northern provinces of Mexico in 1847. To accomplish this, Scott explained that a strong Federal army would advance down the river capturing or turning Confederate strongpoints, much the way that he had advanced through central Mexico outmaneuvering and defeating enemy forces. If these measures proved inadequate, he envisaged striking deep into the Confederate heartland, again reminiscent of his campaign against Mexico City.

These moves would create such an overpowering advantage, thought Scott, that the South would realize that further opposition was useless; if it did not immediately reach this conclusion, then its gradual strangulation would ultimately force it to that realization. Scott also remembered that in 1846–47 the use of water for transport between New Orleans and Mexico provided a secure supply line. His 1861 plan facilitated the use of water for secure lines of communications and supply by exploiting the Confederacy's lack of naval assets. Referred to as the Anaconda Plan, the strategy sought to "envelop the insurgent States and bring them to terms with less bloodshed than by any other plan."[11] It was a different time with different circumstances, but Scott instinctively saw the relevance of past experience.

This volume suggests connections like those alluded to above, with the contributors having identified similarities that point to cause-and-effect relationships between the two wars. Because circumstances were different, Mexican War influences are at times easier to infer than they are to document. Making the task more difficult is the fact that Civil War generals rarely, if ever, cited their Mexican War experience as a reason for taking a certain course of action. But the perceptive observer can find clues that suggest Mexican-American War influences on the Civil War. It may not always be the case that new lessons were learned in Mexico so much as old lessons were confirmed or reinforced. In other words, what had been merely theory prior to 1846 became more concrete after practical, hands-on application in Mexico.

A variety of areas might be explored in search of similarities, as the following examples suggest. The war with Mexico demonstrated the efficiency of water transportation. Also, as America's first expeditionary war, the invasion of Mexico offered lessons in the treatment of civilians. In his march to Mexico City, Scott used a sophisticated pacification plan to prevent a general uprising and potential guerrilla war. In the opening battle at Palo Alto, Taylor skillfully used his artillery to help win the engagement, and nine months later at Buena Vista, artillery again proved decisive in a defensive battle against a superior force. Scott used his mounted troops extensively, not to launch attacks but to conduct reconnaissance and to patrol roads in search of guerrillas. In addition, he used his horsemen to pursue the broken Mexican army after Cerro Gordo and Churubusco. On several occasions Taylor and especially Scott demonstrated the primacy of maneuver and flank attacks. At Monterrey Taylor sent a portion of his army in a flank march to attack from the west while launching diversionary attacks on the northeast corner of the city. After gaining a lodgment on both sides of Monterrey, he then used the two elements of his army in a pincer movement to push deeper into the city, the U.S. Army's first experience in urban warfare.

It was Scott, however, who was the master of maneuver. At Cerro Gordo he demonstrated against the Mexican right while the bulk of his army followed a path, which Lieutenant Beauregard and Captain Lee had scouted and prepared, to execute a surprise attack against the enemy's left and rear. Four months later, on the outskirts of the capital city, Scott moved part of his army during the night into the rear of a Mexican force at Contreras, surprising his foe the next morning in a successful battle that lasted seventeen minutes. On a larger scale his final approach on Mexico City was a giant turning movement. Instead of attacking from the east, which General Antonio López de Santa Anna expected, Scott marched his army clockwise around the city, fighting four major battles before entering the capital from the west. These are examples of tactical turning movements, but in his conception of the campaign, Scott executed a strategic maneuver by changing the entire front of the war from northern Mexico to central

Mexico. He also utilized the concept of strategic concentration by halting other operations and pulling together all available troops under his command for a major and decisive move against the enemy capital, much the way McClellan would attempt to do in Virginia in 1862.

One more element of the Mexico City Campaign warrants notice: Scott's decision to abandon his supply line at Puebla, Mexico, and cover the last seventy-five miles to the capital by living off the land. Perhaps he took inspiration from Hernán Cortés, who over three centuries earlier had burned his ships on the coast of Mexico to signal to his invading army that there was no turning back. Cortés's subjugation of the Aztecs had recently been popularized in William H. Prescott's 1843 book, *History of the Conquest of Mexico*. For five months, as Scott fought his way from Vera Cruz to Puebla, he had been garrisoning towns along the way. By the time his army occupied Puebla, he was defending a supply line that stretched 170 miles back to the coast. Knowing that he would face strong opposition when he arrived at Mexico City, Scott called in all his garrisons so as to strengthen his small army as much as possible and to eliminate the concern about the safety of his vulnerable umbilical cord back to the Gulf. The young officers in the army no doubt took note of this bold move and understood that it was evidence of a resolute and confident commander. One wonders if this 1847 decision was in the back of Grant's mind as he plotted his movements in Mississippi in 1863. Perhaps it factored into Sherman's decision making in Georgia in 1864, for even though Sherman had not been in Mexico, he certainly knew of Scott's daring move.

It was not just battlefields that offered valuable examples for young subalterns. Practical lessons abounded on how to manage an army in the field. Feeding thousands of men and animals everyday was no mean feat. Some Civil War commanders were better administrators than others, and perhaps staff duties in Mexico helped determine one's capabilities in managing an army's supply needs. The ability to gather and interpret intelligence, the propensity to use reconnaissance, and the aptitude for making war on a map were all talents for which Civil War commanders needed a certain level of expertise. Exercising staff duties in Mexico was an excellent way to hone such skills. Moreover, as a few of the following essays will attest, some of the lessons learned in Mexico were negative ones resulting from bad relationships or hard feelings—one of those frictions of war that Carl von Clausewitz wrote about in *On War* (1832).

In this study twelve Civil War scholars have sought to bridge the gap between these two mid-nineteenth-century conflicts by looking at a dozen Civil War generals who were all West Point graduates and Mexican-American War veterans. The subjects of these twelve stand-alone essays commanded either a corps or an army, and they include six U.S. generals and six Confederate, with the former constituting the first half of the essays and the latter the second half. Each author provides his or her own interpretation about how the war in Mexico influenced the officer being examined, and there is an underlying hope that the reader will sense that the Mexican War is the central focus rather than a prerequisite to the main event.

Timothy B. Smith's opening essay asserts that U. S. Grant copied Zachary Taylor in style and personality but learned the art of strategic thinking from Scott. Furthermore, Grant learned basic quartermaster skills in Mexico and also formed relationships with young officers there that would serve him well later when he fought both with and against them in the 1860s. Next, Stephen D. Engle argues that Don Carlos Buell emerged from Mexico with great promise that was not fulfilled in the Civil War. Also, Engle shows how Buell's conciliatory methods in Tennessee in 1862 can be traced back to lessons learned in 1847, while a preference for maneuvering over fighting stemmed, in part, from a serious chest wound received in the assault at Churubusco. In an essay on Joseph Hooker, Ethan S. Rafuse provides a succinct evaluation of the army's antebellum political culture and explains how Hooker came of age as a staff officer in Mexico as he learned to play political games primarily from Gideon J. Pillow's example. He then shows how "Fighting Joe" brought this political gamesmanship to bear in the U.S. Army during the Civil War. Thomas W. Cutrer contends that George B. McClellan's tactical and strategic thinking was shaped in Mexico, and he used the Mexico City Campaign as a blueprint for his Peninsula Campaign in 1862. As a staff officer in Mexico, George G. Meade honed important skills related to mapmaking, planning, and logistics, writes Jennifer M. Murray. It was also in Mexico where Meade developed an "aversion to the powers of the press" as well as his "disdain for political meddling in military affairs" that, Murray shows, he carried over to the Civil War. She also contends that his reputation as a strict disciplinarian resulted in part from his low opinion of volunteers during the 1840s. Rounding out the U.S. generals is Brian Steel Wills's essay on George H. Thomas. Wills provides a detailed account of the Battle of Buena Vista and shows how Thomas's unmovable

nature was developed through his determination as a young artillery officer. While Thomas was known as "Old Slow-Trot," Wills argues that "slow"
should be equated to his persistence and resilience on the battlefield.

The essays on Confederate generals begin with Joseph T. Glatthaar's
appraisal of Robert E. Lee, who used his experience in Mexico to refine ru-
dimentary but crucial skills like reconnaissance and mapmaking. Lee also
learned both positive and negative lessons from Winfield Scott's example:
the former being audacity and the art of operational command, and the
latter being how to maintain a working relationship with superiors. Bold
leadership, Sean Michael Chick observes, was also a lesson that P. G. T.
Beauregard learned as a staff officer in Mexico, where he developed the
ability to conceive an audacious attack but was never quite able to pull one
off during the Civil War. Taken largely from Beauregard's own words in his
Mexican War Reminiscences, Chick also shows how Beauregard's opinion
that he was denied well-deserved credit for his staff duties in Mexico made
him sensitive to this same issue during the Civil War. Cecily N. Zander's
essay on Braxton Bragg reinforces the image of an argumentative martinet,
but his proficient work commanding the new flying artillery in Mexico was
impressive enough to elevate the value of mobile cannons in the minds
of future Civil War commanders. Bragg's performance in Mexico helped
ensure that "the American army could no longer view the artillery arm as
inessential or ineffective," but, as Zander argues, Bragg failed to learn from
his own lesson. Next, Christian B. Keller examines Thomas J. Jackson's
experiences and argues that some of Jackson's most noteworthy Civil War
characteristics took root in Mexico. Some of Jackson's tactical and strategic
thinking was already in an embryonic stage, and Keller notes that some of
his personal traits like humility and submission to God's providence were
already evident as well. Craig L. Symonds demonstrates that it was in Mexico where Joseph E. Johnston's concern over rank and promotion sowed
the seeds that blossomed into a fractious relationship with President Davis
during the Civil War. Finally, in assessing James Longstreet's decision making during the Civil War, Alexander Mendoza uses the general's detached
operation against Knoxville, Tennessee, in 1863 as a case study. His decision
to assault northern forces at Fort Sanders, Mendoza speculates, may have
drawn from the example of the determined assault made by U.S. troops at
Churubusco by Scott, whom Longstreet admired.

These twelve essays are not envisioned as the definitive statement on the origin of Civil War leadership, nor is it suggested to be a comprehensive examination of every important Civil War general. Rather, they are intended as a sampling meant to stimulate critical thought about the role of the Mexican War in the development of Civil War practices. Whether it be strategy, tactics, logistics, or the conduct of relationships, experiences south of the Rio Grande were an important part of leadership development for many of the generals who, by 1865, were nationally known as either heroes or villains. At the very least, this collection should impress upon future Civil War biographers the need to be more attentive to the formative years that their subjects spent as young officers in Mexico.

NOTES

1. This synthesis of the meeting at Appomattox Court House is taken from Horace Porter, "The Surrender at Appomattox Court House," in *Battles and Leaders of the Civil War,* 4 vols., ed. Robert Underwood Johnson and Clarence Clough Buel (New York: Castle, 1887), 4:733–37; Douglas Southall Freeman, *R. E. Lee: A Biography,* 4 vols. (1934; repr., New York: Charles Scribner's Sons, 1962), 4:134–36; U. S. Grant, *Personal Memoirs of U. S. Grant* (2 vols. in 1, Lincoln: University of Nebraska Press, 1996), 629–30. Grant wrote that Lee had, in fact, remembered him.

2. The number of future Civil War generals was compiled by comparing the lists in Timothy D. Johnson, *A Gallant Little Army: The Mexico City Campaign* (Lawrence: University Press of Kansas, 2007), 291; and Felice Flanery Lewis, *Trailing Clouds of Glory: Zachary Taylor's Mexican War Campaign and His Emerging Civil War Leaders* (Tuscaloosa: University of Alabama Press, 2010), 229–35. Because some officers on these lists served under both Taylor and Scott, duplicate names were subtracted.

3. Grant and Jackson quoted in Grady McWhiney and Perry Jamieson, *Attack and Die: Civil War Military Tactics and the Southern Heritage* (Tuscaloosa: University of Alabama Press, 1982), 154–55; Gardner to brother, Oct. 24, 1847, William Montgomery Gardner Papers, Southern Historical Collection, University of North Carolina, Chapel Hill; James Lee McDonough, *William Tecumseh Sherman: In the Service of My Country, a Life* (New York: W. W. Norton, 2016), 124–25.

4. McWhiney and Jamieson, *Attack and Die,* 153–54; McClellan to Col. E. D. Townsend, July 5, 1861, in *The Civil War Papers of George B. McClellan: Selected Correspondence, 1860–1865,* ed. Stephen W. Sears (New York: Ticknor and Fields, 1989), 44–45; Gary W. Gallagher, *Lee and His Generals in War and Memory* (Baton Rouge: Louisiana State University Press, 1998), 121.

5. McWhiney and Jamieson, *Attack and Die;* Earl J. Hess, *The Rifle Musket in Civil War Combat: Reality and Myth* (Lawrence: University Press of Kansas, 2008).

6. Wayne Wei-Siang Hsieh, *West Pointers and the Civil War: The Old Army in War and Peace* (Chapel Hill: University of North Carolina Press, 2009), 8, 72.

7. Archer Jones, *Civil War Command and Strategy: The Process of Victory and Defeat* (New York: Free Press, 1992), 223, 226, 263, 267–72.

8. Ibid., 12–13. For Polk's influence on the army in Mexico, see John C. Pinheiro, *Manifest Ambition: James K. Polk and Civil-Military Relations during the Mexican War* (Westport, CT: Praeger Security International, 2007); Richard Bruce Winders, *Mr. Polk's Army: The American Military Experience in the Mexican War* (College Station: Texas A&M Press University, 1997).

9. Winfield Scott, *Memoirs of Lieut.-General Winfield Scott,* ed. Timothy D. Johnson (Knoxville: University of Tennessee Press, 2015), 308–9.

10. Ethan Allen Hitchcock, *Fifty Years in Camp and Field: Diary of Major-General Ethan Allen Hitchcock, U.S.A.,* ed. W. A. Croffut (New York: G. P. Putnam's Sons, 1909), 284-88; Johnson, *Gallant Little Army,* 148.

11. Timothy D. Johnson, *Winfield Scott: The Quest for Military Glory* (Lawrence: University Press of Kansas, 1998), 226–27; Jones, *Civil War Command and Strategy,* 21; Scott to George McClellan, May 3, 1861, *The War of the Rebellion: A Compilation of the Official Records of the Union and Confederate Armies,* 70 vols. in 128 pts. (Washington, DC: Government Printing Office, 1880–1901), ser. 1, 51(1):369.

GREAT ADVANTAGE TO ME AFTERWARD

Ulysses S. Grant, the Mexican War, and Lessons Learned

TIMOTHY B. SMITH

"I was oblig'd to be in Washington to entertain an old club—of which I was an original member," President Ulysses S. Grant wrote in September 1874. "[It was] formed in the City of Mexico in 1848 during the occupancy of that City by the U.S. Army. We dine together annually—the surviving members of us—so far as we can get together on the 14th of Sept., the anniversary of our entrance into the City." Even though now the chief executive of the United States, Grant still made time for the past. He often dealt with old friends and comrades in arms, no more so than when he attended veterans' reunions and celebrations of old wartimes. Many of the gatherings revolved around the most recent conflict, the Civil War, and Grant was a favorite invitee of various veterans' organizations such as the Society of the Army of the Tennessee and the Society of the Army of the Cumberland. But he was perhaps most interested in his comrades of the earlier war with Mexico in the late 1840s. He and other officers had established the group they named the Aztec Club, and meetings still took place even in the 1870s, when its most famous member lived in the White House.[1]

Grant was even more interested in seeing his old fighting grounds, particularly those in Mexico. He, of course, made a famed world tour of diplomacy and outreach after he left office, but he made other trips as well. He traveled to various Civil War battlefields on occasion—passing through Vicksburg in 1880 and visiting the national cemetery there, for example—but he also made a postpresidency trip to Mexico in 1880 and thoroughly enjoyed himself. His wife, Julia, recalled:

There were many historical and lovely villages in the suburbs of the city. They all brought to the General some interesting reminiscences of the Mexican War. Here was the wall around Molino del Rey where the General (then Lieutenant Grant) found my brother Lieutenant Fred Dent wounded and faint from loss of blood. The General refreshed him from his canteen and dragged him to a place of safety close under the wall. Nearby the General pointed out about the spot where he once backed up a cart against the same walls, thus making a scaling ladder, enabling him with a few followers to enter the Mexican works, which soon surrendered. From here he led us on to the famous San Cosme Gate, where he rendered such signal service in capturing a church cupola and placing in it that fierce, howling little howitzer which brought dismay to the besieged Mexicans and a glorious brevet to my Lieutenant.[2]

Those memories were seemingly a lifetime ago. Indeed, more than twenty years before Grant would lead the United States as president, he had been a strapping young second lieutenant in Mexico, wide-eyed and learning from literally every event in these years of perhaps his most concentrated military education. In fact, he later wrote that his instruction at the U.S. Military Academy had been less than productive when it came to a real military education. He later wrote, "I did not take hold of my studies with avidity, in fact I rarely ever read over a lesson the second time during my entire cadetship." Grant even admitted that when it came to studying the famous European military theorist Henri Jomini, "I have never read it carefully." Rather, he spent more time reading novels "than . . . books relating to the course of studies," although he was careful to point out that the novels were "not those of a trashy sort."[3]

Rather, Grant's real military education came while he was in the regular army, the height of his service being in actual wartime. He later noted that "every officer, from the highest to the lowest, was educated in his profession, not at West Point necessarily, but in the camp, in garrison, and many of them in Indian wars." Then came the Mexican War and the first real combat any of these soldiers had ever seen. Grant added that in the field "a military education was acquired which no other school could have given."[4]

Grant was certainly in a position to learn much from his Mexican War experience simply because he saw the vast majority of that conflict. Recently transferred from the 7th to the 4th U.S. Infantry, he was part of the force that moved southward in Texas under Major General Zachary Taylor to confront what many saw as a border dispute but that President James K. Polk viewed as an opportunity. Although mostly consumed with the idea of marriage to young Julia Dent and never taking a firm stand on the political issues of the day, Grant later wrote that he did not like the obvious land grab; he later explained: "I do not think there was ever a more wicked war than that waged by the United States on Mexico. I thought so at the time, when I was a youngster, only I had not moral courage enough to resign." Young Lieutenant Grant was consequently in the early battles in Texas itself, Palo Alto (May 8, 1846) and Resaca de la Palma (May 9, 1846), where he had his first experience under hostile fire and also his first taste of leading men in combat. Grant later described himself as "a young second-lieutenant who had never heard a hostile gun before" and admitted, "I felt sorry that I had enlisted." Entering battle, his captain moved ahead on detached duty, which left Grant in command of the company itself; he admitted it was "an honor and responsibility I thought very great." Grant led his men in a charge he thought was battle determining but later humorously found that the same ground had already been charged over and won. He was much like the "soldier who boasted that he had cut off the leg of one of the enemy. When asked why he did not cut off his head, he replied: 'Some one had done that before.'"[5]

Nevertheless, young Grant was watching, especially the man who he obviously patterned much of his later command persona on, Zachary Taylor. He was already thinking ahead, wondering about the responsibility of command. "What General Taylor's feelings were during this suspense I do not know," he later admitted, but the low-level officer nevertheless pondered, "as I looked down that long line of about three thousand armed men, advancing towards a larger force also armed, I thought what a fearful responsibility General Taylor must feel, commanding such a host and so far away from friends."[6]

When the victorious American force moved southwestward into Mexico itself, Grant had the dubious duty of being detailed as regimental quartermaster. He was not at all enthused, although the work of supplying men on campaign would teach him a lot about hands-on warfare. At the time, however, the young officer thought it was a bother and yearned to be in the action. "I am not aware of ever having used a profane expletive in my life," Grant later admitted, "but I would have the charity to excuse those who may have done so, if they were in charge of a train of Mexican pack mules at the time."[7]

The 4th Infantry moved with the army in September 1846 toward the city of Monterrey, where the fight soon raged for possession of its outlying defenses and then the city itself. As quartermaster, Grant had been ordered to remain behind at camp, but "my curiosity got the better of my judgement, and I mounted a horse and rode to the front to see what was going on." He added, "I had been there but a short time when an order to charge was given, and lacking the moral courage to return to camp—where I had been ordered to stay—I charged with my regiment." Grant was one of the only officers mounted and later loaned his horse to the regimental adjutant, who was then killed; Grant was then tasked with filling that vacant job as well. Later in the battle when the regiment ran low on ammunition, Grant volunteered to go to the rear to request supplies be sent forward. He made this famous ride hanging on one side of his horse through heavy fire but made it safely, only to soon see his regiment withdrawing.[8]

Taylor ultimately forced the enemy's surrender amid arguable terms then and now. Although the general later proceeded southward and fought at Buena Vista in February 1847, Grant was not at that famous battle. He and many of the other regulars had moved on to participate in the other major thrust toward Mexico City itself. While the politics behind such a move was to clip Taylor's political wings by depriving him of too many battles to win and from becoming too big a military hero, Polk only made Major General Winfield Scott just such a political monster. Indeed, Taylor and Scott would be the next two Whig nominees for president, although only Taylor won. Grant abhorred the politics but reveled in watching a master conduct a campaign. He was with Scott as his army landed at and laid siege to Vera Cruz, then marched inland with the army, which defeated the Mexicans at Cerro Gordo. Despite being sick some of the time, Grant then moved across the mountains to the climactic fighting around Mexico City itself.[9]

Grant participated in most of the battles of the campaign—Contreras, Churubusco, Molino del Rey, and Chapultepec—and later informed Julia that "four of the hardest fought battles that the world ever witnessed have taken place." On the verge of entering the city itself, the young officer made perhaps his biggest mark by hauling a small cannon to the steeple of a church, whose priest had to be convinced to open the doors and let the Americans in. "He began to see his duty in the same light that I did," Grant confessed, "though he did not look as if it gave him special pleasure to do so." When the men had lugged the pieces of the gun up and put it together, Grant himself carrying a wheel, they shelled the gate area: "the shots from our little gun dropped in upon the enemy and created great confusion." Brigade commander Colonel John Garland praised Grant and noted that the gun "annoyed the enemy considerably," adding that the lieutenant "acquitted himself most nobly upon several occasions." The division commander, Major General William J. Worth, was so grateful that he sent a staff officer, John C. Pemberton, to fetch Grant and then sent him back with another cannon to double the fire. Grant did not have the guts to tell his general that another cannon would not fit up in the steeple, but he merely took the gun and left it below while returning to his perch.[10]

With Mexico City captured on September 14, 1847, Grant and his comrades settled down for the negotiated end of the war, which came months later. In the meantime the troops saw the sites but mostly encamped, which put an additional strain on Quartermaster Grant. By this time, although promoted at the death of the company's original first lieutenant, Grant also took on the additional task of commissary. It now fell to him to provide food and equipment, and the lieutenant was busy contracting, renting, and hiring bakers to provide his regiment bread before peace came and the American army returned to the United States.[11]

No human can go through the initial phases of their chosen profession without learning from that figurative rite of passage. And the learning curve is perhaps steeper and thus more pronounced when that hands-on education involves matters of life and death, state building, and government involvement. Grant knew as much, at one point commenting on "the impressions the country made upon my young mind." So, what did Grant learn from his past, particularly from his participation in the Mexican War? In addition to learning that he could act with a level head under extremely dangerous situations (his regimental commander wrote that Grant "behaved with distinguished gallantry" on several days), his answer, in general, was, "my experience in the Mexican War was of great advantage to me afterwards," mentioning numerous "practical" lessons it taught him.[12]

Those unenumerated "practical" lessons were legion, but most have to be discerned between the lines. Rarely did Grant, or many other officers for that matter, come right out and state that they did anything in the Civil War because they had learned it from Taylor or Scott in Mexico. But connecting the dots is the next best thing, and at times Grant gave indications that he at the least compared his Civil War actions with those of the past. For example, he learned of his innate courage and steadiness under fire in 1846, writing of his first battle and how "the balls were whizzing thick and fast about me." He later wrote that "war seems much less horrible to persons engaged in it than to those who read of the battles." Making a connection even during the Civil War, after Belmont in November 1861, Grant issued congratulatory orders to his command: "it has been . . . [my] fortune, to have been in all the Battles fought in Mexico, by Genls. Scott and Taylor, save *Buena-Vista*, and never saw one more hotly contested, or where troops behaved with more gallantry." Of course, the naïve brigadier general would see much worse than Belmont—in fact, one thing Grant apparently did not learn was to dampen his almost lifelong overconfidence, as seen at Belmont, Fort Donelson, Shiloh, and even in later campaigns. He wrote Julia even in November 1845 from Texas that "no doubt the whole affair will be settled by spring and the troops here distributed." He would continue to predict wrongly the near cessation of hostilities, foreshowing his same feeling of confidence but wrong predictions often seen during the Civil War.[13]

Other abstract lessons that foreshadowed his Civil War command experience also developed, even if not mentioned outright or even noticed at the time. One was Grant's seeming heavy dependence on his fiancé and later wife, Julia. His letters from Texas and Mexico gushed with love and need, something he would still display even as an older and more mature husband fifteen years later. At one point he wrote, "when I lay down I think of Julia until I fall asleep hoping that before I wake I may see her in my dreams." His dependence on her as his rock even took the early form of later examples of his seeming instability and thoughts of resignation from the army just to be with her. He of course did just that in 1854, then threatened it on several occasions even during the Civil War itself. In one particularly miserable moment in Mexico, a lovesick Grant opened a letter from Julia in which she had included flowers, "but when I opened your letter the wind blew them away and I could not find them." Similarly, Grant the quartermaster had a couple of episodes in Mexico in which money in his care was stolen, perhaps foreshadowing his later struggle with financial security, especially his risky late-in-life investment that lost everything.[14]

More concretely, it is patently obvious, and even outright stated, that Taylor was an immense influence on Grant as a commander. George G.

Meade later wrote of Grant, "he puts me in mind of old Taylor, and sometimes I fancy he models himself on old Zac." Grant admitted as much, writing of him in 1883, "there was no man living who I admired and respected more highly." Historian Bruce Catton has argued that Taylor "put a lasting imprint on Grant's developing personality," so that one must look no farther than his command persona to see Taylor's influence. "General Taylor never made any great show or parade of uniform or retinue," Grant explained. "In dress he was possibly too plain, rarely wearing anything in the field to indicate his rank, or even that he was an officer; but he was known to every soldier in his army, and was respected by all." In contrasting the styles of Taylor and Scott, Grant could just as easily have been describing himself when he wrote, "General Taylor never wore a uniform, but dressed himself entirely for comfort." He described Scott as much more formal in dress and pomp, neither of which interested Grant years later as a general himself. He added that "both [men] were pleasant to serve under—Taylor was pleasant to serve with." In terms of the clear and concise orders Grant is often noted for, he explained that Scott often wrote his orders not only for contemporary use but also for the eyes of the historian; conversely, "Taylor saw for himself, and gave orders to meet the emergency without reference to how they would read in history." It is not hard to see the influence Zachary Taylor had on Ulysses S. Grant, even if neither knew it was occurring at the time.[15]

The dots can also be connected in Grant's participation in various maneuvers and activities under Scott, such as the water voyage to Vera Cruz, which he described as "a tedious one, . . . many of the troops were on shipboard over thirty days from the embarkation at the mouth of the Rio Grande." One wonders if Grant thought back to this episode as his men steamed up the Tennessee River prior to Shiloh or crossed the Mississippi River at Bruinsburg, Mississippi, during the Vicksburg Campaign. Working with his naval counterparts during the Tennessee River and Vicksburg Campaigns surely also brought thoughts of Scott's close ties with the navy during the Vera Cruz operations. Likewise, the siege of Vera Cruz was a novel new activity no one alive in America had seen in operation. One again wonders if Grant thought back to that time when he encircled Fort Donelson, Vicksburg, or Petersburg; certainly, his mind was on supplies during those operations, and at Vera Cruz Grant the quartermaster admitted to Julia, "I had but little to do except to see to having the Pork and Beans rolled about." Grant had a much narrower view of the proceedings at the time than he did later, but he was obviously watching and learning, and he pondered these events in later years. Grant went so far as to pronounce Scott's activities, especially on certain days, "faultless as I look upon them now, after the lapse of so many years." When the retired Scott died and Grant held the old general's position, he issued an order informing the army of his passing and noted that the Mexico City effort was "a plan of campaign the success of which was as complete as its conception was bold, and which established his reputation as one of the first soldiers of the age."[16]

Similarly, Grant left clues about other lessons learned from watching Taylor and Scott. At one point he mentioned that Scott "hastened on to take personal supervision," something that would likewise become a hallmark of Grant's command mentality, whether it be visiting the front lines frequently at Shiloh or on the dusty roads motioning his men southward during the Overland Campaign in Virginia in 1864. It is likewise telling that Grant made it a point to be at nearly every battle in his approach to Vicksburg, while his counterpart Pemberton, also a Mexican War officer in Grant's same division, was only present at one. Also, the famed maneuver that he utilized so often, whether at Vicksburg or in Virginia, was eerily similar to Scott's entire campaign, Grant remarking about Cerro Gordo on "the reconnaissance [that] was completed, and the labor of cutting out and making roads by the flank of the enemy was effected." Finally, he no doubt also took notice when both Taylor and Scott offered "very liberal terms" to armies that surrendered to them, something he would do as well during the Civil War, most notably at Vicksburg and Appomattox.[17]

The formulation of operational-level campaign plans was also forefront in Grant's mind even as he marched with Scott's army westward toward Mexico City, and it certainly influenced his Civil War activities. There is no doubt that he later pondered Scott's campaign, because even at the time Grant differed with his commander on the best way to approach Mexico City itself. When Scott marched to the south and west, Grant wrote in August and September 1847, "I am wondering whether there is not some other route by which the city could be captured, without meeting such formidable obstructions, and at such great losses." Later he wrote that he was "now more than ever, convinced that the army could have approached the city by passing around north of it, and reached the northwest side, and avoided all the fortified positions." He added, "I had carefully noted on my map" and even "communicated" the information to his superiors, but he did not know whether they acted on it or even if it ever reached Scott. Grant obviously realized he was just a second lieutenant, but the seeds of larger strategic thinking were planted in Mexico and fully blossomed years later when he became general in chief.[18]

Grant supplied more tangible links to other learning activities. In preparation for the Forts Henry and Donelson actions, he confided to his sister, "I have now a larger force than General Scott ever commanded prior to our present difficulties." Similarly, his gathering of supplies from the territory through which his army passed, especially at Vicksburg, has been long touted. But he mentioned in his memoirs that Scott had done the very same thing on the way to Mexico City: "at that point the country is fertile, and an army of the size of General Scott's could subsist there for an indefinite period." Grant also noted that "the troops suffered considerably from heat and thirst," something he would no doubt file away and recall later as an army commander.[19]

The future general perhaps learned the most about logistics when he, as quartermaster for the 4th U.S. Infantry, had to gather and procure those supplies. Grant "respectfully protests against being assigned to a duty which removes me from sharing in the dangers and honors of service with my company at the front"; he later tried to resign the position. The lieutenant's first protest was denied "because of his observed ability, skill and persistency in the line of duty," and when he sought to resign, he was admonished that it was "an *assigned* duty, . . . not an *office* that can be resigned." As an example of his work, Grant later explained that on the march to Mexico City, "I was sent, as quartermaster, with a large train of wagons, back two days' march at least to procure forage." This quartermaster knowledge served him well in the later war; Bruce Catton has argued that "a future army commander could have had no more useful experience." This showed as Grant conducted his Civil War efforts. At the start of that war, when he first began his renewed service, one colonel remarked that "Grant's requisition upon me for supplies seemed to be complete in every detail, for nothing was added to or omitted from the requisition." And Grant said as much while early in the war overseeing bread baking for his command around Cairo, Illinois, writing about "my experience in the management of Bake Houses, as Comy. in the Army."[20]

Yet it was by far—at least insomuch as his correspondence and writings survive to record his thoughts—in the realm of personal connections that

Grant most utilized his knowledge gained in Mexico. He remarked, "besides the many practical lessons it taught, the war [in Mexico] brought nearly all the officers of the regular army together so as to make them personally acquainted." It was at times a two-way journey, as numerous people also sought to use either their connection with Grant personally from the Mexican War or simply their service in that conflict as an entering wedge to receive favors or government jobs. Grant's papers are rife with requests for positions—especially when he was president, of course—but there are also plenty of examples of Grant himself writing other chief executives either before his own presidency or afterward in favor of certain individuals. Most of the time the office seekers mentioned their war service either in the Civil War, the Mexican War, or both. Grant always seemed to thrive on service in that earlier war as well, often mentioning a potential applicant's service in Mexico.[21]

Much of the acquaintance process led to trust for officers on his own side in the later war. While he and William T. Sherman did not begin their touted friendship until later, there were many whom Grant knew and learned to trust in Mexico. He had high esteem for such men as Charles F. Smith and Meade, who he would later command. On lower levels he wrote even during the Civil War of a certain surgeon he wanted for his department. "My services in Mexico brought me in contact with many of the older officers of the Medical Dept.," Grant wrote from Vicksburg. "There is not one of them who I believe possesses all the qualifications for an executive office in an equal degree. . . . He served as Asst. Surgeon with my regiment before, and during a portion of the Mexican War."[22]

Yet Grant gave even more specifics of learning about his future enemies, arguing years later that "the acquaintance thus formed was of immense service to me in the war of the rebellion—I mean what I learned of the characters of those to whom I was afterwards opposed." He went on to qualify this: "I do not pretend to say that all movements, or even many of them, were made with special reference to the characteristics of the commander against whom they were directed. But my appreciation of my enemies was certainly affected by this knowledge."[23]

In terms of specifics, Grant wrote that most people tended to cloak their enemies with almost "super-human abilities." That was certainly the case in the Overland Campaign with the commanders of the Army of the Potomac against Robert E. Lee. But Grant gave them a swift correction by snapping:

"Oh, I am heartily tired of hearing about what Lee is going to do. . . . Some of you always seem to think he is suddenly going to turn a double somersault, and land in our rear and on both of our flanks at the same time. Go back to your command, and try to think what we are going to do ourselves, instead of what Lee is going to do." He later wrote in explanation: "I had known him [Lee] personally, and knew that he was mortal."[24]

Yet no greater example of knowing an opponent from Mexico was that of Gideon Pillow at Fort Donelson. Grant later famously claimed in his memoirs that he had tailored his operations around who he knew was in command: "I had known General Pillow in Mexico, and judged that with any force, no matter how small, I could march up to within gunshot of any intrenchments he was given to hold." He also recounted a conversation between him and friend Simon Bolivar Buckner, who eventually surrendered Fort Donelson: Buckner "said to me that if he had been in command I would not have got up to Donelson as easily as I did. I told him that if he had been in command I should not have tried it the way I did." Grant elaborated:

> Of course there was a risk in attacking Donelson as I did, but I knew the men who commanded it. I knew some of them in Mexico. Knowledge of that kind goes far toward determining a movement like this. If Longstreet or Jackson or even if Buckner had been in command I would have made a different campaign. . . . The Mexican war made the officers of the old regular armies more or less acquainted, and when we knew the name of the general opposing we knew enough about him to make our plans accordingly. What determined my attack on Donelson was as much the knowledge I had gained of its commanders in Mexico as anything else.

Then there was also the account after the surrender in which Buckner told Grant that Pillow had escaped, Pillow being concerned that "you'd rather get hold of him than any other man in the Southern Confederacy." Grant shot back: "If I had got him I'd let him go again. He will do us more good commanding you fellows."[25]

Grant's memoirs do not always match what his correspondence at the time said, but in this case there was proof of his negative view of Pillow. Even before the action in February 1862 along the Tennessee and Cumberland Rivers, Grant joked about Pillow's proclivity for getting slight wounds and making them into nearly mortal injuries, something he had been teased about in Mexico. Grant wrote his father in 1861, "I am not so uncharitable as many who served under him in Mexico" but declared, "as however he would find it necessary to receive a wound, on the first discharge of fire arm[s,] he would not be a formidable enemy."[26]

An article by any officer dedicated to delineating the lessons learned in Mexico and then put into action in the Civil War would be highly instructive and interminably fascinating to read. One from Grant, such a titan in the later war, would be especially valuable. But alas, there is no such article, and the connections and lessons obviously implemented thus must be discerned and distilled from the scraps of evidence and mentions in the general's correspondence and writings. But we know the influence was there, his frequent snippets mentioning something from the Mexican War serving as a skeleton of such a learning process. Grant certainly left enough evidence, both in word and in future actions, to verify that he learned a lot from his experiences during the Mexican War, and we would do well to examine his Civil War exploits partially, at least in theory, through the lens of his Mexico tutorial. After all, he himself admitted that it "was of great advantage to me afterwards."

NOTES

1. John Y. Simon and John F. Marszalek, eds., *The Papers of Ulysses S. Grant*, 32 vols. (Carbondale: Southern Illinois University Press, 1967–2014), 1:388–89, 24:211 25:232–33 (hereafter cited as *PUSG*).

2. *PUSG*, 1:146; John Y. Simon, ed., *The Personal Memoirs of Julia Dent Grant [Mrs. Ulysses S. Grant]* (New York: G. P. Putnam's Sons, 1975), 315–16; John F. Marszalek, David F. Nolen, and Louie P. Gallo, eds., *The Personal Memoirs of Ulysses S. Grant: The Complete Annotated Edition* (Cambridge, MA: Harvard University Press, 2017), 104, 108; Ron Chernow, *Grant* (New York: Penguin, 2017), 894–96. For Grant's travel around the world, see Edwina S. Campbell, *Citizen of a Wider Commonwealth: Ulysses S. Grant's Postpresidential Diplomacy* (Carbondale: Southern Illinois University Press, 2016).

3. John H. Brinton, *Personal Memoirs of John H. Brinton, Major and Surgeon U.S.V., 1861–1865* (New York: Neale, 1914), 239; John F. Marszalek, ed., *The Best Writings of Ulysses S. Grant* (Carbondale: Southern Illinois University Press, 2015), 3–4; Marszalek, Nolen, and Gallo, *Personal Memoirs of Ulysses S. Grant*, 21, 292.

4. Marszalek, Nolen, and Gallo, *Personal Memoirs of Ulysses S. Grant*, 115, 395.

5. John Russell Young, *Around the World with General Grant: A Narrative of the Visit of General U. S. Grant, Ex-President of the United States, to Various Countries . . .*, 2 vols. (New York: American News 1879), 2:447–48; Marszalek, Nolen, and Gallo, *Personal Memoirs of Ulysses S. Grant*, 60, 63–64; *PUSG*, 1:64, 67.

6. Marszalek, Nolen, and Gallo, *Personal Memoirs of Ulysses S. Grant*, 60–61.

7. Ibid., 68–69.

8. *PUSG*, 1:119; Marszalek, Nolen, and Gallo, *Personal Memoirs of Ulysses S. Grant*, 73, 75.

9. *PUSG*, 1:117, 138; Marszalek, Nolen, and Gallo, *Personal Memoirs of Ulysses S. Grant*, 82–115.

10. *PUSG*, 1:146; John H. Gore Report, Jan. 2, 1847 [1848], in *Correspondence between the Secretary of War and Generals Scott and Taylor and between General Scott and Mr. Trist*, H. Exec. Doc. 56, 30th Cong., 1st sess. (1848), 261–63; John Garland Report, Sept. 16, 1847, in *Message from the President . . . at the Commencement of the First Session of the Thirtieth Congress*, H. Exec. Doc. 8, 30th Cong., 1st sess., 169–71; *PUSG*, 24:326–27; Marszalek, Nolen, and Gallo, *Personal Memoirs of Ulysses S. Grant*, 108–9.

11. *PUSG*, 24:393; Marszalek, Nolen, and Gallo, *Personal Memoirs of Ulysses S. Grant*, 111, 124.

12. Francis Lee Report, Sept. 16, 1847, in *Message from the President*, 175–77; Young, *Around the World with General Grant*, 2:448; Marszalek, Nolen, and Gallo, *Personal Memoirs of Ulysses S. Grant*, 132.

13. *PUSG*, 1:63, 71, 73, 85, 97, 104, 3:130.

14. *PUSG*, 1:68, 89, 93, 122–23, 162; Timothy B. Smith, "'I Am Thinking Seriously of Going Home': Mississippi's Role in the Most Important Decision of Ulysses S. Grant's Life," *Journal of Mississippi History* 80, nos. 1 and 2 (Spring/Summer 2018): 21–34.

15. *PUSG*, 31:65; Marszalek, Nolen, and Gallo, eds. *Personal Memoirs of Ulysses S. Grant*, 6593–94; Chernow, *Grant*, 42; Bruce Catton, *U.S. Grant and the American Military Tradition* (Boston: Little, Brown, 1954), 27.

16. *PUSG*, 1:129, 16:213; Marszalek, Nolen, and Gallo, *Personal Memoirs of Ulysses S. Grant*, 82, 84, 99; Ronald C. White, *American Ulysses: A Life of Ulysses S. Grant* (New York: Random House, 2016), 282; Brooks D. Simpson, *Ulysses S. Grant: Triumph over Adversity, 1822–1865* (Boston: Houghton Mifflin, 2000), 46.

17. Marszalek, Nolen, and Gallo, *Personal Memoirs of Ulysses S. Grant*, 88–89; Catton, *U.S. Grant*, 36.

18. Simon and Marszalek, eds., *PUSG*, 1:144–45. The modern U.S. military employs three levels of war: strategic on the national level, operational on the campaign level, and tactical on the battlefield level.

19. Ibid., 4:96; Marszalek, Nolen, and Gallo, *Personal Memoirs of Ulysses S. Grant*, 87, 92.

20. *PUSG*, 1:104, 106–7, 134–35, 3:237–38, 4:96; Marszalek, Nolen, and Gallo, *Personal Memoirs of Ulysses S. Grant*, 87, 92; White, *American Ulysses*, 153; Catton, *U.S. Grant*, 35, 41–42.

21. *PUSG*, 14:117, 15:25, 595, 22:88, 454, 487, 23:362, 24:326, 414, 489, 25:455, 26:502, 27:453–54.

22. Ibid., 9:232, 15:354.

23. Marszalek, Nolen, and Gallo, *Personal Memoirs of Ulysses S. Grant*, 133; Chernow, *Grant*, 24, 51.

24. Marszalek, Nolen, and Gallo, *Personal Memoirs of Ulysses S. Grant*, 133; Chernow, *Grant*, 382.

25. *PUSG*, 28:420; Young, *Around the World with General Grant*, 2:470; Marszalek, Nolen, and Gallo, *Personal Memoirs of Ulysses S. Grant*, 206, 217; William S. McFeely, *Grant: A Biography* (New York: Norton, 1982), 102.

26. *PUSG*, 2:22.

LOFTY EXPECTATIONS

Don Carlos Buell's Mexican-American War Education

STEPHEN D. ENGLE

By the time Don Carlos Buell arrived in Texas in the sweltering summer heat of 1845 as a young officer in Brigadier General Zachary Taylor's Army of Observation, his reputation preceded him. Certainly not a stellar student at the U.S. Military Academy, his greatest achievement was in avoiding being dismissed each year for excessive demerits. His modest academic achievements graduated him thirty-second in a fifty-two-member class four years later. But when he arrived in Florida as a second lieutenant in the 3rd Infantry, Buell was prepared to put into practice the academy's education and training that had outfitted him for field duty. The Second Seminole War (1835–42) had been in progress for five years when the 3rd Infantry landed on Florida's west coast. Although he wrote little of his days in the swamps, his tour quickly schooled Buell beyond anything he had learned in his engineering classes. He gained significant field experience, especially about commanding men in an unusually inhospitable jungle landscape and against guerrilla-type warfare. The Seminoles survived as long as they did because they fought with their entire society, and they not only attacked enemy soldiers and civilians but also killed their own to avoid enslavement. Consequently, army commanders had to rely on scouts and guides and adopt techniques that struck at the Native society's nerve centers: its villages, crops, and herds. Discipline and unit cohesion, Buell learned early on, were the keys to maintaining poise under such conditions and in keeping men together in the jungle. By the time the army departed Florida in the spring of 1843, Buell would long remember his initial baptism by fire. Little did he know that another education awaited him in Mexico.[1]

After an uneventful journey from Port Leon aboard *Ben Franklin,* the 3rd Infantry, commanded by Lieutenant Colonel Ethan Allen Hitchcock, landed in late April at Jefferson Barracks, the country's largest military post, just south of St. Louis, Missouri. The correspondent to the *Army and Navy Chronicle* reported along the way that the men were all in good health. The change from the grueling campaigning in swampy jungles to garrison duty along the Mississippi River proved a welcome reprieve, even though Buell's Florida tour had proven to be a learning experience, as it was for all of the American soldiers. If he learned something of the enemy and his fellow officers, he also discovered something about himself—he had pluck. Not impressive in stature, Buell was nonetheless stout and possessed remarkable strength and a hearty physical endurance. These attributes mirrored a demeanor that appeared almost formidable. Indeed, while he was at Jefferson Barracks, Buell struck an insolent private with his sword, almost severing the man's ear. The incident nearly ended his professional career before it began, but his self-defense plea won him acquittal from a court-martial. It was an odd occurrence, given his own unruly attitude as displayed at the academy, but the episode made Buell legendary among his fellow infantry officers.[2]

By the time Buell's legal drama ended in the summer of 1844, the 3rd Infantry headed for Camp Wilkins, an old Indian reservation in Louisiana, as part of the military buildup in anticipation of the fallout from the U.S. annexation of the Republic of Texas. General Taylor's newly organized Army of Observation, eventually numbering around 3,000 men, the largest assembly of U.S. regulars since the Revolutionary War, watched events unfold for more than a year as President James K. Polk braced for the reaction of Mexico to this acquisition of its former territory. When Texas approved the U.S. annexation proposal in July 1845, Polk sent Taylor's army to Corpus Christi. The 3rd Infantry was the first unit to occupy Texas soil, and Buell arrived as part of an undistinguished but well-trained and proven officer corps. These included Major William W. Lear and Captains Edmund B. Alexander, Henry Bainbridge (under whom Buell served), Philip N. Barbour, Daniel T. Chandler, Lewis S. Craig, William S. Henry, Robert Hazlitt, and Lewis N. Morris. Together these officers molded the soldiers into a professional regiment that merited its legendary fame and the distinction of its regimental commander, Hitchcock, a Vermont native whose last name extended deep in American revolutionary military lore. The regiment traced its lineage to 1784, when it was constituted in the regular army as the 1st American Regiment, consisting of companies from Connecticut, New York, New Jersey, and Pennsylvania.[3]

By midsummer, the War Department redesignated the Army of Observation as the Army of Occupation, a name change that reflected the government's desires in Mexico. Taylor prepared to plant the U.S. flag at Corpus Christi, where he arrived on August 15. It was an arduous task to concentrate the fragmented regiments into something resembling an army in a remote area, and for weeks reinforcements landed daily on the Texas shores, along with an officer corps that would join Buell years later during the Civil War. Already accustomed to crude frontier conditions, Buell's company remained healthy, but by September's end, the weather fluctuated abruptly between sweltering heat during the day and cold piercing winds at night, which took its toll on the rank and file. The exhaustive drilling amid inhospitable conditions that included brackish water and a poor diet led to chronic dysentery, which would ultimately prove more fatal to the army than combat. Worse still, those soldiers who were well enough found outlets at the gambling halls and the grog shops that skirted the camp, which one officer in the 8th Infantry characterized as "the most murderous, thieving, gambling, cut-throat, God-forsaken hole in the 'Lone Star State.'"[4]

As in Florida, Buell kept a tight rein on his men and was careful to keep them from veering into illicit behavior. He possessed tremendous moral restraint and, perhaps realizing as a young man and a professional officer that serving in the U.S. Army would be his lifelong career, established within himself the standard he required from his troops. Buell's conduct reflected an officer wholly devoted to discipline, obedience, and preparation as a means of defense against unpredictability and chaos. Some of this came honestly to him, and some came from observing Hitchcock, in whom he saw a more senior example of himself. The New Englander had played a key role in Buell's court-martial defense at Jefferson Barracks, coming to the aid of a young officer who demanded respect and discipline from his subordinates. Buell saw in him a high-caliber military professional who thrived on discipline and obedience, and he welcomed the opportunity to come under this rigid practitioner's careful eye at Corpus Christi. As commander of the 3rd Infantry, Hitchcock was second to none in bringing order to the ranks, and his junior officers greatly respected his leadership. Buell benefited invaluably from observing his management.[5]

If Buell never mentioned the impetus for the army's looming invasion, he was certainly aware of the political opposition to American operations in Mexico and might have held reservations about Polk's expansionist desires. He was surely aware of Hitchcock's disapproving attitude about the president's ambition, as word trickled through the officer corps. Still, he belonged to the government, and his duty was to fall into line and obey orders no matter the politics involved. He must also have heard and shared reservations about Taylor's "Old Rough and Ready" leadership abilities and shortcomings. Even though some officers admired his pluck, others worried about the general's lack of interest in training the troops and his failure to prepare for potential future operations. Although Buell made his own decisions in such matters, it seems reasonable that he also harbored silent reservations about America's move to Texas as well as Taylor's abilities.[6]

The Mexican expedition began well for Buell, and he relished the return to field duty, especially compared to camp life's monotonous routine. Although soldiers enjoyed the rampant frolicking amid grave military matters, Buell explored the Texas frontier with former academy friends and fellow officers, including those from his Florida and Missouri days. He became friends with Captains Barbour, Craig, and Morris, and together they spent evenings strolling through camp discussing military theory and war. The lieutenant exercised his riding abilities, and, when time permitted, even engaged in horseraces. Still, he was careful to maintain a professional bearing toward and distance from the enlisted men. He never allowed himself to be seen in undignified ways. In these months Buell witnessed the army's massive transformation into one grand military community complete with paymasters, sutlers, provisions, and arms, from artillery and infantry units to dragoons. He learned about the region he was there to defend and how small companies operated as investigative units reconnoitering the foreign landscape while drilling his troops to maintain cohesion for combat preparation. The junior officer was part of something grand—unprecedented as the press reported it—perhaps the greatest professional military force the United States had ever sent to war, but his world extended no farther than his immediate command and the terrain it occupied.[7]

By mid-October 1845, Taylor's army had grown to almost 4,000 soldiers organized into three brigades commanded by Brigadier General William J. Worth, Lieutenant Colonel James S. McIntosh, and Colonel William Whistler. Though there were several West Point–trained junior officers, many of the senior officers lacked formal military instruction, and those who did possess it were dispersed among the several regiments. Heavy rains came that fall, followed by a cold spell in late November, which hampered operations. According to Taylor's own account, the sun did not shine on Corpus Christi Bay for the first two weeks in December. Conditions in the ranks worsened as the soldiers huddled together under the sullen Texas skies to escape the driving wind and rain. Soon troops became irritable, and Buell watched them turn to grog shops, gambling, horseracing, drinking, and other amusements to pass the time. Taylor had been on orders since arriving at Corpus Christi to be prepared at short notice to move, but the army's presence failed to goad the Mexican army into battle. By January 1846, Congress formally admitted Texas into the Union, and President Polk ordered Secretary of War William L. Marcy to direct Taylor to march southward to the Rio Grande to push the U.S. boundary as far south and west as possible. In early March the army started out on the 150-mile journey to the old Spanish city of Matamoros. Hitchcock had fallen ill before the march commenced, and Captain Morris assumed temporary command of the 3rd Infantry. Because Captain Bainbridge was on detached service, command of Company F fell to Buell.[8]

The soldiers passed through magnificent western terrain, but the trail itself was difficult for those unaccustomed to long marches and torturing thirst. Yet by late March, Taylor's army reached the Rio Grande opposite Matamoros and hoisted the Stars and Stripes to demonstrate U.S. military strength and to compel the Mexican government to recognize the great river as the formal boundary between the two countries. Buell, like many officers, believed that before the army reached the river, they would have a fight, so he kept his men alert. Battling severe diarrhea and convalescing along the march, Hitchcock penned in his diary, "my heart is not in this business; I am against it from the bottom of my soul as a most unholy and unrighteous proceeding; but, as a military man, I am bound to execute orders." Still, he was confident in his regiment, boasting that he could do "anything with the 3d Infantry, for every officer and every man knows his place and his duty."[9] Lieutenant Robert Hazlitt agreed, writing that "a better little army than this never took the field."[10]

What Hitchcock called an "important move for good or evil," the Americans were 200 miles from a U.S. base, and rumors from anxious outposts that Mexican soldiers had crossed the Rio Grande to the northern side alarmed them. The arrival of 3,000 Mexican troops at Matamoros, threatening war unless there was an American withdrawal to the Nueces River within twenty-four hours, darkened the hovering war clouds. One officer remarked, "the Mexicans over the river are very angry, and will have nothing to say to us."[11] Hitchcock's health was so poor by this time that physicians recommended sixty days leave, and he returned to St. Louis. On April 23 the Mexican government declared war on the United States, and immediately General Anatastio Torrejón with 1,600 cavalrymen crossed the Rio Grande a few miles upstream of Taylor's camp. When the Mexicans ambushed an American patrol, Taylor reported to Secretary of War Marcy, "hostilities may now be considered commenced."[12]

By early May, the armies maneuvered into combat positions, and Mexican artillery opened two days of battle at Palo Alto and Resaca de la Palma, which the Americans won decisively. These victories, however, hardly ended the war; in fact, the U.S. government had not even declared war. On May 12 Congress consented to Polk's war declaration without knowledge that Taylor had already won a decided victory against the Mexicans. In these first battles the 3rd Infantry lived up to its reputation as an exceptionally well-trained regiment. In his official report Taylor commended the unit for its gallantry in holding the right wing. Buell's combat performance proved him a brave but not reckless soldier. He received two flesh wounds during the first battle, and for his gallantry in leading a charge at the second one, he received his first-lieutenant bar. These battles marked Buell's first large-scale combat and taught him valuable lessons. First and foremost, courage came with a heavy price. He had been in skirmishes with Indians but not in large numbers. While the Seminole War had frustrated his learned abilities, the Battles of Palo Alto and Resaca de la Palma allowed Buell some practical opportunities to combine his military training and previous combat experience in waging more traditional warfare. The prairie's underbrush and ravines determined much about how the soldiers fought the battle, and he learned a lesson in adapting tactics and strategy in a new terrain. The young officer came to appreciate that strict discipline and precise movements usually predicted success.[13]

After Palo Alto and Resaca de la Palma, Taylor prepared to head to Monterrey, Mexico, but delays kept the army at Matamoros for weeks while the United States mobilized for war and Congress called for volunteers to reinforce the army. As part of a small officer corps, Buell, Barbour, Morris, Craig, Hazlitt, and others attempted to build comradeship among the rank and file. Buell was attuned to the soldiers' hardships, disease, and camp-life monotony, which often gave way to gambling, stealing, and fighting. Still, he found drilling a way to keep his men focused on the tactical maneuvers needed in combat. He emphasized cleanliness, sobriety, and virtue while instilling behavioral instincts that that would prove to be lifesaving measures on the battlefield.[14]

Although troop and supply shortages delayed the 100-mile American journey to Monterrey for over a month, the influx of short-term volunteers presented Taylor with more immediate problems. Three thousand volunteers had come for "glory and good time" but arrived without weapons, little immunity from disease, and a natural resistance to military discipline. Several war correspondents noted the appreciable difference between the regulars and the volunteers. The *Niles National Register* correspondent characterized these recruits as the most "graceless and lawless spirits" in the army.[15] Although he commanded a small professional unit, Buell was aware of these differences, and the volunteers' slovenliness and defiance to regular-army discipline appalled him. Like most West Pointers, he held an inherent distrust about their reliability, but he would soon come to appreciate their combat pluck and courage under fire, a lesson he would carry with him into the Civil War.[16]

The army moved out for Monterrey in late June, heading northwest along the Rio Grande and arriving at Camargo in early August. The village's inhospitable location and the suffocating heat and humidity made marching and camp conditions insufferable. One Philadelphia correspondent traveling with the army could hardly tell the difference between the soldiers and their officers, all were so bedraggled. Taylor, he reported, was a "very plain, shabbily dressed old gentleman, of rather small stature, about sixty years of age, and who looked by his hardy appearance, as if he had been camping out all his life."[17] It was no surprise that the grizzled veteran endured campaign fatigue and privations better than most soldiers, especially since he had lived an army existence for more than thirty-eight years. Although just a junior officer, Buell appreciated his commanding general's leadership and tenacity even if he deplored his appearance. Taylor divided his 3,200 regulars into two divisions under Brigadier General David L. Twiggs and Worth, with 3,000 volunteers to follow. Twiggs commanded the First Division, comprising the 3rd and 4th Infantry Regiments, and made Buell his acting assistant adjutant general. The promotion to Twiggs's staff reflected the favorable impression the lieutenant had made on the general. Like Buell, Twiggs had a dour manner but could get the most out of his men, and he no doubt saw a young, proficient officer who had the same ability. Whether Buell welcomed the change from company commander to serving on the general's staff, he surely recognized that the opportunity to assume more responsibility reflected the confidence Twiggs had in him.[18]

By mid-September, Taylor's army came upon Monterrey, perched in a bend of the Santa Clara River that ran along the southern length of the city before turning north and skirting the city's eastern edge. To the 7,200 Americans, the place appeared a solid fortress. More alarming to Taylor than the city's appearance, however, was the report that Mexican troops there had swelled to about 7,300 soldiers. Taylor considered Monterrey a key objective in his campaign in northern Mexico, so he deployed for battle. On September 20 he ordered Worth's division to undertake a daring flanking movement against the western defenses while Taylor himself commanded the remainder of the army in its demonstration against the Citadel, which Americans called the "Black Fort," and the eastern approaches along the river. Amid torrents of rain, the American army moved into position, then spent a miserably cold and eerie night anxious about the looming battle. The following day dawned clear and hot, and soon Worth's sweeping march— characterized by a series of sharp, bloody, and confused engagements— opened the way to the Saltillo Road, which entered the city from the west.[19]

Taylor, meanwhile, suffered heavy losses as the infantry fought gallantly but in vain to move forward against the Black Fort. Realizing that the only hope for success was to commence shelling the stronghold, Taylor ordered his batteries to unleash a tremendous barrage on the monstrous structure. The 3rd Infantry tried to find cover in the cornfields but found none, forcing the troops to endure tremendous fire. Lieutenant William S. Henry declared that in their "utter ignorance of . . . locality, we had to stand and take it."[20] The barrage killed Buell's good friend and fellow officer Barbour and severely wounded the 3rd Infantry's commander, Major William Lear. The Americans suffered heavy casualties but pressed on, which apparently surprised the Mexicans, who began to waver just as Taylor called up reinforcements. For the next several hours, the bloody fight continued, and the Americans finally gained a foothold in the northeast corner of the city. On September 22 Worth continued the assault and advanced into the city from the west, forcing the Mexicans out during the night. His soldiers had given a masterfully courageous exhibition and expected to finish the battle the next day. Although the previous days' combat exhausted both armies, Taylor launched a massive offensive using both wings the following day, which resulted in vicious close combat and forced the enemy to surrender the city. The Mexican force left Monterrey on September 26, beaten but not a defeated.[21]

In Monterrey's actual capitulation the Army of Occupation suffered few casualties. The 3rd Infantry, however, "suffered most severely," as one correspondent put it, losing 52 men out of an effective force of 262 and six of its fourteen officers, including the "Old Guard's" Captains Lear, Barbour, and Morris and Lieutenants Douglass Irwin and Hazlitt. Buell was in the thick of the fight but came through the three-day battle unscathed. He witnessed personal bravery as the soldiers and officers tried unsuccessfully to save their comrades and suffered the personal loss of his friends; Lear and Irwin, for example, had served as members of a court-martial that four years earlier had acquitted him. Buell emerged as an officer who reacted skillfully to combat "in exposed positions." It was during the Monterrey Campaign that Lieutenant Cadmus M. Wilcox discussed the impressions the lieutenant had made on his men. "Buell," he wrote, "was frequently seen on horseback, but whether mounted or on foot, the eye always followed him as he passed, attracted by his fine soldierly air and a natural easy dignity of manner."[22]

Twiggs valued Buell's administrative flare, but the lieutenant's combat gallantry impressed him even more. He praised the junior officer for his "valuable and meritorious services" at Monterrey; Buell would be breveted a captain in the months to come. Although he would have preferred that the lieutenant remain on his staff, Twiggs realized that, considering the high numbers of casualties among officers, it would be better if he returned to the 3rd Infantry as regimental adjutant. The command of the regiment reshuffled after Monterrey, and its leadership now fell to Captain Bainbridge, who also had served on Buell's court-martial and was aware of the lieutenant's pluck.[23]

As impressive as Taylor's victories were, they produced no overtures from the Mexican government for peace. Eager to bring the war to a close, President Polk concluded that only Mexico City's capitulation would accomplish the victory he desired. He sent Major General Winfield Scott, the army's senior commander, to arrange an expedition that would advance from the Mexican Gulf coast inland toward the capital city. During the winter months, "Old Fuss and Feathers" requisitioned several regular-army units for his overland march and ordered Taylor to head into the northern region with the volunteers. Although reluctant about the arrangement, Taylor acceded to his superior's plan, and by late February 1847, he defeated General Antonio López de Santa Anna at the Battle of Buena Vista, ending the military campaign in the north. But the war raged on, and Scott decided to take Vera Cruz (the walled city) by land and by sea. He organized his forces into three divisions: Twiggs's and Worth's regulars formed two and Brigadier General Robert Patterson's volunteers the third; Buell fell into line under Twiggs. The entire landing force numbered over 8,500 men, among them Lieutenant Colonel Hitchcock, who had returned to the army. The investment of Vera Cruz took nearly three weeks, with the 3rd Infantry playing an important part in the city's capitulation. While Worth and Patterson initiated the encirclement, Twiggs's troops completed it by hacking their way north toward Vergara and seizing the northwest passage out of Vera Cruz. By the end of the fourth day, Twiggs's soldiers reached the village. For the next two weeks, the siege was a duel between the Mexican and American artillery, but on March 21 Scott ordered the heavy guns of Commodore David Connor's Home Squadron and Commodore Matthew C. Perry's Mosquito Fleet, which had been operating in the Gulf of Mexico, to commence bombarding the city. Mexican and even European authorities requested Scott to cease firing so that foreigners and noncombatants could escape. The general refused, and not until March 27 did the Mexicans formally surrender.[24]

Within two weeks, Scott consolidated his force at Vera Cruz and commenced his westward advance overland along the National Road. This time Twiggs's division was the vanguard commencing the movement. By the time his troops started forward in early April, Santa Anna, having returned from Buena Vista, had united his forces to defend the nation's capital. Concerned by the news that the Americans were advancing, the general himself took command of a 12,000-man Mexican force and guided it to a mountain pass near the small town of Cerro Gordo. Soon, Twiggs reached Cerro Gordo and, joined by the rest of the army, launched a fierce flank attack on April 18. Buell was in the thick of the fighting as infantrymen fought bayonet to bayonet. Mexican artillery responded by unleashing a long series of volleys to which the American guns replied, and a deafening artillery duel commenced across the hilltops of La Atalaya and El Telégrafo. U.S. infantry stormed the heavily defended El Telégrafo and carried the enemy stronghold in what Hitchcock reported as certainly "one of the most extraordinary assaults ever made by any troops." Meanwhile, Scott's remaining forces reached the village and overwhelmed the Mexicans. By 10 o'clock, the Americans had taken both the hill and the village and watched as thousands of Mexicans retreated like "stampeded cattle," hoping perhaps that rain might save them from utter disaster.[25]

Although the Battle of Cerro Gordo lasted only about three hours, the Americans achieved a victory far more overwhelming than even Scott had expected. He boasted to Taylor that Mexico no longer had an army. About 200 Mexicans were killed and almost 3,000 taken prisoner. The Americans suffered about 450 casualties. The 3rd Infantry had nine men killed and twenty-six wounded. In his official report Twiggs expressed his pride in the conduct of his men, at least half of whom were raw recruits. Besides the general good conduct of the 3rd Infantry, he made specific references to Buell, who fought bravely under severe fire. Though he mentioned no specifics, Captain Alexander, now the regiment's commander, wrote, "I cannot speak in too high terms of the gallant bearing throughout the day" of Buell and Captain Craig.[26] Even Scott commended Twiggs's staff officers for their meritorious services.[27]

After Cerro Gordo, Scott's army inched its way to Puebla, 60 miles west of Jalapa and more than 130 miles from Vera Cruz, where he reinforced his army. As these soldiers arrived, his command swelled to almost 14,000 men. Scott made plans for his army's final campaign against Mexico City with an estimated 36,000 men. Major Generals Worth and Twiggs commanded the 1st and 2nd Divisions, followed by the divisions of Major Generals Gideon J. Pillow and John A. Quitman. By early August, his army organized for an advance that would take more than a week. Scott abandoned his guerrilla-plagued supply line and decided to live off the countryside, a bold move in an enemy-occupied region. Buell surely understood the risk involved, especially when it meant keeping civilians from engaging in military affairs, and that it would require ongoing reconnaissance. Yet he had faith in Scott's plan to focus on his army's advance instead of its rear. Besides, this would allow the commander to operate on interior lines and remain in constant divisional communication to make effective use of his engineers. To the Americans, the Mexican capital appeared impregnable. Santa Anna had crowded his troops inside the city and prepared his defenses. The capital lay amid a series of marshes and lakes, with three strongly fortified causeways as the only entry routes. Scott's forces would have to seize the causeways before advancing to the city's gates. Santa Anna fixed his sights on defending those entries. The army approached from the south until reaching an impassable dried lava bed called the Pedregal, when Scott turned to his engineers to find alternative routes in the rugged terrain. Santa Anna's base, Churubusco, lay on the field's northern edge; Scott's base, San Agustín, lay on the southern edge. In two days of fighting, August 19–20, Worth fought his way around the eastern side of the Pedregal toward San Antonio and Churubusco while Twiggs's and Pillow's divisions cut their way around the southwest side near Contreras. The stormy night of the nineteenth caused Santa Anna to withdraw northward from his advanced position to San Angel, while the Americans moved closer to battle.[28]

At dawn on the morning of the twentieth, Twiggs's and Pillow's men surprised the Mexicans with a brief but murderous assault. The soldiers showed no mercy as they chased the fleeing defenders out of the small village and down the turnpike to Coyoacan. The Battle of Contreras ended almost before the day began. One officer pulled out his watch and declared, "It has taken just seventeen minutes" to affect this rout.[29] When Scott arrived at San Angel, he ordered the troops to press on to Churubusco to support Worth. By late afternoon, according to Hitchcock, a "tremendous fight came off." Worth secured the Churubusco bridge, while Twiggs's forces under Captain Alexander seized by bayonet the strongly fortified Convent of San Mateo (San Pablo), from which they could draw cover. Two other brigades crossed to the north side of the Churubusco River and secured both the village of Portales and a main causeway to Mexico City. The Battles of Contreras and Churubusco had achieved at least one of Scott's objective— the seizure of a main causeway—but at a heavy cost to his army.[30]

Santa Anna suffered a devastating defeat, losing an estimated 4,000 men killed, wounded, and missing and 3,000 others captured. The Americans also sustained their highest numbers of casualties since coming to Mexico, over 1,000 men either killed, wounded, or missing. Twiggs's division was in the thick of the fighting, and Scott commended the gallant efforts of Buell's regiment in his official report. Buell had been in the fierce and close fighting in front of the works surrounding the convent. Apparently when others hesitated to overtake the enemy positions, he scaled the redoubt and was hit by a musket ball passing through the upper part of his chest near the right shoulder. Upon witnessing this courageous act, Captain Alexander allegedly said, "there has fallen the bravest man in the army."[31] Many years after the war, Daniel F. Frost, a lieutenant in the Regiment of Mounted Rifles, which was with Buell's outfit at Churubusco, recalled that although the "Mexicans got the best of us that day," Buell displayed tremendous courage. "The Mexicans were in a large field of corn which was higher than our heads," he reported, "and we did not know what kind of fortifications they were behind and there was no chance to find out. Finally, Buell climbed on top of an adobe house and reconnoitered. We kept yelling to him to come down, and when he dropped we felt sure that he was killed. We afterward found that he was shot through the body. It was not expected that he would live, but in six weeks he was on duty again."[32] Buell's actions so impressed Lieutenant Frost that even years later he remarked, "I have never known but one man whom I thought was absolutely ignorant of what it was to be afraid." He continued: "That person was . . . Buell, who I am certain, was the bravest man it was ever my fortune to know. . . . [H]e was a magnificent specimen of manhood and was strong as a person could find in a day's journey."[33]

For his performance that day, Buell became universally known among the junior officers in his regiment as "the bravest of the brave." Indeed he was. Even his superiors were impressed with his actions. Both Twiggs and Brigadier General Persifor F. Smith credited Buell for displaying a "coolness and activity under the circumstances."[34] Although he was not among those comrades in September who advanced and ran up the U.S. flag in Mexico City, signaling the end of the military conflict, his courage and combat valor in the war had distinguished him, and his reputation preceded him in the coming years. For the moment, however, his wound was painful and slow to heal. Indeed, it was in great measure due to his physical strength that he survived at all. Buell had been among the first to step foot on Mexican soil and had endured the prairie's rigors. He had witnessed considerable and intense combat and no doubt wanted to witness the Mexican capital's capitulation by a victorious U.S. army—a testimony to the services of thousands of soldiers like himself. The Mexican War did not formally end until February 10, 1848, when U.S. and Mexican officials signed the Treaty of Guadalupe Hidalgo, restoring peace between the two countries.[35]

Buell spent the winter months with his regiment in Mexico City, but in early March 1848 he returned to the United States and made his way to Marietta, Ohio, to his family's farm. As a soldier wounded in a war so distant, he may have wanted to relieve his mother's anxiety about his well-being. Whatever the case, the seclusion and serene pastoral atmosphere along the banks of the Muskingum River was a welcome reprieve from the last two years. By this time, his combat exploits in the war had made him famous among the townspeople, and word of his gallantry had preceded him. Buell would remember several immediate details about the war, not the least of which was the loss of his horse—a companion of almost six years. Even Congressman Amos Lane, who recommended Buell to West Point, knew of the loss of this horse and offered to replace it.[36]

The more Buell distanced himself from Mexico, the more impressive the war became and the more valuable was his experience in being part of something militarily grand. Several months convalescing impressed upon the young officer that he had survived a war that left numerous comrades behind. As an officer, he shouldered the responsibility for being a servant-leader and required of his men nothing he was not prepared to do himself. That meant leading in combat, learning how to stay in the fight while remaining cool, and standing ground under fire. He learned that frontal assaults were a frightful, bloody, but necessary part of war and that superior skill would win the day. A contributing factor to these lessons was his experience at Churubusco, where the Mexicans were in a strongly fortified position anchored by the San Mateo Convent. The soldiers fought more tenaciously there than in any battle of the campaign. His own chest wound was a vivid example of how difficult it was to breech fortifications. The tenacity of this battle might have influenced Buell's generalship fifteen years later, as he fell under the spell of maneuvering rather than fighting for success, which he believed to be a better means to an end.

He came away with reinforced notions of fortifications, discipline in the ranks, unit cohesion under fire, utilizing environmental and terrain advantages, importance of reconnaissance, and other practical lessons of maneuvering for battlefield success. He saw the value in having good leaders around him. Taylor's and Scott's military leadership provided him with broad and impressive lessons. Lieutenant Buell learned that capturing and occupying strategic places rather than destroying armies was the key to success. At Monterrey Taylor was content to hold on to the city and allow the Mexican army to march away intact under an armistice. Likewise, Scott's campaign was all about capturing strategic points without necessarily destroying the enemy forces. The general demolished the Mexican army at Cerro Gordo, but that was not his objective. In the same way that Buell was an observer of these examples, he later instituted essentially the same philosophy in capturing and occupying the strategically important city of Nashville and large swaths of Middle Tennessee in 1862.

Perhaps more than anything, he came to appreciate the difference between making war on a government versus making war on its people. Scott's conciliatory and pacification policies, his declaration of martial law and strict discipline for his own troops, and his lenient treatment toward Mexican civilians were all intended to minimize insurgencies and guerrilla activities. Buell learned something about cultural revenge that frequently turned people violent and their actions into guerrilla warfare. Depredations committed by American soldiers appalled him, and he tried to curb his own men from engaging in such activities, fearing reprisals from enraged civilians. Established rules of warfare spurned pillaging and committing atrocities, and Buell came away with the knowledge that such depredations had deadly consequences. The pacification policy that he observed in Mexico he used in 1862 to pacify Tennesseans, reflecting his desire to limit bloodshed and to win civilian hearts and minds. Scott's policies had reinforced in him the determination to avoid waging war on the people while waging war on the government's combatants.

If he turned a blind eye to the war's cause, Buell was bound to execute his orders and his mission as effectively as possible and disassociate himself with terrorizing tactics. Because the Americans were the invading army, he learned the logistical importance involved in long overland marches and, more especially, what it meant to live off the countryside in hostile territory. Scott's pacification plan in Mexico imposed order on the local people to squelch insurgency against his invading army. His approach favoring limited war for limited goals had so impressed Buell that years later, now a general and occupying hostile soil in Tennessee, Mississippi, and Alabama, he imposed conciliatory policies on the citizenry having earlier experienced a practical lesson in crafting guidelines that established military policies to govern and appease civilians in enemy-occupied territory. Scott's was a course in distinguishing between occupying enemy soil and enemy citizens while waging war against combatants.[37]

For someone who had made the army his life's career, the Mexican War was a series of defining moments in Buell's maturation as an officer and a leader, as it was for so many officers and soldiers. It was a kind of military laboratory in which he learned invaluable practical lessons by trial and error, and his superiors certainly noticed his conduct. For his gallantry at

Churubusco, he received a major's brevet. Buell emerged from the war a skillful combat soldier who had earned the respect of his fellow soldiers and understood more clearly the troublesome tactical and logistical burdens of moving an army through a hostile countryside. He prided himself on being a strict disciplinarian and became universally known in the army as a professional officer, perhaps even a martinet to some. Even when compared to Hitchcock, Twiggs, and Worth—masters of discipline—Buell's efforts on and off the battlefield seemed to measure up to his superiors' expectations. The professional pride and manner of his senior officers made a great impression on him. And to those in the regular army whom he impressed, Buell was a fine example of character and devotion to duty.[38]

In many ways Buell epitomized in camp and in battle the professionalism of the army that marched into Mexico as the most proficient force that the United States had ever sent to war. One fellow officer said that Buell's Mexican War exploits were in accordance with his true character, "nothing slighted, no attempts at blazonry, a brave honest soldier, performing all the duties of his position." He continued, "His record was not brilliant but honorable. . . . [H]e did whatever duty was assigned him faithfully and well, and not with a vein to personal distinction, but personal honor."[39] It was not just that the men expected nothing less from a West Point–trained Seminole War veteran, but Buell's character and professional bearing epitomized the honorable citizen-soldier turned professional. He was one among many West Point graduates who filled many of the company and field commands as well as key staff positions in Taylor's and Scott's armies. Many were long-service volunteers, hardened by frontier experience, but they maintained discipline and morale throughout the ordeal. Some scholars feel that the Mexican War served as an apprenticeship, and the conflict made war seem too easy and painless to these future generals, thus contributing to the bloodbath that began in 1861. It was truly the regular army's war; although there were sizeable numbers of volunteers, most of the combat was done by regulars. The U.S. Army typically fought offensively, and an unbroken string of victories taught young officers to seize the initiative by being aggressive on the battlefield.[40]

Unlike many Civil War commanders, Buell's Mexican War career was his finest moment as a combat leader and perhaps as an officer, inspiring his soldiers to follow him by what he did rather than by the rank he possessed. There was little complexity to his demeanor and almost nothing flamboyant about his personality, but once on the battlefield, Buell proved his mettle and gallantry on several occasions by his heroic performances. Among the many junior officers who emerged from the conflict, Buell had demonstrated he was the most promising of all, destined for military greatness. More than ten years later, however, the splendid tactician and polished, high-minded, clear-headed, no-nonsense career officer had turned cold and taciturn, his genteel manner having become completely uncompromising. Other than his role in helping secure a northern victory at the Battle of Shiloh (April 6–7, 1862), his Civil War career had few highlights. Perhaps had he ended the war in uniform among the handful of high-ranking commanders, contemporaries and scholars might have trumpeted his Mexican War exploits more prominently. A supremely capable organizer and administrator, Buell's reputation as a daring and gallant officer became near legendary in Mexico and gave every indication that he was destined for military greatness should another conflict break out. After a frustrating tenure in leadership as a major general who tried to bend the war to his ways, however, he resigned from the army in 1864, refusing to accept a command he thought was beneath him. Consequently, Buell's Mexican War exploits became a footnote in history. It was an ironic end to a commander destined for greater accolades.[41]

NOTES

1. Stephen D. Engle, *Don Carlos Buell: Most Promising of All* (Chapel Hill: University of North Carolina Press, 1999), 15–65. On the Second Seminole War, see John K. Mahon, *History of the Second Seminole War, 1835–1842* (Gainesville: University Press of Florida, 1967); and C. S. Monaco, *The Second Seminole War and the Limits of American Aggression* (Baltimore: Johns Hopkins University Press, 2018).

2. *Army and Navy Chronicle* reports as found in *Boston Atlas*, May 2, 1843, and *National Intelligencer* (Washington, DC), May 20, 1843; Engle, *Don Carlos Buell*, 24–29; Buell's Defense, June 19, 1843, Buell Court-Martial File, Record Group 153, National Archives and Records Administration, Washington, DC (hereafter cited as RG #, NARA).

3. William S. Henry, *Campaign Sketches of the War with Mexico* (New York: Harper and Brothers, 1847), 11–26; Ulysses S. Grant, *Personal Memoirs of U. S. Grant*, 2 vols. (New York: Charles L. Webster, 1885–86), 1:45; K. Jack Bauer, *The Mexican War, 1846–1848* (New York: Macmillan, 1974), 32; *Niles National Register*, Sept. 20, 1845, 36; Darwin Payne, "Camp Life in the Army of Occupation: July 1845–March 1846," *Southwestern Historical Quarterly* 72 (1970): 326–29; Ethan Allen Hitchcock, *Fifty Years in Camp and Field: Diary of Major-General Ethan Allen Hitchcock, U.S.A.*, ed. W. A. Croffut (New York: Putnam's, 1909), 195; Cadmus M. Wilcox, *History of the Mexican War* (Washington, DC:

Church News, 1892), 630–32; Theophilus Rodenbough and William Haskin, *The Army of the United States* (New York: Maynard, Merrill, 1896), 438; Army Returns, July–Aug. 1845, RG 94, NARA; *Army and Navy Chronicle*, Feb. 29, 1844, 257–78; Doc. 71 in *Public Documents Printed by Order of the Senate of the United States, First Session of the Twenty-Eighth Congress, December 4, 1843*, 7 vols. (Washington, DC: Printed by Gales and Seaton, 1844), 2:1–62; *The Old Guard: History of the Third Infantry Regiment* (Washington, DC: Government Printing Office, 1955), 3–5; Peter Guardino, *The Dead March: A History of the Mexican-American War* (Cambridge, MA: Harvard University Press, 2017), 31–34; Robert W. Johannsen, *To the Halls of the Montezumas: The Mexican War in the American Imagination* (New York: Oxford University Press, 1985); Engle, *Don Carlos Buell*, 28–33.

4. Justin H. Smith, *The War with Mexico*, 2 vols. (New York: Macmillan, 1919), 1:140–43; K. Jack Bauer, *Zachary Taylor: Soldier, Planter, Statesman of the Old Southwest* (Baton Rouge: Louisiana State University Press, 1985), 11–19, 118–19; *Niles National Register*, May 23, Sept. 3, Oct. 25, Nov. 22, 1845; Edward Wallace, *General William Jenkins Worth: Monterrey's Forgotten Hero* (Dallas, TX: Southern Methodist University Press, 1953), 66; Army Returns, Dec. 1845, RG 94, NARA; General Orders No. 14, Taylor's Army of Occupation, Sept. 26, 1845, AGO, ibid.; George W. Smith and Charles Judah, *Chronicles of the Gringoes: The U.S. Army in the Mexican War, 1846–1848* (Albuquerque: University of New Mexico Press, 1968), 274–76; Daniel H. Hill, "The Army in Texas," *Southern Quarterly Review* 9 (Apr. 1946): 448–50; Felice Flanery Lewis, *Trailing Clouds of Glory: Zachary Taylor's Mexican War Campaign and His Emerging Civil War Leaders* (Tuscaloosa: University of Alabama Press, 2010), 1–30.

5. Buell Court-Martial File, RG 153, NARA; Engle, *Don Carlos Buell*, 30–36.

6. Wallace, *General William Jenkins Worth*, 66; Smith, *War with Mexico*, 1:144; Hitchcock, *Fifty Years*, 195–203; *Niles National Register*, Jan. 3, 1846, 273; Eba Anderson Lawton, ed., *An Artillery Officer in the Mexican War, 1846–7* (New York: G. P. Putnam's Sons, 1911), 44–49; Lewis, *Trailing Clouds of Glory*, 1–25; Engle, *Don Carlos Buell*, 30–35.

7. Buell to James Grant Wilson, Nov. 22, 1896, Buell Papers, The Filson Historical Society, Louisville, KY (hereafter cited as FHS); Mrs. Alma Lane to Mr. Buell, Feb. 21, 1913, June 28, 1914, Don Carlos Buell Papers, Shelia Tschumy Private Collection, Dallas, TX; Wallace, *General William Jenkins Worth*, 66–67; Bauer, *Mexican War*, 34–35; Henry, *Campaign Sketches*, 46; Wilcox, *History of the Mexican War*, 632–33; Payne, "Camp Life," 338–40; Engle, *Don Carlos Buell*, 30–35.

8. Bauer, *Mexican War*, 33–43; Henry, *Campaign Sketches*, 52–59; John Frost, *The Mexican War and Its Warriors* (New Haven, CT: H. Mansfield, 1850), 11–12; Army Returns, Mar. 1846, RG 94, NARA; Army of Occupation, General Orders Nos. 14, 15, Sept. 26, 28, 1845, ibid.; Hitchcock, *Fifty Years*, 210; Bauer, *Zachary Taylor*, 124–27; Wallace, *General William Jenkins Worth*, 65–71; Jeannie Heidler, "The Military Career of David Emmanuel Twiggs" (Ph.D. diss., Auburn University, 1988), 80–83; Guardino, *Dead March*, 34–47; Engle, *Don Carlos Buell*, 30–36.

9. Hitchcock, *Fifty Years*, 213–14, 221–23; Henry, *Campaign Sketches*, 56–57; *Niles National Register*, May 26, 1846, 182–83; Rodenbough and Haskin, *Army of the United*

States, 436; Bauer, *Mexican War,* 38–39; Philip Norbourne Barbour, *Journals of the Late Brevet Major Phillip Norbourne Barbour . . . ,* ed. Rhoda Van Bibber Tanner Doubleday (New York: Putnam's, 1936), 17; Smith, *War with Mexico,* 1:145–50; Bauer, *Zachary Taylor,* 147; Lewis, *Trailing Clouds of Glory,* 38–45; Guardino, *Dead March,* 76–77; *North American* (Philadelphia), Mar. 27, 1846.

10. Robert Hazlitt to Sister, Apr. 22, 1846, Robert Hazlitt Papers, Special Collections, U.S. Military Academy Library, West Point, NY (hereafter cited as USMA).

11. *Cleveland Daily Herald,* Apr. 22, 1846; Hitchcock, *Fifty Years,* 213–17, 221–23; Army Returns, Mar.–Apr. 1846, RG 94, NARA; Bauer, *Mexican War,* 41; Smith, *War with Mexico,* 1:148–49; Barbour, *Journals,* 27, 36; Wilcox, *History of the Mexican War,* 42–46; Taylor to Adjutant General, Apr. 26, 1846, in *Mexican War Correspondence,* H. *Exec. Doc.* 60, 30th Cong., 1st sess., 141, 288–89; Bauer, *Zachary Taylor,* 149–50; *Niles National Register,* May 16, 1846, 161–64; Guardino, *Dead March,* 47–58; *National Intelligencer* (Washington, DC), Apr. 3, June 13, 1846; *North American* (Philadelphia), Mar. 27, 1846.

12. Hitchcock, *Fifty Years,* 213–14, 221–42; Army Returns, Mar.–Apr. 1846, RG 94, NARA; Bauer, *Mexican War,* 41; Smith, *War with Mexico,* 1:148–49; Barbour, *Journals,* 27, 36; Wilcox, *History of the Mexican War,* 42–46; Taylor to Adjutant General, Apr. 26, 1846, in *Mexican War Correspondence,* 141, 288–89; Bauer, *Zachary Taylor,* 149–50; *Niles National Register,* May 16, 1846, 161–64; Guardino, *Dead March,* 47–58; *National Intelligencer* (Washington, DC), Apr. 3, June 13, 1846; *North American* (Philadelphia), Mar. 27, 1846; Engle, *Don Carlos Buell,* 30–42.

13. Hitchcock, *Fifty Years,* 225, 230–32; Report of Taylor, May 17, 1846, RG 94, AGO, NARA; Heidler, "Military Career of David Emmanuel Twiggs," 89–91; *Chicago Inter-Ocean,* Nov. 20, 1898, newspaper clipping, Buell Papers, FHS; *Niles National Register,* May 23, June 6, 20, July 4, 1846; *Daily Union* (Washington, DC), Aug. 24, 1846; Army Returns, May 1846, RG 94, NARA; Bauer, *Mexican War,* 52–71; Smith, *War with Mexico,* 1:158–96; *Congressional Globe,* 29th Cong., 1st sess., 782–804; Wilcox, *History of the Mexican War,* 53–58; Guardino, *Dead March,* 80–84; *North American* (Philadelphia), May 8, 1846; Engle, *Don Carlos Buell,* 30–42.

14. Hazlitt to Sister, June 23, July 28, 1846, Hazlitt Papers, USMA; Barbour, *Journals,* 62–68, 73–75, 99–100; Bauer, *Zachary Taylor,* 171–74; Bauer, *Mexican War,* 81–87; Smith, *War with Mexico,* 1:204; Wilcox, *History of the Mexican War,* 78–86; *Niles National Register,* June 20, July 11, 1846; Rodenbough and Haskin, *Army of the United States,* 436; Army Returns, May–June 1846, RG 94, NARA; Guardino, *Dead March,* 96–110. See also Amy Greenberg, *Manifest Manhood and the Antebellum American Empire* (New York: Cambridge University Press, 2005); and *North American* (Philadelphia), May 12, 1846.

15. *Niles National Register,* July 25, 1846; *Boston Atlas,* May 15, Sept. 21, 1846; Smith, *War with Mexico,* 1:207; Wilcox, *History of the Mexican War,* 78; Hazlitt to Sister, June 23, 1846, Hazlitt Papers, USMA.

16. Henry, *Campaign Sketches,* 124–25; Smith, *War with Mexico,* 1:204–11; *Niles National Register,* July 11, 1846; Hazlitt to Sister, Aug. 16, 1846, Hazlitt Papers, USMA.

17. *South Carolina Temperance Advocate*, reprinting item from *Philadelphia Enquirer*, May 21, 1846; Army Returns, July–Sept. 1846, RG 94, NARA: General Orders No. 36, Aug. 12, 1846, AGO, ibid.; Buell to Adjutant General, May 6, 1846, AGO, Letters Received, ibid.; Rodenbough and Haskin, *Army of the United States*, 436–37; Wilcox, *History of the Mexican War*, 81–90; *Weekly National Intelligencer* (Washington, DC), Oct. 3, Nov. 28, 1846; Barbour, *Journals*, 90–91; Bauer, *Mexican War*, 88–89; Heidler, "Military Career of David Emmanuel Twiggs," 91–95; Wallace, *General William Jenkins Worth*, 80–83; Guardino, *Dead March*, 134–43; Engle, *Don Carlos Buell*, 30–42.

18. Army Returns, July–Sept. 1846, RG 94, NARA; General Orders No. 36, Aug. 12, 1846, AGO, ibid.; Rodenbough and Haskin, *Army of the United States*, 436–37; Wilcox, *History of the Mexican War*, 79–90; *Weekly National Intelligencer* (Washington, DC), Nov. 28, 1846; Barbour, *Journals*, 90–91; Bauer, *Mexican War*, 88–89; Henry, *Campaign Sketches*, 124–25; Smith, *War with Mexico*, 1:211; *Niles National Register*, Oct. 3, 1846; Bauer, *Zachary Taylor*, 175; Henry, *Campaign Sketches*, 153–55; Buell to Adjutant General, May 6, 1846, AGO, Letters Received, RG 94, NARA; Heidler, "Military Career of David Emmanuel Twiggs," 91–95; Hazlitt to Sister, Aug. 16, 24, 1846, Hazlitt Papers, USMA; Wallace, *General William Jenkins Worth*, 80–83; Guardino, *Dead March*, 134–43.

19. Barbour, *Journals*, 106–8; Smith, *War with Mexico*, 1:230–40; Bauer, *Mexican War*, 92–96; Wallace, *General William Jenkins Worth*, 85–89; Henry, *Campaign Sketches*, 190–91; *Boston Atlas*, Oct. 14, 1846; Daniel Harvey Hill Diary, 36–38, Southern Historical Collection, Wilson Library, University of North Carolina, Chapel Hill (hereafter cited as UNC).

20. Henry, *Campaign Sketches*, 194; Smith, *War with Mexico*, 1:250–54; Bauer, *Zachary Taylor*, 179–81; Heidler, "Military Career of David Emmanuel Twiggs," 96; *Boston Atlas*, Oct. 14, 1846.

21. Wallace, *General William Jenkins Worth*, 96–99; Henry, *Campaign Sketches*, 194–205; Smith, *War with Mexico*, 1:243–54; Bauer, *Zachary Taylor*, 179–82; Wilcox, *History of the Mexican War*, 91–110, 632–33; Bauer, *Mexican War*, 98–101; *Niles National Register*, Oct. 17, 24, 1846; *Boston Atlas*, Oct. 14, 1846; *North American* (Philadelphia), Oct. 30, 1846; Army Returns, Sept., Dec. 1846, RG 94, NARA; Heidler, "Military Career of David Emmanuel Twiggs," 96–97; Hill Diary, 35–39, UNC.

22. Wilcox, *History of the Mexican War*, 118; *Boston Atlas*, Oct. 29, 1846; Heidler, "Military Career of David Emmanuel Twiggs," 95, 105; Army Returns, Oct., Dec. 1846, RG 94, NARA: Don Carlos Buell, Statement of Military Service, Mar. 13, 1890, AGO, ibid. (hereafter cited as Buell's Statement); Report of Twiggs, Sept. 29, 1846, ibid. Timothy D. Johnson, *Winfield Scott: The Quest for Military Glory* (Lawrence: University Press of Kansas, 1998), 171–209; *North American* (Philadelphia), Oct. 30, 1846; *National Intelligencer* (Washington, DC), Oct. 26, 29 1846; Hill Diary, 45, UNC; Henry, *Campaign Sketches*, 195–200; Engle, *Don Carlos Buell*, 30–42.

23. Army Returns, Dec. 1846, Feb. 1847, RG 94, NARA; Rodenbough and Haskin, *Army of the United States*, 437; Report of Twiggs, Sept. 29, 1846, RG 94, AGO, NARA; Henry, *Campaign Sketches*, 195–200; Smith, *War with Mexico*, 1:259–61, 494–96; *Niles*

National Register, Oct. 17, 24, 1846; *Daily Union* (Washington, DC), May 20, 1847; Engle, *Don Carlos Buell,* 30–42.

24. Smith, *War with Mexico,* 1:262, 2:17–46; Bauer, *Mexican War,* 204–5, 235–39, 240–53; Hitchcock, *Fifty Years,* 242–48; Bauer, *Zachary Taylor,* 188–206; Smith and Judah, *Chronicles of the Gringoes,* 188–89, 194–95; Guardino, *Dead March,* 148–93; Army Returns, Jan.–Feb. 1847, RG 94, NARA; Heidler, "Military Career of David Emmanuel Twiggs," 99–100, 109; Wallace, *General William Jenkins Worth,* 116–19; *National Intelligencer* (Washington, DC), Apr. 13, 17, 1847; *Boston Atlas,* Apr. 16, 1847; Johnson, *Winfield Scott,* 171–209.

25. Hitchcock, *Fifty Years,* 249–53 (quote); Smith, *War with Mexico,* 2:37–59; Wallace, *General William Jenkins Worth,* 126–27; Bauer, *Mexican War,* 259–70; *Niles National Register,* Apr. 24, May 15, 1847; Heidler, "Military Career of David Emmanuel Twiggs," 113; Isaac I. Stevens, *Campaigns of the Rio Grande and of Mexico* (New York: D. Appleton, 1851), 55–56; George C. Furber, *The Twelve Months Volunteer; or, Journal of a Private in the Tennessee Regiment of Cavalry in the Campaign in Mexico, 1846–47* (Cincinnati: J. A. and U. P. James, 1848), 579–600; Guardino, *Dead March,* 148–93; Engle, *Don Carlos Buell,* 30–42.

26. Report of Alexander, Apr. 20, 1847, AGO, RG 94, NARA; Army Returns, Apr. 1847, ibid.; Engle, *Don Carlos Buell,* 30–32.

27. Report of Scott, Apr. 23, 1847, AGO, RG 94, NARA; Report of Twiggs, ibid.; Smith, *War with Mexico,* 2:47–59; Rodenbough and Haskin, *Army of the United States,* 438; Bauer, *Mexican War,* 267–68; *Niles National Register,* May 22, 29, 1847.

28. Wallace, *General William Jenkins Worth,* 143–56; Smith, *War with Mexico,* 2:99–110; Bauer, *Mexican War,* 279–98; Hitchcock, *Fifty Years,* 272–79; Heidler, "Military Career of David Emmanuel Twiggs," 123; Report of Twiggs, Aug. 23, 1847, RG 94, AGO, NARA; *Niles National Register,* Nov. 27, 1847; Wilcox, *History of the Mexican War,* 358–79; George H. Gordon, "The Battles of Contreras and Churubusco," in *Papers of the Military Historical Society of Massachusetts,* vol. 13 (Boston: Military Historical Society of Massachusetts, 1913), 577–97; Guardino, *Dead March,* 193–202; Timothy D. Johnson, *A Gallant Little Army: The Mexico City Campaign* (Lawrence: University Press of Kansas, 2007), 150–55.

29. Smith, *War with Mexico,* 2:109; Johnson, *Gallant Little Army,* 178–94.

30. Report of Twiggs, Aug. 23, 1847, RG 94, AGO, NARA; Heidler, "Military Career of David Emmanuel Twiggs," 126–29; Hitchcock, *Fifty Years,* 277–83; Wilcox, *History of the Mexican War,* 387–89; Bauer, *Mexican War,* 296–301; Furber, *Twelve Months Volunteer,* 617–18; Smith, *War with Mexico,* 2:99–110; *New Orleans Daily Picayune,* Sept. 23, Oct. 8, 14, 1847; *New York Herald,* Sept. 16, 17, 19, 23, 1847; Gordon, "Battles of Contreras and Churubusco," 577–97; *National Intelligencer* (Washington, DC), Oct. 13, 1847; Johnson, *Gallant Little Army,* 178–94.

31. Unidentified newspaper clipping, Buell Papers, FHS; Charles Keeny to Buell, Feb. 10, 1848, enclosed with Buell to Adj. Gen. Roger Jones, Apr. 26, 1848, AGO, Letters Received, RG 94, NARA; *New York Times,* Nov. 12, 1861; Gordon, "Battles of Contreras and Churubusco," 577–97.

32. *St. Louis Globe-Democrat,* Nov. 20, 1898; Dana O. Jensen, "Daniel Frost's Memoirs," *Missouri Historical Society Bulletin* 3 (Apr. 1970): 221; Engle, *Don Carlos Buell,* 30–42.

33. Jensen, "Daniel Frost's Memoirs," 221.

34. Report of Smith, Aug. 23, 1847, RG 94, AGO, NARA; Report of Twiggs, Aug. 23, 1847, ibid.; Report of Scott, Aug. 28, 1847, ibid.; unidentified newspaper clippings, Buell Papers, FHS; *Niles National Register,* Nov. 20, 27, 1847; Wilcox, *History of the Mexican War,* 387–89; *New York Times,* Nov. 12, 1861; George W. Kendall, *The War between the United States and Mexico* (New York: Appleton, 1851), 31–33; Engle, *Don Carlos Buell,* 30–42.

35. Army Returns, RG 94, NARA; Buell's Statement; unidentified newspaper clipping, Buell File, USMA; Jensen, "Daniel Frost's Memoirs," 221. Buell was not a member of the Aztec Club. See "Original List of Members Belonging to the Aztec Club Founded in the City of Mexico, A.A., 1847, by the Officers of the Army of the U.S.," 1879, USAMHI; Guardino, *Dead March,* 222–326.

36. Buell's Statement; Lane to Buell, Dec. 14, 1847, Buell Papers, FHS; Buell Family Genealogy Records, Buell Papers, Tschumy Private Collection; Army Returns, RG 94, NARA: Buell to Adj. Gen. Roger Jones, Apr. 26, 1848, AGO, Letters Received, ibid.; George Lane to Buell, Dec. 14, 1847, Buell Papers, FHS; Engle, *Don Carlos Buell,* 30–44.

37. Engle, *Don Carlos Buell,* 38–43; Johnson, *Gallant Little Army,* 148–49, 267–71; Johnson, *Winfield Scott,* 195–209.

38. Engle, *Don Carlos Buell,* 38–43.

39. *Reunion of Society of the Army of the Cumberland, Twenty-Eighth Reunion, Detroit, Michigan, Sept. 26–27, 1899* (Cincinnati: Robert Clarke, 1900), 99–100.

40. Spencer Tucker, James R. Arnold, and Roberta Wiener, eds., *The Encyclopedia of the Mexican-American War: A Political, Social, and Military History* (Santa Barbara, CA: ABC-CLIO, 2013), 1:xxv–xxvii; Martin Dugard, *The Training Ground: Grant, Lee, Sherman, and Davis in the Mexican War, 1846–1848* (New York: Little, Brown, 2008); Ian C. Hope, *A Scientific Way of War: Antebellum Military Science, West Point, and the Origins of American Military Thought* (Lincoln: University of Nebraska Press, 2015).

41. *Portland Oregonian,* Sept. 1, 1898; *National Tribune,* Mar. 29, 1906; Engle, *Don Carlos Buell,* passim.

PLAYING GAMES

Joseph Hooker and the Politics of Command

ETHAN S. RAFUSE

In January 1863 Major General Ambrose Burnside turned over command of the Army of the Potomac after a decidedly rough two months for the Union war effort in Virginia, highlighted by a bruising battlefield defeat at Fredericksburg (December 13, 1862). Throughout his time in charge, bitter conflict had so wracked the army's high command that Burnside undoubtedly felt some measure of relief at having the burdens of a position he had not wanted lifted from his shoulders. To his displeasure, though, President Abraham Lincoln appointed Major General Joseph Hooker as his replacement, doing so only a few days after Burnside had declared Hooker "unfit to hold an important commission during a crisis like the present, when so much patience, charity, confidence, consideration, and patriotism are due from every soldier in the field." Indeed, Burnside was convinced Hooker must be "dismissed [from] the service of the United States," for the army could not endure a man "guilty of unjust and unnecessary criticisms of his superior officers, and of the authorities and . . . by the general tone of his conversation, endeavored to create distrust in the minds of officers who have associated with him . . . , habitually speaking in disparaging terms of other officers."[1]

While Burnside made his fair share of misjudgments during the war, he was right about Hooker, for that officer was never shy about criticizing fellow officers or "playing games" in Washington with an eye on advancing his own interests and views. (The term "playing games" is taken from a 1971 essay by political scientist Morton Halperin analyzing why members of bureaucracies, which the nineteenth-century U.S. Army—though small relative to what it would one day be—most certainly was, act in what seem to be unsavory ways to get what they want.)[2] Indeed, few if any generals were such a persistent thorn in the side of other members of the Union high command as Hooker, who was constantly, as John Gibbon wrote after the war, "in the habit of talking very freely and did not hesitate to criticize not only his brother-officers, but his commander." For his part, Ulysses S. Grant declared Hooker "a dangerous man. He was not subordinate to his superiors. He was ambitious to the extent of caring nothing for the rights of others."[3] Hooker, of course, did not see his conduct negatively but rather as rooted in a sense of duty, explaining to a postwar interviewer, "I was too earnestly in the War to look on blunders approvingly, or silently."[4] Hooker's conduct is also, if not commendable, a bit more understandable if one considers what he had seen as an officer during the war with Mexico. During that conflict, there had also been intense friction within the U.S. high command, shaped in part by tensions in American society, rooted in the emergence of an officer corps that came to view itself as a profession during the first half of the nineteenth century. These tensions would also shape the Civil War in Virginia.

Historians seeking to understand the conduct of the American Civil War have, not surprisingly, devoted considerable time and energy to studying the antebellum U.S. Army. After all, as David Petraeus observes in a 1986 essay analyzing how the U.S. Army at that time perceived the lessons of the Vietnam War, "Political scientists, organizational psychologists, and historians have assembled considerable evidence suggesting that one reason decision-makers behave as they do is that they are influenced by lessons they have derived from certain events in the past, especially traumatic events during their lifetimes." Such events, especially if they occur early in an individual's professional life, he notes, can become such a significant part of "the 'intellectual baggage' that policymakers carry into office and draw on" that they come to "exercise unwarranted tyranny over the minds of decision-makers."[5]

The question of how the war with Mexico influenced the men who led the armies of the Union and Confederacy has naturally been of interest to students of American military history.[6] It was, of course, one of the rare instances before the Civil War in which the U.S. government assembled forces larger than a regiment in the field and the only time between 1815 and 1861 that it conducted conventional operations against armies constructed along European lines. Both conflicts also served as tests of a decades-long effort

by leaders of the U.S. Army after 1815 to improve its organizational efficiency and professionalize the officer corps, while senior leaders in Mexico
like Winfield Scott and Zachary Taylor offered models for junior officers to
emulate as they developed their own command styles and methods. In 1861
George B. McClellan declared Scott "the General under whom I first learned
the art of war" and sought to "prove that the great soldier of our country can
not only command armies himself but teach others to do so." For his part, in
April 1864 George G. Meade said Ulysses S. Grant "puts me in mind of old
Taylor, and sometimes I fancy he models himself on old Zac."[7]

Both wars were also waged in the aftermath of the transformation of
American political life associated with the rise of Andrew Jackson. By the
1840s, the political culture of the early republic had given way to political
democracy (at least for white males) and bitter political conflict between
the Democratic and Whig Parties in which, one observer of northern politics exclaimed, "politics seem to enter into everything."[8] Yet among the
objectives of the army reform movement after the War of 1812 were the
professionalization of the army and diminishing the influence of partisan
politics on military affairs. The curriculum and culture at the U.S. Military
Academy after 1815 was in part designed to detach officers from prewar
identities, attitudes, and loyalties and to encourage them to embrace the
culture of the army and an attitude toward politics that conflicted with
what was happening in the rest of American society. "By the 1820s and
1830s, officers had begun to distinguish consistently between the military
and political worlds," in the words of historian William B. Skelton, with "the
professed ideal . . . an apolitical officer corps and a rigid separation between
the civilian and military spheres." In part due to the near-monopoly West
Point graduates secured over new commissions in the regular army after
1815, considerable progress was made before 1846 in developing an officer
corps whose members viewed themselves as apolitical servants of the national state, accountable and subordinate to civil authority regardless of
the party in power.[9]

Yet however much American officers may have paid homage to the ideal
of being separate from the sordid world of partisan politics, in reality the
influence of politics on their lives was constant and inescapable. While the
officer corps was not subjected to the "spoils system" that Jackson brought
to Washington to the degree that other government agencies were, the U.S.
Army was an intensely political animal. All West Point cadets, including

Hooker, owed their appointments to the academy, and thus their commissions, to members of Congress. Moreover, they were often joined by blood, marriage, or mutual self-interest to figures of political prominence. Consequently, it was not unusual for officers to "play games" and work through political channels to advance the interests of the army, their particular communities within the military, and their individual careers.[10] Moreover, officers were acutely aware that, while it fell to the regular army to conduct dirty and thankless constabulary operations on the frontier, should the country find itself in a major war, the army would swell in numbers. This ensured that there would be opportunity for rapid promotion as well as intense competition for it.

Also exerting an influence on U.S. military affairs in nineteenth-century America was a popular attachment to the idea of the citizen-soldier and amateur general. This was especially strong in many quarters due to Jackson's example and his supporters' celebration of the "common man." Consequently, in much of the country there was a deep skepticism toward standing armies and the officer corps. The regular army, West Point, and its officer corps frequently found themselves under attack and accused of being—not completely without justification—elitist institutions that drew too heavily on European models and harbored ethos and attitudes that were not in line with the values of a democratic republic. The tensions produced by the ethos of Jacksonian democracy and its clash with that of the institutional army emerging by the 1840s ensured there would be much of interest for junior officers to take away from the conflict with Mexico regarding the politics of command. Both the Mexican-American War and the American Civil War would powerfully illustrate Carl von Clausewitz's observation that war is "a true political instrument, a continuation of political intercourse, carried on with other means" that is profoundly shaped by "the character of the state involved."[11]

Born in Hadley, Massachusetts, in November 1814, Hooker arrived at West Point in July 1833 and graduated four years later, along with such future notables as William H. French, John Sedgwick, Braxton Bragg, and Jubal A. Early. Shortly after being assigned to the 1st U.S. Artillery, Hooker accompanied his unit to Florida and saw service in operations against the Seminole Indians before being dispatched to the Canadian border during the summer of 1838. With the exception of a three-month stint as adjutant at West

Point, he spent the next few years in New England. There the army's job was to maintain peace along the border with Canada as the United States and Great Britain worked out boundary disputes—a good place, as historian Samuel J. Watson has observed, for a young officer to see how intertwined the political and military realms could be.[12]

In May 1846 the "young, ambitious, and belligerent" Hooker welcomed news of the outbreak of hostilities with Mexico, an early biographer exclaimed, "with an intense joy that would have horrified his Puritan fathers if they could have been cognizant of it."[13] Shortly thereafter Hooker learned he had been appointed to the staff of Brigadier General Persifor F. Smith. Grandson of a hero of the Battle of Brandywine (September 11, 1777), after relocating from Philadelphia to Louisiana, Smith's prominence in the legal community and local militia led to his appointment to command troops Louisiana sent to Florida to participate in the Second Seminole War (1835–42). Smith proved an able officer whose performance in Florida impressed Major General Winfield Scott and others in the army. Nonetheless, Hooker's appointment was made with the expectation that his possession of the West Point education and staff experience Smith lacked would ensure a sufficient level of professional rigor and regular-army discipline in the workings of his command. When Hooker arrived at Smith's camp on the Rio Grande, however, he found himself reassigned to the staff of Brigadier General Thomas L. Hamer, an amateur soldier who owed his rank to his prominence in the Democratic Party in Ohio—and who a few years earlier had been responsible for securing an appointment to West Point for Hiram Ulysses Grant. Hooker's appointment as Hamer's chief of staff was undoubtedly made with the expectation that he would provide that unit the professional direction its commander needed more than Smith did.[14]

This expectation was fulfilled at the September 1846 fight for Monterrey, in which Hamer commanded a brigade in Major General William O. Butler's division. Although Butler had served with distinction during the War of 1812, his appointment was also due to politics, as he left the army after the war and served as a U.S. congressman and a leader of the Democratic Party in Kentucky. At Monterrey Major General Zachary Taylor directed Butler's command to advance against the city's northeastern defenses, while Brigadier General William J. Worth's troops maneuvered to attack from the west. After three days of heavy fighting, the Mexican commander decided on September 23 that he had had enough and asked for an armistice. Although the victory had mainly been won by Worth, the capture of Monterrey boosted talk among Whigs of Taylor's potential as a presidential candidate in 1848.[15]

Taylor was not the only one who won attention for what happened at Monterrey. Hamer had nothing but praise for Hooker. "I am in particular obligations to the Chief of my Staff, Lieut. J. Hooker," the general declared in his official report, "his soldierly conduct and fine military acquirements . . . has been invaluable to me during the whole campaign; and his coolness and self[-]possession in battle set an example to both officers & men." In November Hamer personally wrote to President James K. Polk to appeal for Hooker's promotion to captain. "He is undoubtedly," declared Hamer, "one of the most accomplished young officers in the Army."[16] Butler was impressed as well. After Hamer died from dysentery in December 1846, Hooker accepted Butler's invitation to join his staff as aide-de-camp. The months that followed, however, brought dull occupation duty at Monterrey and Saltillo. Eager for more active service, Hooker happily accepted appointment in April 1847 as chief of staff for Brigadier General George Cadwalader, whose brigade was ordered to join the American army at Vera Cruz. Like Smith and Hamer, Cadwalader was an amateur soldier whose general's commission was largely due to his political prominence. His command reached Vera Cruz in June and immediately pushed inland to join the rest of Winfield Scott's army at Puebla in early July. Shortly thereafter, Cadwalader's brigade was assigned to the division led by Major General Gideon J. Pillow. It did not take long for Pillow to decide that Hooker, now a brevet captain, was the sort of man he wanted on his own staff and appointed him assistant adjutant general for the entire division.[17]

Pillow was not a West Point graduate. Instead, he owed his position to his friendship and political affiliation with the president, and he understood that Polk possessed an intense suspicion of both the regular army and the commander of the American army at Puebla, Major General Scott. Everyone knew that Scott, despite being a regular officer, was a partisan Whig with political ambitions and had had a decidedly problematic relationship with the Democratic Party's great hero Andrew Jackson. Old Hickory also happened to have been the mentor, friend, and close political ally of William Carroll, who as Tennessee governor had taken Pillow on as a protégé and appointed him adjutant general of the state militia in 1833. Like Jackson,

Carroll was an enthusiast of the ideal of the untrained amateur soldier, and his views, in the words of Pillow's biographers, "strongly influenced the military and political thought of young Pillow."[18]

Scott's problematic relationships with Jackson, Polk, and Pillow were in part a manifestation of the ongoing debate over the country's needs in terms of military leadership. Although he owed his own initial commission in the army to Jeffersonian politics and personally harbored political ambitions, Scott was among the most important champions of the professionalization of the officer corps. Firmly believing the country needed to move away from the "Cincinnatus" model of military leadership and what he deemed an outdated exaltation of the amateur general, after 1815 he had worked tirelessly to improve the army's management and foster an ethos among junior officers that contrasted conspicuously with the attitudes Jackson and his supporters brought to politics and war. In Scott's vision, officers should earn their positions not through party politics, but by embracing apolitical professional standards that could only be fully developed through long-term service in uniform. The general was an especially enthusiastic champion of West Point and presented himself to cadets as a personal example of the professional-soldier ideal. Years later Ulysses S. Grant, even though he chafed at a good deal of the program at the military academy and did not share Scott's love of pageantry and uniforms, could not deny the power of the image Scott projected. "With his commanding figure, his quite colossal size and showy uniform," Grant declared, "I thought him the finest specimen of manhood my eyes had ever beheld, and the most to be envied."[19]

Jackson, on the other hand, a friend and political mentor to Polk (who embraced the moniker "Young Hickory"), personified the citizen-soldier ideal and had brought to Washington the "spoils system," which tied appointments to government offices to partisan loyalty. Embracing the ideal of the amateur commander that Jackson personified, when war broke out with Mexico, many of Old Hickory's followers possessed an intense suspicion of the regular army and its officer corps. This was evident in the spirit Polk brought to his duties as commander in chief, declaring in his first annual message to Congress that the maintenance of a "large standing army" in peacetime was "contrary to the genius of our free institutions, would impose heavy burdens on the people and be dangerous. . . . [R]eliance for protection and defense on the land must be mainly on our citizen soldiers."[20]

To ensure he had allies in the army tasked with fighting the war with Mexico, Polk used his authority to appoint general officers whose loyalties, both politically and in respect to the debate over the primacy of regulars versus citizen-soldiers, rested with the president rather than Scott. In all, historian Richard Bruce Winders notes, Polk would appoint thirteen volunteer general officers, all of whom "had one trait in common—all were loyal Democrats with years of service to the party."[21] Polk, not surprisingly, viewed Scott with suspicion, declaring after a meeting in May 1846: "Gen'l Scott did not impress me favourably as a military man. He has had experience . . . but I thought was rather scientific and visionary in his views." (He did not mean that as a compliment.) It did not take long for Polk and Scott to find themselves in conflict, and the president decided to keep the general chained to a desk in Washington, where there would be no opportunities for personal distinction.[22]

Then, however, Taylor's victories in northern Mexico aroused talk among Whigs of making "Old Rough and Ready" their presidential candidate in 1848. This, the unwillingness of the Mexican government to agree to a satisfactory political settlement, and the failure to get Congress to pass legislation creating a new rank that would enable him to appoint a political ally above Scott finally compelled Polk to gratify the general's desire to command in the field. To keep an eye on him and ensure affairs were managed in line with the president's way of thinking and interests, Polk looked to his friend Pillow. Scott and other regulars, not surprisingly, were dubious about Pillow's competence and loyalties, with one West Pointer later scorning him as "a twenty-fifth rate country lawyer."[23]

Having Hooker on the staff would, Scott and other regulars no doubt anticipated, ensure there would be someone at Pillow's headquarters who would furnish, "it was generally understood and felt," an early student of Hooker's career later wrote, "all the brains" and "energy and industry" necessary to prevent the volunteer general's shortcomings from being fatal to the campaign.[24] Pillow, with a degree of modesty and self-awareness that was uncharacteristic of him, accepted the arrangement and appreciated Hooker's talents enough to reportedly tell the young captain: "When you see occasion for issuing an order, give it without reference to me. You understand these matters." Just as Polk made his selection of generals with an eye on keeping a check on Scott and the regulars, Scott and the regulars as-

signed staff to keep an eye on generals like Pillow. Indeed, Scott's approach
echoed the Prusso-German system of assigning general-staff officers to the
staffs of units commanded by members of the nobility, producing such notable "military marriages" as those between Gebhard von Blücher and August
von Gneisenau, Johann von Thielmann and Carl von Clausewitz, Frederick
III and Count Leonhard von Blumenthal, and August von Mackensen and
Hans von Seeckt.[25]

In early August 1847 Scott ordered his army to advance west from Puebla
toward Mexico City. Drawing advice from his staff of West Point graduates,
he then decided to swing his army of about 11,000 men to the left and approach the Mexican capital from the south. By the time Scott's command
reached San Augustin on August 17, though, the Mexican high command
had positioned forces at San Antonio to block the road to Mexico City running between Lake Xochimilco and a large lava field, El Pedregal. Captain
Robert E. Lee of Scott's staff, however, was able to find a mule path through
the field that led to a high hill known as Zacatepec, from where it was possible to see the road that ran along the western edge of El Pedregal, and to
learn that Mexican forces commanded by General Gabriel Valencia were
posted near the village of Padierna (although Lee misidentified it as Contreras). Scott decided he wanted the path turned into a road and assigned
the task to Lee and a working party of about five hundred men from Pillow's
division, with the rest of Pillow's men and Brigadier General David Twiggs's
division protecting them as they worked. Shortly before 1 p.m., Pillow and
the road workers had reached the base of Zacatepec when two English-
speaking residents made their way to the general's position and reported
that Valencia's force "consisted of twenty-eight pieces of artillery, and six
thousand of infantry."[26]

Pillow promptly ordered Hooker to relay the information to headquarters at San Augustin, from whose church steeple the sight of the two sides
exchanging fire near Padierna could clearly be seen. Scott, already aware of
the presence of enemy troops, Hooker later recalled, received Pillow's report
coolly, "stating, in substance, that he did not send General Pillow out there
to fight a battle, but to make a road." Scott also read to Hooker a note he had
dispatched to the general before his arrival, underscoring "that it was not
the intention of General Scott to fight a battle on that day." Hooker promptly
returned to Pillow, who after hearing what the staff officer had to say about
Scott's intentions directed him to talk to the senior engineer officer on the

field regarding the suitability of the road over which artillery and wagons would have to pass. After doing so, he returned to Pillow, who had already decided to ignore Scott's admonition for caution and ordered forces forward to push Valencia's skirmishers out of Padierna.[27]

After Hooker returned from his meeting with the engineer, Pillow, having received directions from Scott to push Colonel George Morgan's regiment forward, directed him to find the unit and have it join Cadwalader's brigade in a move to the right along with Colonel Bennet Riley's and Brigadier General Persifor Smith's brigades. On his return to the hill where Pillow had his command post, Hooker learned that Scott was on his way from San Augustin, Pillow directing him to find the commanding general and bring him there. After doing this, he listened in as the two generals discussed the situation at around 4:00 p.m. Scott was not pleased that Pillow had violated his express orders not to initiate an engagement, but Hooker later recalled that Scott responded to Pillow's account of events with words "expressive of approbation of what had been done."[28]

Shortly before sundown, Hooker and Pillow departed. While traveling through the lava field, they fell in with a party that included Twiggs and proceeded through darkness and rain that fell "at times," in Hooker's words, "with great violence." After occasionally losing their way and at one point wandering close enough to the enemy's lines to hear "the shrill blasts of his bugles," Hooker and Pillow finally reached San Augustin at around 11:00 p.m. and found rest in a house on the plaza. Scott sent orders directing Pillow to remain there until morning, which the "wet and completely exhausted" general made no objection to. "From Pillow's perspective," writes historian Timothy Johnson, "it was probably a well-deserved opportunity for rest, but from Scott's view, it was likely just a diplomatic way of keeping Pillow out of the way." At sunrise he told Hooker it was time to return to the field. By then, however, what became known as the Battle of Contreras was in the process of being settled. That morning three American brigades delivered a devastating blow to Valencia's command and quickly sent it, along with forces General Antonio López de Santa Anna had sent forward in a futile attempt to assist, fleeing north and west, eventually rallying with the forces Santa Anna had directed to fall back from San Antonio to Churubusco.[29]

At Churubusco the Mexican leader positioned his forces in a line anchored by a Franciscan convent and a *tête de pont* south of the Churubusco River. Eager to follow up his victory at Contreras, Scott ordered an assault on these defenses and personally followed Pillow's troops as they approached them. Hooker would not miss the fight on August 20. He personally directed the advance of the mixed force of infantry and cavalry tasked with assaulting the Mexican position at the convent. Fierce resistance and the open nature of the ground, however, blunted the attack and compelled the captain to position the force behind the cover of a church. He then made his way to Pillow, and the two men were between the convent and the bridgehead when the pressure of American attacks finally rendered the Mexican positions untenable. When the forces defending the convent showed a white flag, Pillow directed Hooker to receive it, although the honor of receiving the surrender of the Mexican garrison fell to Captain J. M. Alexander of the 3rd U.S. Infantry instead. Nonetheless, Pillow made a point in his report on the battle of calling to General Scott's attention as "worthy of his special notice" the performance of Hooker and the rest of his staff, which was distinguished by "fearless and gallant conduct, as well as by their judgment and skill."[30]

After a failed armistice and a costly victory at Molino del Rey on September 8, Scott decided to assault the "Castle of Chapultepec," which one observer described as "built upon a knob or mound which rises high and abrupt from the plain . . . approached by a road which winds around the mount. On all sides the hill is steep and in many places inaccessible." Scott noted that it was "strongly fortified at its base, on its acclivities and heights." The general continued, "Besides a numerous garrison, here was the military college of the republic, with a large number of sub-lieutenants and other students."[31] Early on September 13, under the cover of American artillery fire, the assault began, with Hooker in the thick of the fight. Along with the rest of the assault force, he rushed forward and helped seize the outer Mexican works. When the attack stalled at the walls protecting the top of the hill, Hooker went back to hurry forward scaling ladders. On reaching the wounded Pillow's command post, the captain took care of getting the ladders moving forward and offered to lead another assault with a fresh regiment from Worth's division. Pillow approved, and once again Hooker went forward. Though the regiment's effort to reach the Mexican position faltered, Hooker continued forward personally and watched as U.S. forces finally broke the enemy line. The following day the American army took possession of the Mexican capital.[32]

Both Scott and Pillow were eminently pleased with Hooker's performance. In his September 18 report on the operations against Mexico City, Scott included the captain on the lengthy "list of individuals of conspicuous merit" for having "won special applause, successively, on the staff of Pillow and Cadwalader." In his report on Chapultepec, Pillow declared: "I cannot adequately express . . . the sense of obligation I feel to my personal staff for its distinguished gallantry and patient endurance of the dangers and fatigues. . . . Captain Hooker, my adjutant general, and chief of my staff, was greatly distinguished throughout this action by his extraordinary activity, energy, and gallantry."[33]

Unfortunately, the capture of Mexico City and agreement regarding the merits of Joseph Hooker were insufficient to heal the rift between Scott and the administration, as Polk was determined to undermine any prestige the general might reap from military victories so remarkable that no less than the Duke of Wellington reportedly proclaimed Scott "the greatest living soldier" and his campaign "unsurpassed in military annals."[34] It was not just his personal fortunes that Polk sought to undercut, but the notion that the professional concept of military leadership the general represented had been validated by the war. (Indeed, generations of West Point cadets would memorize Scott's "fixed opinion, that but for our graduated cadets, the war between the United States and Mexico might, and probably would have lasted some four or five years, with, in its first half, more defeats than victories falling to our share; whereas, in less than two campaigns, we conquered a great country and a peace without the loss of a single battle or skirmish.")[35] Fortunately for Polk, he had an ally in the army to support his effort and who agreed that whatever political benefits the war produced must go where they properly belonged—with the administration and its volunteer generals, not with Scott and his regulars.

In his reports on the battles around Mexico City, Pillow disparaged Scott's generalship and elevated the importance of his own efforts in the victories. Not surprisingly, Scott, acutely aware of his subordinate's agenda, disapproved these reports and was decidedly displeased when private letters echoing them began appearing in newspapers friendly to the Polk administration. Regarding Contreras, an August 27 account of the battle penned by "Leonidas" that appeared in the *New Orleans Daily Delta* on September 10, 1847, proclaimed that Pillow's generalship compared favorably with

Napoleon's at Ulm in 1805. The amateur general had, "Leonidas" declared, *"evinced on this, as he has done on other occasions, that masterly military genius and profound knowledge of the science of war, which has astonished so much the mere martinets of the profession."*[36]

Scott responded in November by reminding the army of regulations for-bidding the writing and sending of such letters but could not resist, though he did not name names, stating: "It requires not a little charity to believe that the principal heroes of the scandalous letters . . . did not write them, or specially procure them to be written. . . . False credit, may no doubt, be obtained at home, by such despicable self-puffing and malignant exclu-sions of others, but at the expense of the just esteem and consideration of all honorable officers."[37] Pillow, who had also been subjected to a court of inquiry for being in possession of two Mexican howitzers seized at Cha-pultepec in violation of regulations, responded by writing to Polk of his troubles. He also made a point of ensuring that the president was aware of who his friends in the army were—and that they were not overlooked in the distribution of honors. "I have never had a truer or better friend than Hooker," Pillow advised Polk that same month and warned that failure to acknowledge the captain's services with a brevet promotion would produce feelings of "secret triumph & exultation of Scott and his *coterie*."[38]

Finally, after Secretary of War William L. Marcy presented him with official notification that Scott had arrested and charged Pillow and two other officers for their conduct, Polk acted. He had Marcy issue orders re-moving Scott from command, releasing Pillow and the other two officers from arrest, and directing that Scott's conduct be subjected to a court of inquiry. The court, which began at Puebla in March 1848, placed Hooker in a decidedly ticklish situation. As Pillow's chief of staff, his take on matters would naturally be a matter of interest to the court. Yet presenting them placed him at risk of antagonizing Pillow and the president or Scott and the West Point clique that idolized the general, disdained Pillow and an-ticipated his discrediting, and resented the Polk administration's attitudes toward and meddling in military affairs.[39] Nonetheless, in March and April 1848, Hooker took the stand. When finished, he had provided the court with nothing that prevented it from ending the proceeding with Polk and his allies satisfied that they had done what they set out to do. While Hooker said little that could be construed as critical of Scott, the general treated the captain as a hostile witness and, in the words of historian Jack Ballard, "ac-

cused Hooker of having been coached in his testimony before the court and
. . . demanded the names of persons dictating Hooker's statements." In his
June 1848 defense before the court, Pillow made clear he was pleased with
his staff officer's testimony. It certainly did the captain no favors with Scott
and his supporters that Pillow saw fit to cite Hooker's testimony multiple
times as vindicating his take on matters.[40]

To Pillow's—and Polk's—satisfaction, the general who conquered Mexico City would not be a threat to the Democratic ambitions of holding the
Executive Mansion after 1848. Four years later Scott would get a turn as the
Whig candidate for president, but by that point the party was falling apart,
with the general destined to be its last presidential candidate. The Whig
Party's problems, which included the emerging issue of slavery's future in
the western territories, and Scott's shortcomings as a candidate (his image
as Old Fuss and Feathers was a decided obstacle to his ability to effectively
appeal to the American electorate), combined to produce the general's defeat at the hands of Franklin Pierce.[41]

Thus, Scott's focus returned to his duties as commanding general of the
army, which Hooker, tarred by his association with Pillow, could not have
looked at as a good thing. In 1849 Hooker had been ordered to California
and assumed the position of adjutant general of the Pacific Division. That
same year, however, would see the appearance of one of the first significant
histories of the war by Capt. Roswell Ripley, who had also been a member of
Pillow's staff. Not surprisingly, given that Pillow closely supervised Ripley's
efforts (and even may have written part of the book himself), its take on
events was in line with his and not Scott's viewpoint. This prompted Isaac
Stevens, who had served on Scott's staff, to publish his own work two years
later to refute Ripley's arguments. Meanwhile, Hooker began looking for
opportunities beyond the army (in part because the costs of living in California made survival on an officer's salary difficult), acquiring a ranch near
Sonoma and engaging in several business ventures. Finally, in February
1853 Hooker decided that the time had come to leave the army. This was
prodded in part by a bitter court-martial over his handling of contracts.
Though found not guilty by the court, the episode further sowed seeds of
conflict between Hooker and Scott loyalists among the army's West Point–
educated officers. Two of his principal antagonists were Lieutenant Colonel
Ethan Allen Hitchcock, who had been a member of Scott's staff in Mexico
and a fierce defender of his chief in the Pillow court of inquiry, and Captain

Henry W. Halleck, a fellow admirer of Scott who served as chief prosecutor in the case. After leaving the army, Hooker would remain in California until the outbreak of rebellion in 1861.[42]

During the American Civil War, few generals would "play games" with more vim and vigor than "Fighting Joe" Hooker. He arrived in Washington during the summer of 1861 just as Union forces were preparing for offensive operations against Confederate forces at Manassas Junction. Lacking a formal appointment, Hooker accompanied Washington notables who followed the Union advance into northern Virginia and witnessed its defeat at First Manassas. Not surprisingly, many in the army, not least Scott and George B. McClellan, believed the defeat was the result of politicians in Washington, ignorant of military affairs, pushing for a campaign before Union volunteer forces had received sufficient training, discipline, and professional leadership. Hooker offered a different take, one more appealing to the administration and its allies. The problem was not, as he saw it, that bellicose politicians had demanded a fight in 1861, but that the men in uniform had failed. Shortly after First Manassas, Hooker managed to secure a personal meeting with President Lincoln and wasted little time tearing down others, declaring, "I was at the battle of Bull Run the other day, and it is no vanity in me to say I am a damned sight better general than you had on that field."[43]

In the weeks that followed, Lincoln placed Hooker's name on a list of eleven officers submitted to the U.S. Senate for a brigadier general's commission; by the end of 1861, Hooker commanded a division in the Army of the Potomac. Then, in March 1862 that army's divisions were organized into corps, with Lincoln appointing corps commanders who were friendlier to Republicans in Washington than to the army's commander, McClellan. Hooker found his division assigned to the Third Corps. Its commander, Samuel P. Heintzelman, had graduated from West Point in 1826—the same year McClellan was born—and by March 1862 had come to share the resentment of Republicans in Washington toward McClellan's habit of keeping decisions about organization and operations close to his vest and giving preference to general officers like Fitz John Porter and William B. Franklin. This was not just because McClellan and his coterie were younger and had less experience in uniform than their military critics. By early 1862, a suspicion had begun to take hold among politicians in Washington and officers who were outside McClellan's inner circle that the Army of the Potomac commander and those around him had taken too much to heart the methodical engineering mentality—echoing Polk's critique of Scott's "rather scientific and visionary" views—that West Point had sought to cultivate and consequently had insufficient appreciation for the virtues of "fighting generals." In making officers with a jaundiced view of the army commander (but having good relationships with Washington politicians) McClellan's principal subordinates, Lincoln to a certain extent was following Polk's precedent. By doing so, he made a major contribution to the development of friction within the Army of the Potomac's high command and provided encouragement to those with a beef with their commanding officer to seek an audience for their complaints, creating an optimal climate for Hooker to "play games."[44]

Heintzelman's frustration with McClellan only grew as the army advanced to the environs of Richmond in 1862—and it came to be shared by his subordinates. At Yorktown Heintzelman bristled at efforts by McClellan to work around the corps organization and ensure that the greatest responsibilities (and opportunities for laurels) went to younger division commanders like Porter, Franklin, and William F. Smith. Then came the May 1862 battle at Williamsburg. Hooker's division bore the heaviest combat, but "Little Mac" extolled the efforts of Winfield Scott Hancock in his initial report. As McClellan learned more about the battle, he endeavored to correct this, but Hooker was enraged and took up his pen to fume to friendly senators and other political associates about what he complained was the commanding general's "determination to award merit only to favorites." So too did Philip Kearny, the other division commander in the Third Corps, a non–West Pointer who like Heintzelman brought to his duties greater experience in the field than McClellan and who like Hooker possessed an aggressiveness and taste for combat that seemed conspicuously lacking in McClellan and his favorites, whom Kearny disdained. By the time the grand campaign against Richmond came to a desultory close that summer, the hard-fighting Third Corps had become a bastion of anti-McClellan sentiment within the Army of the Potomac.[45]

Hooker's emergence as one of the eastern army's leading generals was mainly due to his excellent performances as a division commander. It was also a consequence of the fact that he embraced, encouraged, and benefited from a critique of McClellan and other West Point–educated officers that emerged in the North in 1862 and enjoyed particular resonance among Republicans. McClellan and his fellow travelers were, the critique held, a drag on the army and an obstacle to its success. In their "idea of what an army ought to be," as Hooker put it, they placed too much emphasis on "strategy," a methodical approach to war that emphasized logistics, engineering, and fortifications. Consequently, they failed to adequately appreciate the virtues of aggressive operations and combat. "General McClellan," Lincoln at one point complained, "thinks he is going to whip the rebels by strategy; and the army has got the same notion. They have no idea that the war is to be carried on and put through by hard, tough fighting. . . . [N]o headway is going to be made while this delusion lasts." The president continued, "The army has not settled down into the conviction that we are in a terrible war that has got to be fought out—no; and the officers haven't either. . . . General McClellan is responsible for the delusion that is untoning the whole army—that the South is to be conquered by strategy."[46] After John Pope's defeat with his Army of Virginia at Second Manassas, no officer in the eastern theater would work more assiduously or effectively than Hooker to convince McClellan's critics in Washington that he was the man to reverse the "untoning" of the Army of the Potomac and inject into the Union war effort in the East the sort of spirit they thought Little Mac lacked.

After a strong performance during the Second Manassas Campaign, Hooker further burnished his reputation as a general with a taste for hard fighting in Maryland, driving the Confederates from high ground around Turner's Gap in South Mountain and spearheading the Union attack at Antietam on September 17, 1864. Yet just as his command had driven the Confederates from their positions defending the Miller Cornfield, East Woods, and Dunker Church, the general fell wounded. Shortly thereafter, he made a beeline for Washington and undertook a campaign to cultivate support within the administration and on Capitol Hill by presenting himself as the pro-emancipation, hard-fighting alternative to McClellan that the North needed. Hooker's game playing was aided by the fact that a correspondent from the *New York Tribune* accompanied his staff at Antietam and ensured that the general's aggressive performance received plenty of attention in initial accounts of the battle. Before long, Hooker's ambition, opportunism, and eagerness to please Washington Republicans had become a subject of commentary in the letters of other officers. A few weeks after Antietam, George G. Meade, a division commander under Hooker in Maryland, detected the shadow of events of the 1840s in Fighting Joe's endeavors. Hooker, he noted in a letter, "injured himself in Mexico by attaching himself to Pillow and his clique. . . . Now he is made, and his only danger is the fear that he will allow himself to be used by McClellan's enemies. . . . Hooker is a Democrat and anti-Abolitionist—that is to say he was. What he will be when command of the army is held out to him is more than any one can tell."[47]

Hooker, however, was unable to recover from his wounds before Burnside was chosen as McClellan's successor, with one of Burnside's motives in accepting the command being to ensure Hooker would not get the position. Throughout Burnside's time in command, Hooker, as commander of one of the army's three "grand divisions," confirmed Burnside's reservations about his ambitious, game-playing subordinate. Hooker persistently and openly questioned his commander's competence and second-guessed his plans, with one officer who observed his behavior at Fredericksburg proclaiming his conduct "ungentlemanly if not unpatriotic." When he appeared before friendly members of Congress after the battle, Hooker justified his unwillingness to execute Burnside's orders to continue what had become fruitless attacks on the Confederate position by acidly declaring, "I felt I had lost all the men my orders required."[48]

Instead of being punished for "playing games," Hooker was rewarded by selection as Burnside's replacement. Hooker did a remarkable job restoring the army's morale and fitness in early 1863, which led him to declare to an interviewer after the war, "I did some handsome things for the country . . . but I never did my country better service than when I reorganized the Army of the Potomac during the winter of 1862-3." He also pleased Washington politicians by favoring and heavily relying on the counsel of non–West Point graduates Daniel Butterfield and Daniel Sickles. Sickles's appointment as commander of the Third Corps and subsequent service as a Hooker stalwart and thorn in Meade's side after the latter, a West Point–educated officer in the methodical McClellan mold, succeeded Hooker as commander of the Army of the Potomac further cemented that corps's distinctive place within the army.[49] Hooker's choice of allies, however, aroused suspicion among generals with backgrounds in the regular army that McClellan, like Scott in Mexico, had been a victim of antiarmy politicians and a game-playing general. After the Union defeat at Chancellorsville (May 1–4, 1863), they decided to employ Hooker's own methods against him, undermining his authority and scheming for his replacement. Finally, after a dispute with General in Chief Henry W. Halleck, Hooker was removed from command of the Army of the Potomac in June 1863.[50]

That Halleck and Hooker would clash surprised no one. Like McClellan and other officers Hooker tangled with, Halleck was a product of the post-1815 push for military professionalization and was viewed as one of its outstanding products, with his contributions to antebellum military literature (Lincoln was among their readers) winning him the nickname "Old Brains." Both Scott and Dennis Hart Mahan, the dominant figure at West Point during the decades before the Civil War, supported his rapid rise early in the conflict and appointment as general in chief in 1861–62.[51] Making matters worse for Hooker, as previously noted, he and Halleck had crossed paths in California during the 1850s, a time when Halleck thrived as a lawyer and businessman, while Hooker struggled financially and personally. Service as prosecutor on Hooker's court-martial there was but one of several events that led Halleck to develop a personal "grudge," in the words of his biographer John F. Marszalek, "against Joseph Hooker. . . . Hooker owed him money and more generally because he disapproved of Hooker's reputation for drinking too much and carousing with loose women." Their relationship was so poor that, on his appointment to command in January 1863, Hooker received authorization from Lincoln to bypass Halleck and communicate with him directly—the president explicitly revoked it after Chancellorsville. Soon thereafter, Halleck provoked a confrontation over control of the Union garrison at Harpers Ferry, Virginia, that resulted in Hooker submitting his resignation as commander of the Army of the Potomac, which Halleck happily persuaded Lincoln to accept.[52]

Later that year Hooker was given an opportunity to redeem himself in the West. Unfortunately, he brought his penchant for Pillowesque backbiting and game playing with him, leading one man to describe him as possessing "an unfortunate state of mind for one who has to co-operate . . . faultfinding, criticizing, dissatisfied." A bitter relationship with Major General William T. Sherman resulted in the final blow being delivered to Fighting Joe's career in the field. With the Union army at the outskirts of Atlanta, Sherman shed no tears when Hooker, insulted by his decision to choose another officer for a position the latter believed (with some justice) his performance merited, angrily asked for "removal from an army in which rank and service are ignored." Sherman frankly declared years later, "I did feel a sense of relief when he left."[53]

As was the case with Halleck, that Hooker would become an enemy of Sherman, in light of the attitude fostered by his experiences in Mexico, was not surprising. Sherman was a protégé of Halleck's who shared his mentor's and Scott's commitment to their military professional vision. Despite being the foster son, son-in-law, and brother of prominent members of the U.S. Senate, Sherman was intensely suspicious of politicians and bitterly resented intrusions by them into matters he believed were the proper responsibility of professional officers. Like Scott, Halleck, and McClellan, he had a decided preference for West Point–educated products of the regular army who followed the professionalist ethos and was suspicious of officers drawn from civilian life who might carry with them a willingness to play Pillowesque political games, as was evident when he selected Oliver O. Howard to take James B. McPherson's place as commander of the Army of the Tennessee instead of Hooker or political general John Logan. After the war Sherman would serve as commanding general of the Army from 1869 to 1883, during which his commitment to furthering the development of the army in the direction Scott had laid out after 1815 (and was evident in McClellan's and Halleck's efforts during their time in that office) was evident in his traveling overseas to study the organization of European armies and how they developed their officers, sponsoring Emory Upton's labors, and establishing the School of Application for Infantry and Cavalry at Fort Leavenworth, Kansas. During those same years, an embittered Logan returned to politics and argued for the Jackson-Polk-Pillow tradition of the citizen-soldier and political general in his 1887 work, *The Volunteer Soldier of America*, which historian Russell Weigley describes as "a 700-page diatribe against the undemocratic exclusiveness of the Regular Army and its West Pointers, calling for military reliance on a citizen army and the native military genius of American citizens in the tradition of Andrew Jackson."[54]

When he appointed Hooker commander of the Army of the Potomac in January 1863, Lincoln deemed it necessary to write him a personal letter that "in later years," writes historian Mark E. Neely Jr., "became quite famous," with historians from T. Harry Williams to James McPherson to Matthew Moten lauding it as, in Williams's words, "one of the best of his war letters."[55] The president advised the general that it was not for his willingness to play games that he was receiving the command, but despite it. He also warned, "I fear the spirit which you have aided to infuse into the Army, of criticizing their Commander, and withholding confidence from him, will now turn upon you." Hooker had certainly helped infuse "the spirit" into the army, and after Chancellorsville, it certainly did turn upon him. Yet Lincoln—not least by seeming to reward Hooker in January 1863 for his behavior—had done much to infuse it as well. Moreover, in declaring that he believed the general "did not mix politics with your profession," Lincoln was far from correct.[56] The "spirit" he lamented was a consequence of the fact that leaders of the Union army—in part because the Civil War, like all wars, was an extension of policy—could not avoid mixing politics with their profession. The army was an inherently political organization, organized for a political purpose, and thus invariably shaped by both partisan and what in later years would be referred to as bureaucratic politics. Thanks in large part to the tensions between the attitudes toward military affairs held by the professionalized officer corps and those held by significant segments of the larger American society it has served, "the spirit," as Hooker saw vividly in Mexico, Virginia, and Georgia, was there all along.

NOTES

1. General Orders No. 8, Jan. 23, 1863, *The War of the Rebellion: A Compilation of the Official Records of the Union and Confederate Armies*, 70 vols. in 128 pts. (Washington, DC: Government Printing Office, 1880–1901), ser. 1, 21:998–99 (hereafter cited as *OR*, all references to ser. 1 unless otherwise stated).

2. In his essay, which appeared two years after he stepped down as deputy assistant secretary of defense for international security, Morton Halperin (whose work earned him a place on Richard Nixon's "enemies list") emphasized the ability of organizations in the national security world to instill in their members perspectives on matters that reflect, among other things, an organization's desire for autonomy in the execution of its responsibilities, its desire to maintain and exercise influence, and its notion of what its essential roles and missions are—all of which they sincerely believe are critical to the nation's security interests. This can, he noted, lead officials to approach issues on an assumption that "since, in general, I know how to protect the nation's security interests, whatever increases my influence is in the national interest." Halperin, "Why Bureaucrats Play Games," *Foreign Policy* (Spring 1971): 70–90 (quote, 73).

3. John Gibbon, *Personal Recollections of the Civil War* (New York: G. P. Putnam's Sons, 1928), 107; John F. Marszalek, David S. Nolen, and Louis P. Gallo, ed., *The Personal Memoirs of Ulysses S. Grant: The Complete Annotated Edition* (Cambridge, MA: Harvard University Press, 2017), 754.

4. Hooker to Bates, Apr. 2, 1877, Box 3, Samuel Penniman Bates Collection, 1875–79, Pennsylvania Historical and Museum Commission, Harrisburg.

5. David H. Petraeus, "Lessons of History and Lessons of Vietnam," *Parameters: The US Army War College Quarterly* 15 (1988): 43–44.

6. In his effort to link the experiences of officers in Mexico with their endeavors during the Civil War, Kevin Dougherty provides a brief chapter on Hooker that connects lessons learned while serving on staffs in Mexico to his effectiveness in restoring the Army of the Potomac's administrative rigor in 1863. Dougherty, *Civil War Leadership and Mexican War Experience* (Jackson: University of Mississippi, 2007), 91–95.

7. McClellan to Scott, May 7, 9, 1862, in *The Civil War Papers of George B. McClellan: Selected Correspondence, 1860–1865*, ed. Stephen W. Sears (New York: Ticknor and Fields, 1989), 16, 17; Meade to his wife, Apr. 24, 1864, in *The Life and Letters of George Gordon Meade, Major-General United States Army*, ed. George Gordon Meade, 2 vols. (New York: Charles Scribner's Sons, 1913), 2:191.

8. Quoted in William E. Gienapp, "Politics Seem to Enter into Everything: Political Culture in the North, 1840–1860," in *Essays on American Antebellum Politics, 1840–1860*, ed. Stephen E. Maizlish and John J. Kushma (College Station: Texas A&M University Press, 1982), 39.

9. William B. Skelton, *An American Profession of Arms: The Army Officer Corps, 1784–1861* (Lawrence: University Press of Kansas, 1992), 283–85.

10. Ibid., 287–96.

11. Carl von Clausewitz, *On War*, trans. and ed. Michael Howard and Peter Paret (1832; Princeton, NJ: Princeton University Press, 1984), 81, 87.

12. Walter H. Hebert, *Fighting Joe Hooker* (1944; repr., Lincoln: University of Nebraska Press, 1999), 17–24; Jack L. Ballard, "General Joseph Hooker: A New Biography" (Ph.D. diss., Kent State University, 1994), 1, 4–16; Samuel J. Watson, "Army Officers Fight the 'Patriot War': Reactions to Filibustering on the Canadian Border, 1837–1839," *Journal of the Early Republic* 18 (Fall 1998): 485–519.

13. William F. G. Shanks, *Personal Recollections of Distinguished Generals* (New York: Harper and Brothers, 1866), 167.

14. Herbert, *Fighting Joe Hooker*, 25–26; Ballard, "General Joseph Hooker," 18–20; Felice Flanery Lewis, *Trailing Clouds of Glory: Zachary Taylor's Mexican War Campaign and His Emerging Civil War Leaders* (Tuscaloosa: University of Alabama Press, 2010), 92, 119. Now going by the name Ulysses S. Grant due to a paperwork error, Lieutenant Grant served in Hamer's command in Mexico and would deeply lament the general's death in December 1846. Marszalek, Nolen, and Gallo, *Personal Memoirs of Ulysses S. Grant*, 1:67–68.

15. Lewis, *Trailing Clouds of Glory*, 128–57.

16. Ballard, "General Joseph Hooker," 23–28.

17. Lewis, *Trailing Clouds of Glory*, 150; Hebert, *Fighting Joe Hooker*, 26–29; Ballard, "General Joseph Hooker," 29–35.

18. Nathaniel Cheairs Hughes Jr. and Roy P. Stonesifer Jr., *The Life and Wars of Gideon J. Pillow* (Chapel Hill: University of North Carolina Press, 1993), 4–5, 9, 22–28.

19. Marszalek, Nolen, and Gallo, *Personal Memoirs of Ulysses S. Grant*, 1:23–24. For excellent accounts of Scott's life prior to the war with Mexico that effectively chronicle his efforts to shape the army, see Timothy D. Johnson, *Winfield Scott: The Quest for Military*

Glory (Lawrence: University Press of Kansas, 1998), 7–148; and Allan Peskin, *Winfield Scott and the Profession of Arms* (Kent, OH: Kent State University Press, 2003), 1–131.

20. James K. Polk, "First Annual Message," Dec. 2, 1845, in James Richardson, *A Compilation of the Messages and Papers of the Presidents,* 11 vols. (Washington, DC: Government Printing Office, 1904), 4(3):413.

21. Richard Bruce Winders, *Mr. Polk's Army: The American Military Experience in the Mexican War* (College Station: Texas A&M Press, 1997), 37.

22. Allan Nevins, ed., *Polk: The Diary of a President, 1845–1849* (New York: Longmans, Green, 1929), 93 (May 14, 1846).

23. McClellan to Sturgeon, Oct. 20, 1847, in *The Mexican War Diary and Correspondence of George B. McClellan,* ed. Thomas Cutrer (Baton Rouge: Louisiana State University Press, 2009), 136.

24. Shanks, *Personal Recollections of Distinguished Generals,* 167.

25. Hebert, *Fighting Joe Hooker,* 29. The role and uses of a staff in the Civil War is a subject that merits more attention, though there is much of value in R. Steven Jones, *The Right Hand of Command: Use and Disuse of Personal Staffs in the Civil War* (Mechanicsburg, PA: Stackpole Books, 2000). For an interesting discussion of how one Civil War general used members of his staff in ways that had parallels with the Prusso-German approach, see Richard L. DiNardo, "Southern by the Grace of God but Prussian by Common Sense: James Longstreet and the Exercise of Command in the U.S. Civil War," *Journal of Military History* 66 (Oct. 2002): 1011–32.

26. Scott to Marcy, Aug. 19, 1847, in *Message from the President of the United States to the Two Houses of Congress at the Commencement of the First Session of the Thirtieth Congress, January 8, 1848, Executive Document 8* (Washington, DC: Wendell and Van Benthuysen, 1848), 303–4; Timothy D. Johnson, *A Gallant Little Army: The Mexico City Campaign* (Lawrence: University Press of Kansas, 2007), 160–62; Pillow to Scott, Aug. 24, 1847, *Message from the President,* 334; Smith to Scott, Aug. 27, 1847, ibid., 350; Hooker testimony, Apr. 11, 1848, in "Senate No. 65: Proceedings of the Two Courts of Inquiry in the case of Gideon Pillow," in *Executive Documents Printed by Order of the Senate of the United States during the First Session of the Thirtieth Congress . . . ,* vol. 8 (Washington, DC: Wendell and Van Benthuysen, 1847), 162 (hereafter cited as "Senate No. 65").

27. Allan Peskin, ed., *Volunteers: The Mexican War Journals of Private Richard Coulter and Sergeant Thomas Barclay, Company E, Second Pennsylvania Infantry* (Kent, OH: Kent State University Press, 1991), 142–43; Hooker testimony, Apr. 11, 1848, in "Senate No. 65," 162; Scott to Marcy, Aug. 19, 1847, in *Message from the President,* 305; Johnson, *Gallant Little Army,* 162–63.

28. Johnson, *Gallant Little Army,* 163–68; Hooker testimony, Apr. 11, 1848, in "Senate No. 65," 162–63.

29. Pillow to Scott, Aug. 24, 1847, in *Message from the President,* 335; George W. Kendall, *Dispatches from the Mexican War,* ed. Lawrence Delbert Cress (Norman: University of Oklahoma Press, 1999), 329; Johnson, *Gallant Little Army,* 170–76; Hooker testimony, Apr. 11, 1847, in "Senate No. 65," 162–63, 165, 167.

30. Scott to Marcy, Aug. 28, 1847, in *Message from the President*, 308–9, 311; Pillow to Scott, Aug. 24, 1847, ibid., 338, 340; Hebert, *Fighting Joe Hooker*, 31–32; Ballard, "General Joseph Hooker," 45–49; Hooker testimony, Apr. 11, 1847, in "Senate No. 65," 168.

31. Peskin, *Volunteers*, 165; Scott to Marcy, Sept. 18, 1847, in *Message from the President*, 377.

32. Hebert, *Fighting Joe Hooker*, 32–33; Ballard, "General Joseph Hooker," 55–59.

33. Scott to Marcy, Sept. 18, 1847, in *Message from the President*, 380; Pillow to Scott, Sept. 18, 1847, ibid., 407.

34. Peskin, *Winfield Scott and the Profession of Arms*, 191.

35. *Bugle Notes: The Handbook of the United States Corps of Cadets* (West Point, NY: U.S. Military Academy, 1929), 24.

36. "Leonidas" to Editors, *New Orleans Daily Delta*, Aug. 27, 1847, in "Senate No. 65," 388.

37. Peskin, *Winfield Scott and the Profession of Arms*, 198–99.

38. Pillow to Polk, Nov. 2, 4, 1847, quoted in Hughes and Stonesifer, *Life and Wars of Gideon Pillow*, 116.

39. Pillow's "conduct has been of the most unblushing character," 1838 West Point graduate Theodore Laidley, speaking for many others who shared his background, declared. "Direct falsehood can too easily be proved on him. The Army generally is with Genl. Scott." Laidley to My dear Father, Mar. 22, 1848, in *"Surrounded by Dangers of All Kinds": The Mexican War Letters of Lieutenant Theodore Laidley*, ed. James M. McCaffrey (Denton: University of North Texas Press, 1997), 151.

40. *Defence of Major Gen. Pillow before the Court of Inquiry at Frederick, Maryland, against the Charges Preferred against Him by Maj. Gen. Winfield Scott* (N.p., June 1848), 7, 9, 14, 28–29, 35, 51; Ballard, "General Joseph Hooker," 70–71.

41. Johnson, *Winfield Scott*, 213–17; Michael Holt, *The Rise and Fall of the American Whig Party: Jacksonian Politics and the Onset of the Civil War* (New York: Oxford University Press, 1999), 681–92, 695–762.

42. Hughes and Stonesifer, *Life and Wars of Gideon Pillow*, 122–23; R. S. Ripley, *The War with Mexico*, 2 vols. (New York: Harper and Brothers, 1849); Robert W. Johannsen, *To the Halls of the Montezumas: The Mexican War in the American Imagination* (New York: Oxford University Press, 1985), 253–55; Ballard, "General Joseph Hooker," 101–49.

43. Shanks, *Personal Recollections of Distinguished Generals*, 182–83.

44. Hebert, *Fighting Joe Hooker*, 50–54, 72. Indeed, on learning of his elevation to corps command, Heintzelman expressed as much gratification at seeing others denied corps command as he did with his own appointment. Samuel P. Heintzelman Diary, Mar. 7, 8, 1862, Samuel Peter Heintzelman Papers, Manuscript Division, Library of Congress, Washington, DC (hereafter cited as LC), reel 7; Jerry Thompson, *Civil War to the Bloody End: The Life & Times of Major General Samuel P. Heintzelman* (College Station: Texas A&M Press, 2006), 3–9, 146–47, 150–51.

45. Hooker to Ten Eyck, May 16, 1862, Schoff Collection, University of Michigan, Ann Arbor; Hooker to Nesmith, July 11, 1862, James Nesmith Papers, Oregon Historical Society,

Portland; Stephen R. Taaffe, *Commanding the Army of the Potomac* (Lawrence: University Press of Kansas, 2006), 19–21.

46. Hooker interview, *Brooklyn Eagle*, n.d., newspaper clipping, Ezra Ayers Carman Papers, LC; Mary A. Livermore, *My Story of the War: A Woman's Narrative of Four Years Personal Experience as Nurse in the Union Army, and in Relief Work at Home, . . . during the War of the Rebellion . . .* (Hartford, CT: A. D. Worthington, 1888), 556–57, 558; Mark E. Neely Jr. *The Union Divided: Party Conflict in the Civil War North* (Cambridge, MA: Harvard University Press, 2002), 66–89.

47. Ballard, "General Joe Hooker," 671–93; George W. Smalley, *Anglo-American Memories* (New York: G. P. Putnam's Sons, 1911), 141–50; Meade to his wife, Oct. 12, 1862, in Meade, *Life and Letters*, 2:319.

48. Herbert M. Schiller, ed., *Autobiography of Major General William F. Smith, 1861–1864* (Dayton, OH: Morningside, 1990), 60, 64; George C. Rable, *Fredericksburg! Fredericksburg!* (Chapel Hill: University of North Carolina Press, 2002), 256; Hooker testimony, Dec. 20, 1862, Joint Committee on the Conduct of the War (1863), 1:668, 670.

49. "Fighting Joe Hooker: He Fights the Battle of Chancellorsville over Again," *San Francisco Chronicle*, May 23, 1872. For an outstanding examination of the dynamics within the Army of the Potomac under Hooker, see John J. Hennessy, "We Shall Make Richmond Howl: The Army of the Potomac on the Eve of Chancellorsville," in *The Chancellorsville Campaign: The Battle and Its Aftermath*, ed. Gary W. Gallagher (Chapel Hill: University of North Carolina Press, 1996), 1–35.

50. Ethan S. Rafuse, "'The Spirit Which You Have Aided to Infuse': A. Lincoln, Little Mac, Fighting Joe, and the Question of Accountability in Union Command Relations," *Journal of the Abraham Lincoln Association* 38 (Summer 2017): 32–38; Stephen W. Sears, *Lincoln's Lieutenants: The High Command of the Army of the Potomac* (New York: Houghton Mifflin, 2017): 520–24, 538–41.

51. Mahan to Chase, Oct. 22, 1861, Salmon P. Chase Papers, LC, reel 15; Russell F. Weigley, *The American Way of War: A History of United States Military Strategy and Policy* (New York: Macmillan, 1973), 82–87; John F. Marszalek, *Commander of All Lincoln's Armies: A Life of General Henry W. Halleck* (Cambridge, MA: Harvard University Press, 2004), 22–27, 34–46, 107; Ian C. Hope, *A Scientific Way of War: Antebellum Military Science, West Point, and the Origins of American Military Thought* (Lincoln: University of Nebraska Press, 2015), 184–90.

52. Marszalek, *Commander of All Lincoln's Armies*, 95, 165–66, 173–75; Rafuse, "Spirit Which You Have Aided," 31–32, 37–38.

53. Dana to Stanton, Oct. 27, 1863, *OR*, 31(1):72; Hooker to Whipple, July 27, 1862, *OR*, 38(5):273; William T. Sherman, *Memoirs of General William T. Sherman*, 2 vols. (1875; repr., New York: Da Capo, 1984), 2:86.

54. Mark R. Grandstaff, "Preserving the Habits and Usages of War: William T. Sherman, Professional Reform, and the U.S. Army Officer Corps, 1861–1881," *Journal of Military History* 62 (July 1998): 521–37; Russell F. Weigley, *History of the United States Army* (New York: Macmillan, 1967), 270–71.

55. Mark E. Neely Jr., "Wilderness and the Cult of Manliness: Hooker, Lincoln, and Defeat," in *Lincoln's Generals*, ed. Gabor S. Boritt (New York: Oxford University Press, 1994), 55; James M. McPherson, *Tried by War: Abraham Lincoln as Commander in Chief* (New York: Penguin, 2008), 163–64; Matthew Moten, *Presidents & Their Generals: An American History of Command in War* (Cambridge, MA: Harvard University Press, 2014), 124–26; T. Harry Williams, *Lincoln and His Generals* (New York: Alfred A. Knopf, 1952), 212–13.

56. Lincoln to Hooker, Jan. 26, 1863, in *The Collected Works of Abraham Lincoln*, ed. Roy P. Basler et al., 9 vols. (New Brunswick, NJ: Rutgers University Press, 1953–55), 6:78–79.

A STEPPING STONE TO SOME FUTURE AND GREATER WAR

George B. McClellan's Mexican War Apprenticeship

THOMAS W. CUTRER

George Brinton McClellan, among the foremost of the junior officers who won their spurs in Mexico, was destined to lead one of the most distinguished public lives of his era: as chief engineer of the Illinois Central Railroad, as commander of the Army of the Potomac and general in chief of the U.S. Army, as president of the Ohio and Mississippi Railroad, as governor of New Jersey, and as the Democratic candidate for president of the United States in 1864, winning 45 percent of the popular vote against Abraham Lincoln. McClellan was born in Philadelphia, Pennsylvania, on December 3, 1826, the son of a highly distinguished physician, George McClellan, and his socially prominent wife, Elizabeth Steinmetz (Brinton) McClellan. After attending the University of Pennsylvania, he entered the U.S. Military Academy at West Point on July 1, 1842, and was graduated, at the age of twenty, second in the class of 1846. Among his classmates were no fewer than seventeen cadets who were to become general grade officers in the northern and southern armies during the Civil War: Jesse Lee Reno, Darius Nash Couch, Samuel Davis Sturgis, George Stoneman Jr., Dabney Herndon Maury, David Rumph Jones, Cadmus Marcellus Wilcox, Samuel Bell Maxey, and the redoubtable Thomas Jonathan Jackson; George Edward Pickett was the class "goat," graduating in fifty-ninth place.[1]

To the rigorous education that the cadets received at West Point Major General Winfield Scott, general in chief of the U.S. Army and commander of the force that was to capture Mexico City, attributed his army's success.

"I give it as my fixed opinion that but for our graduated cadets the war between the United States and Mexico might, and probably would, have lasted some four or five years, with, in its first half, more defeats than victories falling to our share."[2]

Already in 1846–48, one may clearly see in the newly commissioned McClellan the talent, the ambition, and the arrogance that characterized the engineer, businessman, soldier, and politician he was to become. He was indefatigable in planning and organization, superbly intelligent, and able to draw to him close personal loyalties. His was also a character contemptuous of those of lesser talents than his own, quick to see conspiracies where none existed, and ready to place upon others the blame for his own shortcomings and to take credit for actions performed by others.

McClellan was also guilty of a social snobbery that later manifested itself in his reference to the baseborn Lincoln as "the original gorilla" and in his breathtaking snub of his commander in chief when, on November 13, 1861, the young general sent his porter to inform him that he was not receiving guests when the president and the secretary of war called at his home.[3] In Mexico he was also "perfectly disgusted" to find himself outranked by older volunteer officers, "a soldier of yesterday, a miserable thing with buttons on it," in the new lieutenant's estimation. To caption a sardonically humorous sketch that he made in his wartime diary in Mexico, McClellan wrote, "*M. le President a fait ce que le bon Dieu ne peut pas*" (the President has done what the Lord did not) in regard to making a general of Gideon J. Pillow.

McClellan's well-known ambition might best be illustrated by a diary entry, written while at the Rio Grande during his first weeks with the army in 1846. "I came down here with high hopes," he wrote, "with pleasing anticipations of distinction, of being in hard fought battles and acquiring a name and reputation as a stepping stone to a still greater eminence in some future and greater war." He found not only distinction and promotion but also bitter frustration with superiors who did not measure up to his standard of excellence. And the energetic officer was introduced to the methodical plodding of a military establishment too slow for his mercurial temperament.[4]

With the outbreak of fighting along the Rio Grande in May 1846, Cadet McClellan wrote to his sister, Frederica M. English: "Hip! Hip! Hurrah! War at last sure enough! Ain't it glorious! . . . Well it appears that our wishes have at last been gratified and that we shall soon have the intense satisfaction of fighting the crowd—musquitos and Mexicans. . . . You have no idea in what a state of excitement we have been here [at West Point]."[5]

Upon receiving his commission as a brevet second lieutenant of engineers, McClellan was granted a furlough to be spent in Philadelphia. Having been there but a few days, however, he received orders to return to West Point to assist in the organization and training of what was to become Company A, Engineer Troops, the first unit of enlisted sappers and miners in the U.S. Army.[6] McClellan was to be the junior of the three officers to lead the company, with Alexander J. Swift as its captain and his friend Gustavus W. Smith its first lieutenant. Assignment to this unit was "all that I could hope, ask, or expect," McClellan wrote to his sister; "it is exactly what I desired."[7]

The company was first assigned to Brigadier General Zachary Taylor's army at Matamoros. Following the indecisive Battle of Monterrey in September 1846, however, the Polk administration determined that further operations in northern Mexico would be of no use in bringing the war to an end and authorized Major General Winfield Scott—next to Andrew Jackson the great hero of the War of 1812—to make a landing at Vera Cruz on the Gulf coast and from there to march to Mexico City. To compose his army, Scott drew heavily on Taylor's command, with those units selected to join the expedition, including Company A of the Engineer Troops, ordered to march to a staging area at Tampico.

Excellent as his education at West Point had been, the second half of McClellan's preparation as a soldier began under Scott, who would introduce him to the practical arts of strategy and tactics. So great was Scott's influence that at the beginning of the Civil War, McClellan referred to him as "the general under whom I learned my first lessons in war."[8] His Mexico City Campaign was cautiously executed but eminently successful, outflanking Mexican defenders when possible and keeping casualties at a minimum; McClellan would follow his example in Virginia and Maryland, although with less satisfactory results. Scott's landing below Vera Cruz on March 9, 1847, according to a correspondent for the *New Orleans Bulletin*, was "accomplished in a manner that reflects the highest credit on all concerned; and the regularity, precision, and promptness with which it was effected has probably not been surpassed, if it has been equaled, in modern warfare."[9]

When Scott's army splashed ashore, the engineer company was among the first to land, with McClellan in the van.[10] It conducted reconnaissance to determine the best position for Scott's siege lines, began to excavate trenches and earthworks, and placed the heavy batteries with which to reduce the Mexican stronghold. As Lieutenant Colonel Ethan Allen Hitchcock, Scott's inspector general, observed, under the supervision of the engineers, "everything has proceeded according to known rules of the Art of War." But a strong sense of urgency impelled Scott's army, for the dreaded yellow-fever season was only a few weeks away, making the reduction of the city and its castle and a move to higher ground inland imperative before the onset of the deadly *vomito*.[11]

By the afternoon of March 22, the army's mortars and a battery of naval ordnance were trained on the enemy defenses, and Scott demanded the city's capitulation. General Juan Morales, the commander of the Mexican army in Vera Cruz, rejected his terms. Within half an hour, the American artillery began to knock the city's walls into rubble. For two days the garrison and citizens of Vera Cruz withstood the terrible bombardment while Scott's lines crept closer. The end of the twenty-day operation came on March 29. "When the white flag was shown," McClellan's classmate Second Lieutenant Maury recalled, "we were overjoyed and greatly comforted." An important victory had been obtained at very slight cost in blood.[12]

Scott's chief engineer, Colonel Joseph G. Totten, was rightfully proud of Company A's contribution to the American cause during the siege, writing of "the highly meritorious deportment and valuable services of the sappers and miners."[13] Moreover, he reported to Secretary of War William L. Marcy, "the great exertions and services" of the company had been "animated by, and emulating the zeal and devotion of its excellent officers, Lieutenants Smith, McClellan, and Foster."[14] Nevertheless, McClellan felt that he had not received the credit he was due.

Foreshadowing his behavior in later years, McClellan's exaggerated sense of self-worth was piqued when, following the Mexican surrender, the commanding general failed to continue to sing his praises. During the siege, "we were needed and remembered," he wrote in a characteristic fit of overweening ego, but "the instant the pressing necessity passed away we were forgotten," and Scott did not recall that "such a thing existed as an Engineer Company."[15]

Even so, fourteen years later as commander of the Army of the Potomac, when confronted with the fortified city of Yorktown on the Virginia Peninsula, McClellan was to replicate Scott's tactic to force the Rebels from their stronghold with engineering finesse and overwhelming firepower rather than suffer the needless casualties that seizing the city by a *coup de main* would have entailed.

McClellan played a distinguished role in all the engagements of the Mexico City Campaign, not only fulfilling his duties as an engineer but also seeing action as a combat infantry officer and as an artillery officer and winning brevets through the rank of captain. Finding life in the peacetime army too tedious, however, in 1857 he resigned his commission to become the chief engineer of the Illinois Central Railroad. With the outbreak of the Civil War, he rejoined the army as a major general of Ohio volunteers. His chance for "greater eminence" came on the morning of July 22, 1861, when Brevet Lieutenant General Winfield Scott informed McClellan that "a panic seized McDowell's army" at Bull Run, the first battle of the Civil War, and that it was "in full retreat on the Potomac. A most unaccountable transformation into a mob of a finely-appointed and admirably-led army."[16]

The army was not alone in its sense of demoralization. As Sir William Howard Russell, special correspondent of the *London Times*, recorded in his diary, Scott was "quite overwhelmed by the affair, and is unable to stir." So disheartened was the old general that later that day Secretary of War Simon Cameron ordered McClellan to Washington. "Circumstances make your presence here necessary," he wired. "Come hither without delay."[17]

Lieutenant Charles B. Haydon of the 2nd Michigan Infantry was far from alone in his belief that McClellan was "undoubtedly the man on whom the United States are hereafter to lean as a military chieftain." Scott, he noted in his diary, was "unmistakably past taking the field. His advice is good but the field requires a much younger man."[18]

Scott hailed McClellan's arrival at the capital as "an event of happy consequence to the country and the Army," later claiming, "if I did not call for him, I heartily approved of the suggestion, and gave him the most cordial reception and support."[19] Consequently, in a July 27 letter to his wife, the "Young Napoleon" boasted that the president, the cabinet, and Scott himself were "all deferring to me. I seem to have become the power of the land."[20] Indeed, on August 20 President Lincoln named McClellan commander of what was soon to become the Army of the Potomac. "My previous life," the general wrote to his wife, "seems to have been unwittingly directed to this great end."[21]

The close bond between senior and subordinate that had been forged in Mexico was cruelly shattered in the trying months that followed, the trouble between the two generals, McClellan declared with unintended irony, having arisen from Scott's "eternal jealousy of all who acquire any distinction." Whatever the root of the imbroglio, on October 6 McClellan wrote to his wife that Scott had "become my inveterate enemy!"[22]

Scott for his part accused his former protégé of having "prided himself in treating me with uniform neglect, running into disobedience of orders."[23] When McClellan, as commander of the Union's principal army, began to communicate directly with the president and various cabinet secretaries, completely and deliberately cutting the general in chief out of the chain of command, Scott responded on September 16 by informing the secretary of war that McClellan's "arrest and trial before a court-martial would probably soon cure the evil."

At the close of what Secretary of the Navy Gideon Welles characterized as "an unpleasant interview" attended by the president, several cabinet secretaries, and the two generals in early October, Scott told McClellan: "You were called here by my advice. The times require vigilance and activity. I am not active and shall never be again. When I proposed that you should come here to aid, not supersede, me, you had my friendship and confidence. You still have my confidence."[24]

Only because "a conflict of authority near the head of the Army" would likely strengthen the Confederate cause had Scott exercised his "long forbearance" in disciplining his headstrong subordinate. Believing, however, that Lincoln had ordered Major General Henry W. Halleck to Washington to supersede him as general in chief, thus giving him "increased confidence in the safety of the Union," Scott postponed his retirement from the army and deferred any move that he might have made against McClellan.[25] Halleck's appointment did not come to pass until July 1862, however, and on November 1, 1861, McClellan replaced his former mentor as general in chief of the U.S. Army. McClellan's mandate was now to capture the Confederate capital at Richmond, Virginia, and crush the rebellion. By April 1862, he predicted to J. Gordon Bennett of the *New York Herald* that he would lead Union arms to "the Waterloo of the rebellion."[26]

Despite the bitter parting of ways between the Young Napoleon and his former mentor, McClellan's tactics in his first Civil War battle and his strategy for the capture of the Confederate capital were in fact applications of lessons learned in Mexico. Modeling his campaign on Scott's, McClellan planned to lead an amphibious operation against the Confederate capital, thus avoiding the arduous and dangerous overland advance through enemy territory, with the navy maintaining the army's line of communications. Both the Peninsula Campaign of 1862 and the Mexico City Campaign of 1847 were strategic turning movements, flanking the enemy out of strong positions and designed, as Scott wrote of his earlier venture, to "strike effectively, at the vitals of the nation."[27]

As Scott had landed largely unopposed at Vera Cruz, adroitly flanking the Mexican army out of position and leaving Antonio López de Santa Anna to deal with a smaller force under Taylor at Buena Vista, so McClellan sailed down the Chesapeake to land his Army of the Potomac—130,000 soldiers, 15,000 horses, 1,100 wagons, and forty-four artillery batteries—at Fortress Monroe on the tip of the Virginia Peninsula, formed by the York River to the north and the James River to the south. As had Scott, McClellan met the huge logistical challenge of transporting an army by sea, conducting an amphibious landing on hostile soil, and then marching west in what he hoped would be a rapid campaign.

Scott had avoided direct confrontation with the enemy at Cerro Gordo by outflanking Santa Anna's army. Likewise, McClellan sought to conduct a campaign of maneuver rather than of assault. Soon, however, his plans confronted a reality that checked his advance.

Major General John B. Magruder positioned his 13,600-man Army of the Peninsula so as to delay McClellan's juggernaut. Although he had graduated in the middle of the West Point class of 1830 and had been assigned to the infantry rather than to the more prestigious engineers, Magruder made the best of a naturally strong position that stretched between the York and the James, anchored on its left by the city of Yorktown. As he described the so-called Warwick Line, redoubts were linked "by long curtains and flanked by rifle-pits," and the Warwick River, "a sluggish and boggy stream, twenty or thirty yards wide, and running through a dense wood fringed by swamps," covered its front. In addition, Magruder utilized a series of dams to "back up the water along the course of the river, so that for nearly three fourths of its distance its passage is impractical."[28] McClellan's chief engineer, Brigadier General John G. Barnard, considered the Warwick defenses to be "one of the most extensive known to modern times."[29]

Although General Joseph E. Johnston expressed his opinion that "no one but McClellan could have hesitated to attack" in view of this imposing obstacle, the Federal commander, like Scott at Vera Cruz, invested the city with formal siege lines and called up 103 pieces of heavy artillery, including naval guns, to bombard the defenses and silence the Confederate batteries. At Yorktown, however, the enemy's apparent strength was largely a sham, and its "artillery" was to a great extent only so-called "Quaker cannons," logs painted black and placed in embrasures by the Rebels. Magruder, moreover, added to this subterfuge by constantly marching his greatly inferior force back and forth along the line, creating the illusion of a much larger military presence.[30]

Magruder, wrote the noted diarist Mary Boykin Chesnut, "played his ten thousand before McClellan like fireflies," utterly deluding the Federal commander.[31] The success of this *coup de théâtre* added almost the entire month of April to McClellan's schedule for the capture of Richmond, giving Johnston—by then convinced that the principal threat to Richmond came from the east rather than from the north—time to march from the Rappahannock River, bringing the total number of Confederates on the Peninsula to 56,600 men.

By April 27, however, Johnston learned that McClellan's batteries would be in place in five or six days to open on Magruder's position. "The fight for Yorktown must be one of artillery," Johnston concluded, "in which we cannot win. The result is certain; the time only doubtful." He therefore elected to withdraw all Confederate forces toward Richmond. McClellan, still deceived by Magruder's *ruse*, declared himself "fully satisfied of the correctness of the course I have pursued" in achieving a nearly bloodless capture of Yorktown. "The success is brilliant," he boasted, "and you may rest assured that its effects will be of the greatest importance." But his timidity in the face of greatly inferior numbers along the Warwick surely cost the North its best opportunity to take Richmond early in the war and exemplified a lesson from the master imperfectly learned.[32]

If Vera Cruz had been McClellan's practical introduction to siege craft, Cerro Gordo was to be his first lesson the art of the set-piece battle; he attempted to apply this experience during his 1862 campaigns in western Virginia and on the Peninsula. With his base and line of communications secure, Scott had marched inland, reaching the strategically vital pass at Cerro Gordo, the gateway to the Mexican highlands and ultimately Mexico City, on April 18, 1847. There, Santa Anna had fortified the naturally strong positions on El Telégrafo and La Atalaya in anticipation of holding the Yankee invaders on the fever-ridden coastal plain.

Scott determined to fix Santa Anna's forces in place with a feint along his front by Brigadier General Pillow's volunteer brigade while turning the enemy's left flank and cutting the Mexicans' line of retreat with his regulars under Major General David E. Twiggs. Much to McClellan's disgust, he was attached to Pillow's brigade, which he derisively called the "Duck Creek Fencibles."[33]

Although Pillow totally bungled his assignment, ordering a headlong charge into the well-fortified Mexican front rather than merely making the demonstration that Scott had instructed, thus needlessly sacrificing the lives of many men in his brigade, the flanking movement executed by Twiggs's regulars was a stellar success. As U. S. Grant succinctly observed, "The attack was made, the Mexican reserves behind the works beat a hasty retreat, and those occupying them surrendered."[34]

McClellan recorded in his diary Scott's praise for the charge of Twiggs's "rascally Regulars," calling it "the most beautiful sight that he had ever witnessed."[35] The debacle on Pillow's front, on the other hand, further solidified McClellan's already ingrained prejudice against volunteers, especially against volunteer officers. Scott "evidently was not much surprised and not much 'put out' that Pillow was thrashed, and attached no importance to his future movements," but McClellan considered the commanders of the volunteer regiments to be "deficients of the Mil. Academy, friends of politicians, & bar room blaguards." What administration, he asked rhetorically, "having at its disposal men trained to be soldiers from their boyhood who were educated expressly for the army, and probably the best Military Academy in the world, passes over these men . . . and goes behind the curtain, in to country courthouses, and low village bar rooms" to commission its officers? This bias was to reiterate itself when he became commander of the Army of the Potomac.[36] For "the really serious work" of leading troops in combat, he wrote to his wife on July 31, 1862, McClellan trusted only officers from the regular army and a few "educated soldiers" from European armies. Of the volunteer officers who he commanded, the general maintained that "the most useless thing imaginable is one of these 'highly educated' civilians."[37]

Despite Pillow's poor performance at Cerro Gordo, the victory there was so brilliant and absolute and its memory so vivid that fourteen years later McClellan attempted to employ Scott's tactics in his first battle. Before his rise to prominence while commander of the Department of Ohio, McClellan had faced Confederate forces in western Virginia in the summer of 1861.

Recalling the useless sacrifice of Pillow's men in their haphazard assault on enemy entrenchments, he vowed to "repeat the manoeuvre of Cerro Gordo" against Brigadier General Robert S. Garnett's Confederates at Rich Mountain. "No prospect of a brilliant victory shall induce me to depart from my intention of gaining success by manoeuvring rather than by fighting," he assured Scott. "I will not throw these men of mine into the teeth of artillery and intrenchments, if it is possible to avoid it."[38]

When he found Garnett's forces entrenched on Laurel Hill, he planned to "turn the position from the south, and thus occupy the Beverly Road in his rear. If possible," he assured Scott, "I will repeat the maneuver of Cerro Gordo."[39] The battle did not go exactly as McClellan had planned largely because of his hesitancy, a flaw that was to reassert itself in the campaigns on the Peninsula and in Maryland, but clearly his intention had been to emulate Scott's tactics.

During the Peninsula Campaign in 1862, McClellan, of course, failed to achieve the objective that Scott had won—namely, the capture of the enemy capital. General Robert E. Lee's vigorous counterattacks during the Seven Days' Battles before Richmond (June 25–July 1, 1862) drove the Army of the Potomac back down the Peninsula toward the safety of the Federal gunboats at Harrison's Landing on the James River in what McClellan euphemistically referred to as a "change of base." Even after his artillery bloodily repulsed the poorly coordinated Confederate attacks on his lines at Malvern Hill on July 1, he failed to resume the offensive, instead embarking on his transports on August 16 and returning to Washington. In retreating, however, McClellan attempted to shift the blame, insisting that he bore no responsibility for the defeat because "the Government has not sustained this army." On June 28 he wrote to Secretary of War Edwin M. Stanton: "If I save this army now, I tell you plainly that I owe no thanks to you or to any other persons in Washington. You have done your best to sacrifice this army."[40]

Whatever he might have learned from his old commander, McClellan lacked Scott's moral courage and the ability to carry on in the face of adversity. "Are you not over-cautious when you assume that you cannot do what the enemy is constantly doing?" President Lincoln famously asked him.[41] Also relevant is the fact that in the campaign for Richmond, McClellan faced another of Scott's old pupils, Robert E. Lee, who had perhaps learned the lessons of the Mexico City Campaign better than had his northern opponent.

NOTES

1. John C. Waugh, *The Class of 1846: From West Point to Appomattox: Stonewall Jackson, George McClellan, and Their Brothers* (New York: Warner Books, 1994).

2. T. Harry Williams, ed., *With Beauregard in Mexico: The Mexican War Reminiscences of P. G. T. Beauregard* (Baton Rouge: Louisiana State University Press, 1956), 46; Scott quoted in Russell Weigley, *History of the United States Army* (New York: Macmillan, 1967; repr., Bloomington: Indiana University Press, 1984), 185.

3. Stephen W. Sears, ed., *The Civil War Papers of George B. McClellan: Selected Correspondence, 1860–1865*, ed. (New York: Ticknor and Fields, 1989), 135–36, 323; Michael Burlingame and John R. Turner Ettlinger, eds., *Inside Lincoln's White House: The Complete Civil War Diary of John Hay* (Carbondale: Southern Illinois University Press, 1997), 32.

4. Thomas W. Cutrer, ed., *The Mexican War Diary and Correspondence of George B. McClellan* (Baton Rouge: Louisiana State University Press, 2009), 48.

5. Ibid., 5.

6. War Department, "General Regulations for the Army, 1841," Article 75, paragraph 878, 159; Steven W. Sears, *George B. McClellan: The Young Napoleon* (New York: Ticknor and Fields, 1988), 13.

7. Cutrer, *Mexican War Diary and Correspondence of George B. McClellan*, 10.

8. *The War of the Rebellion: A Compilation of the Official Records of the Union and Confederate Armies*, 70 vols. in 128 pts. (Washington, DC: Government Printing Office, 1880–1901), ser. 1, 51:1, 373 (hereafter cited as *OR*, all references to ser. 1 unless otherwise stated); Sears, *Civil War Papers of George B. McClellan*, 17.

9. *New Orleans Bulletin*, Mar. 27, 1847.

10. Hazard Stevens, *The Life of Isaac Ingalls Stevens*, vol. 1 (Boston: Houghton Mifflin, 1900), 216–17.

11. Ethan Allen Hitchcock, *Fifty Years in Camp and Field: Diary of Major-General Ethan Allen Hitchcock, U.S.A.*, ed. W. A. Croffut (New York: G. Putnam's Sons, 1909), 241.

12. Dabney Herndon Maury, *Recollections of a Virginian in the Mexican, Indian, and Civil Wars* (New York: Charles Scribner's Sons, 1894), 34; Bradley T. Johnson, ed., *A Memoir of the Life and Public Service of Joseph E. Johnston* (Baltimore: R. H. Woodward, 1891), 291.

13. Joseph G. Totten to Winfield Scott, Mar. 28, 1847, quoted in G. S. Hillard, *Life and Campaigns of George B. McClellan* (Philadelphia: J. B. Lippincott, 1865), 17.

14. Totten's annual report to the secretary of war, quoted in Hillard, *Life and Campaigns of George B. McClellan*, 21; Stevens, *Life of Isaac Ingalls Stevens*, 116; Williams, *With Beauregard in Mexico*, 30–31.

15. Stevens, *Life of Isaac Ingalls Stevens*, 119.

16. *OR*, 2:752–54.

17. Quoted in Townsend, *Anecdotes of the Civil War in the United States*, (New York: D. Appleton, 1884), 62; *OR*, 2:752–53; William Howard Russell, *My Diary North and South*, ed. Fletcher Pratt (New York: Harper and Brothers, 1954), 233–34; Allan Nevins

and Milton Halsey Thomas, eds., *The Diary of George Templeton Strong*, vol. 3 (New York: Macmillan, 1952), 169.

18. Stephen W. Sears, ed., *For Country, Cause, and Leader: The Civil War Journal of Charles B. Haydon* (New York: Ticknor and Fields, 1993), 77.

19. Scott to Simon Cameron, Oct. 4, 1861, *OR*, 51:1, 491–92.

20. Sears, *Civil War Papers of George B. McClellan*, 70.

21. Ibid., 112–13.

22. Ibid., 105–6.

23. *OR*, 51:1, 492.

24. Gideon Welles, *Diary of Gideon Welles: Secretary of the Navy under Lincoln and Johnson*, vol. 1 (Boston: Houghton Mifflin, 1911), 241–42.

25. *OR*, 51:1, 492; E. D. Townsend, *Anecdotes of the Civil War in the United States* (New York: D. Appleton, 1884), 66.

26. Sears, *George B. McClellan*, 130.

27. Timothy D. Johnson, "McClellan and Mentor," *MHQ: The Quarterly Journal of Military History* 13, no. 2 (Winter 2001): 89–95; Winfield Scott, *Memoirs of Lieut.-General Scott, 2 vols. (New York: Sheldon, 1864)*, 1:404–5.

28. *Southern History of the War: Official Reports of Battles* (New York: Charles B. Richardson, 1864), 518.

29. *OR*, 11:1, 16.

30. Ibid., 456.

31. C. Vann Woodward, ed., *Mary Chesnut's Civil War* (New Haven, CT: Yale University Press, 1981), 401.

32. *OR*, 11:3, 135.

33. Hillard, *Life and Campaigns of George B. McClellan*, 18–19.

34. U. S. Grant, *Personal Memoirs of U. S. Grant*, 2 vols. (New York: Charles L. Webster, 1885–86), 1:133.

35. Cutrer, *Mexican War Diary and Correspondence of George B. McClellan*, 120.

36. Ibid., 135; Sears, *George B. McClellan*, 17.

37. Sears, *Civil War Papers of George B. McClellan*, 379.

38. Ibid., 45.

39. *OR*, 2:198.

40. *OR*, 11:1, 61.

41. Roy P. Basler et al., eds., *The Collected Works of Abraham Lincoln*, vol. 5 (New Brunswick, NJ: Rutgers University Press, 1953), 460–61.

NINETEEN MONTHS IN MEXICO

George Gordon Meade Develops His Philosophy of War, 1845–1847

JENNIFER M. MURRAY

At 1:07 p.m. on the afternoon of July 3, 1863, a single artillery shot pierced the air from a Confederate signal gun posted in a peach orchard owned by Joseph Sherfy in the small Pennsylvania town of Gettysburg. What became known as Pickett's Charge had begun.[1] When Major General George Gordon Meade arrived on the battlefield sometime after midnight on the morning of July 2, the army commander made his headquarters in a small farmhouse owned by a widow, Lydia Leister. Located about 300 yards east (or behind) the Federal line on Cemetery Ridge, the Leister home quickly became an unintended target of overshooting enemy artillery. In now his sixth day in command of the Army of the Potomac, Meade stood calmly in the doorway amid the chaos of solid shot and exploding shell. One round came uncomfortably close to hitting the general, and believing it safer being completely outside, Meade and his staff moved into Leister's small garden.[2]

As Meade paced about, he observed several aides clinging to the leeward side of the small wooden house, desperate to find any measure of protection. He paused, smiled assuredly, and then queried, "Gentlemen, are you trying to find a safe place?" Then, Meade proceeded to recount an amusing anecdote from the Battle of Palo Alto, fought on May 8, 1846. He told his aides they reminded him of the driver of the ox-team carrying ammunition onto the plains at Palo Alto, who, finding himself in range of Mexican artillery, overturned his cart and used it for cover. Just then, by Meade's telling, "General Taylor came along, and seeing this attempt at shelter, shouted, 'You damned fool, don't you know you are no safer here than anywhere else?' The driver replied, 'I don't suppose I am, general, but it kind o' feels so.'"[3]

By July 1863, the forty-seven-year-old Army of the Potomac commander was no stranger to the perils of combat, serving in all of that army's major campaigns since receiving his commission as a brigadier general in the volunteer army on August 31, 1861. But perhaps it is surprising that when attempting to calm his panicked staff during the artillery bombardment that hot, sunny afternoon in Pennsylvania, Meade offered an anecdote from his experiences in a battle fought seventeen years earlier. Indeed, the Battle of Palo Alto (May 8, 1846) was Meade's *"bapteme de fue."*[4] As a young second lieutenant in the Corps of Topographical Engineers, he spent nineteen months in Mexico, September 1845 until March 1847, serving the bulk of his time on the staff of General Zachary Taylor. Lieutenant Meade, of course, would not be the only soldier serving under Taylor who would rise to prominence during the American Civil War. Indeed, at least 173 men who served in the Army of Occupation became general officers during the sectional crisis. Although Meade did not serve for the duration of the Mexican War—his departure in March 1847 meant that he missed the war's culminating campaign against Mexico City—this conflict proved formative for the young officer.[5]

Meade's experience in Mexico came through the lens of a topographical engineer on Taylor's staff. Unlike Ulysses S. Grant and James Longstreet, who served as young lieutenants in the infantry, or John F. Reynolds and Braxton Bragg, who saw service in the artillery, as a staff officer rather than a line officer, Meade did not lead troops into battle nor was he called upon to demonstrate tactical prowess in the face of the enemy; those opportunities would come years later fighting, not Mexicans but fellow Americans.[6] Yet with nearly two years of service in Mexico, which included participation in the Battles of Palo Alto, Resaca de la Palma, and Monterrey (September 20-24, 1846) as well as witnessing the siege at Vera Cruz (March 9-24, 1847), Meade observed much about war, the men who made it, and those who fought it. He articulated an unfavorable but not uncommon opinion of volunteer soldiers, an aversion to the powers of the press, and a deep-seated disdain for political meddling in military affairs. On the battlefield, Lieutenant Meade observed the importance of reconnaissance, advance planning, and logistics; the imperative of leadership; and the consequences of battlefield victory. Each of these attributes emerged during the Civil War—some to a greater extent—underpinning Meade's leadership in the Army of the Potomac.

On August 12, 1845, Lieutenant Meade, then stationed in Philadelphia, Pennsylvania, working on the construction of lighthouses in Delaware Bay, received orders to report to Brevet Brigadier General Zachary Taylor at Aransas Bay, Texas. At twenty-nine years old, Meade bid farewell to his wife, Margaret, and three young children, then began the long journey to Texas.[7] Although he had been born in Cadiz, Spain, in 1815, his family returned to Philadelphia in 1817. Thus, the young American officer did not speak Spanish, a fact that he would come to regret.[8]

Propelled by the Texas Congress voting in favor of annexation that June, events were unfolding along the border. In late August Taylor had moved his forces, then named the Army of Observation, to Corpus Christi, just over thirty miles from Aransas Bay and situated north of the Nueces River.[9] It was here that Lieutenant Meade met the general on September 15, 1845. He found his new commanding officer to be a "plain, sensible, old gentleman." The young lieutenant described Taylor as a "stanch Whig," a political sentiment that Meade would have found welcoming, considering his own Whiggish persuasions and family connections. Indeed, his Whig tendencies were not uncommon among regular-army officers, and some, Meade included, expressed reservations about the nation's policy of expansion and annexation. Meade considered the war an "injustice to a neighbor" but, once President James K. Polk committed forces, urged that the war should be prosecuted vigorously to bring it to a quick resolution. No doubt these political sensibilities underscored some of his criticism of the Democratic president's administration of the war. The Mexican War was a highly politicized conflict, and one that provided Meade with a preview of the infusion of politics into warfare.[10]

Until January 1847, Meade would serve on Taylor's staff as a topographical engineer, sometimes the only one. Although the composition of the Corps of Topographical Engineers officers assigned to Taylor's staff would vary during the war, Meade's responsibilities remained unchanged: he was to complete vital surveying and mapmaking work. These were meticulous and often dangerous undertakings. He surveyed and sketched maritime and land routes, detailed lines of march for the army, accompanied working parties to repair roads, selected campsites, and identified suitable water crossings as well as positions for the army's artillery guns.[11]

When Polk received a declaration of war from Congress on May 13, 1846, he proceeded to call for 50,000 volunteers to serve for one year or the duration of the war.[12] Indeed, volunteers would constitute the majority of American soldiers during the Mexican War. Although regular-army officers frequently bemoaned their utility, Polk championed the value of the citizen-soldier.[13] Modern historians frame the unruliness of the volunteers as rooted in the philosophies of the period; as historian Richard Bruce Winders explains, "The product of Jacksonian America, Polk's army carried its view of democracy to the land of the Montezumas."[14] Meade graduated from West Point in 1835, and although he had temporarily left the army for civilian pursuits, membership in what Alexis de Tocqueville termed the "aristocratic army" framed his perception of the volunteers, not only during the Mexican War but also during the early months of the Civil War.[15]

Meade arrived in Texas imbued with the philosophies of an antebellum army officer, foremost among them a disdain for volunteer soldiers. To this point he had minimal experience with the nation's citizen-soldiers, briefly serving alongside volunteers and militiamen during the Second Seminole War in Florida in 1836.[16] What he witnessed in Mexico only amplified this distaste, but by no means were Meade's perceptions exceptional. Writing of the regular-army officer corps during the Mexican War, historian William B. Skelton has summarized, "No opinion was as wide-spread in the army as contempt for citizen-soldiers." Two specific characteristics permeated Meade's description of the U.S. volunteers: undisciplined and helpless. "They are perfectly ignorant of discipline, and most restive under restraint. They are in consequence a most disorderly mass," he groused. The young lieutenant speculated they would give the army "more trouble than the enemy." Excessive drinking seemed endemic. Drunken officers and enlisted men roamed throughout camp and in the streets of the local communities. Too often these *"volontarios"* initiated brawls with the local civilians, a behavior that Meade found particularly distasteful.[17] One specific incident merited recounting in a letter to Margaret. With volunteers arriving regularly, Taylor endeavored to establish some level of control and had explicitly prohibited the firing of weapons in camp, then situated at Matamoras, just across the Rio Grande. Ignoring Taylor's order, groups of volunteers would walk to the riverbank, across from army headquarters, and discharge their weapons. Meade sardonically recorded, "bullets come whizzing by us as thick as in an action, and I really consider spending a day in my tent, uninjured, equivalent to passing through a well-contested action."[18]

In addition to a stark lack of discipline, Meade found the volunteers feckless. He reserved special criticism for slaveowning southerners, men who arrived at camp expecting their basic needs to be attended to by the regulars. Accustomed to a life of privilege, these upper-class southerners recoiled at performing labor like cutting wood or drawing water required for camp life.[19] "They cannot take care of themselves; the hospitals are crowded with them, they die like sheep; they waste their provisions, requiring twice as much to supply as regulars do," Meade grumbled.[20] Officers were no better. The root of the problem was organizational, however, as the enlisted elected their officers, a deeply respected tradition of the citizen-soldier model.[21] These problems could be remedied if "Colonel Polk," who Meade identified as being biased against professional officers, had authorized the expansion of the regular army.[22]

Meade carried this unfavorable opinion of volunteers into the Civil War. In mid-September 1861, Brigadier General Meade arrived at Camp Tennally, Maryland, to take command of the Second Brigade of Pennsylvania Reserves. This was his first command, with some 3,600 men falling under his authority. He spent no more than a month with his brigade before grumbling about the quality of men responding to President Abraham Lincoln's call for volunteers, writing, "Soldiers they are not in any sense of the word."[23] But this condemnation changed rapidly in the months that followed, as Meade's soldiers fought tenaciously during the Peninsula Campaign and at Turner's Gap, Antietam, and Fredericksburg, accumulating a distinguished service record that Meade felt particularly proud of.[24] General Meade held the respect of his men and stridently enforced order in his command. No doubt targeting behavior witnessed in Mexico, Meade quickly earned a reputation as a stern disciplinarian. His strict style was not uncommon for Civil War officers, particularly those trained within the regular army. One incident during the Battle of Antietam offers an example. On the morning of September 17, 1862, when Meade observed a private in the 7th Pennsylvania Reserves digging underneath a large tree root to escape the raining artillery fire, he barked at the sergeant to get the man back in the ranks. Unmoving, Meade "furiously" rode up to the private and smacked him with the broad side of his sword, prodding the soldier into line. This act of brandishing the sword was intended to curb battlefield cowardice or stymie any similar erosion of discipline.[25]

The volunteers' lack of discipline most clearly manifested itself in their disregard for civilian property. War, Meade reasoned, should be limited

to belligerent armies and nations; civilians, whether Mexican or southern, were to be left alone. With the prolonged presence of the U.S. Army
in Matamoros in the summer of 1846, American *"volontarios"* unleashed
considerable destruction on civilian property, crops, and fences. They stole
cattle, robbed civilians of their corn, and acted, as Meade described, "more
like a body of hostile Indians than of civilized whites." The volunteers, he
reported, "commenced to excite feelings of indignation and hatred in the
bosom of the people, by their outrages against them."[26]

Within the year, Meade's estimation of the volunteers had marginally
improved, particularly after their hard-fought victory at Monterrey. But
their proclivity for unwarranted destruction of civilian property remained
problematic. "They are a set of Goths and Vandals," he observed. Men
plundered "everything they can lay their hands on" and remained prone to
get into drunken brawls with civilians. This behavior did not go unnoticed,
but the volunteer officers had no effective form of control over their recruits.
General Taylor tried to curb the plundering, going so far as to threaten
courts-martial, but even this had little effect.[27]

Meade's denigration of the volunteers' conduct was more than an effort to herald the discipline of a professionalized regular army. Indeed, he
understood that the unwarranted destruction of civilian property and unfavorable treatment of the region's inhabitants had consequences for the
trajectory of the war. If American soldiers became a "terror to innocent
people," Meade believed that the Mexican civilians would take up arms,
either directly or indirectly, against U.S. forces, thus prolonging the war.
The volunteer troops needed to act with restraint (or be restrained) to con-
tinuously demonstrate to the civilians that the U.S. Army did not desire to
disrupt their daily existence but only to make war on the Mexican army and
its government.[28] Indeed, Meade believed that the U.S. government held an
obligation to protect the citizens within the territory the army inhabited and
particularly those who had assisted the Americans. "Either let the people
alone, or when you have taken a place, hold it and protect those who com-
promise themselves by serving you," he declared.[29]

Meade carried this philosophy of shielding a belligerent's civilians from
the hardships of war into the Civil War. Although 1860s Americans did not
define the terminology as such, Meade believed in a policy of conciliation.
Particularly prevalent in the first year of the war, conciliation rested on the
belief that most white southerners were opposed to secession, and conse-

quently Federal soldiers needed to minimize the war's effect on these loyal citizens.[30]

An incident in early December 1861 highlights Meade's conciliatory views. After crossing over the Potomac River and marching into Virginia, Brigadier General George McCall's division of Pennsylvania Reserves had settled into a position at Camp Pierpont. This area of northern Virginia, and in particular the small community of Dranesville, figured prominently in U.S. and Confederate reconnaissance missions and small-scale operations in the early months of the war. McCall ordered Meade's brigade to capture two known secessionists accused of killing two Union soldiers and who resided at a small farmstead (owned by Richard Gunnell) two miles north of Dranesville. Once the Pennsylvanians had secured the two men, they were permitted to "bring in the forage" from the farmstead. A train of fifty-seven wagons accompanied Meade's brigade, which the troops filled with grain and various vegetables. The soldiers also rounded up eleven horses, thirty-eight hogs, one ox, and two slaves present on Gunnell's property.[31]

While the mission was an operational success and the orders had permitted foraging, Meade privately condemned the excessive plundering. Although the Gunnells were known secessionists and were actively undermining Federal operations in the area, Meade remained resolute that their private property needed to be protected. He confided to Margaret, "The great difficulty was to prevent the wanton and useless destruction of property which could not be made available for military purposes." The general struggled to restrain his men from destroying everything on the property, reflecting two days after the Gunnell affair, "It made me sad to do such injury, and I really was ashamed of our cause, which thus required war to be made on individuals."[32]

Service in Mexico also laid the foundation for Meade's perceptions of the press and war correspondents, one that would devolve considerably during the Civil War.[33] Meade found the press to be not only prone to inciting falsehoods and rumors but also an instrument in shaping reputations and public views of the war. Writing to Margaret a week after the Battle of Palo Alto, he quipped, "I trust you will receive my previous letters in time to prevent any unnecessary alarm from the thousand wild and extravagant rumors which I see by the papers from New Orleans have been put in circulation."[34] As newspapers circulated throughout camp in the weeks following the battle at Monterrey, Meade found it unfortunate that the press did not "appreciate" the army's victory and its strategic consequences. Monterrey, rather than Palo Alto or Resaca de la Palma, was the war's first significant battle. He pointed out that not only had General Pedro de Ampudia's forces evacuated the city, but they also withdrew over 300 miles southward to San Luis Potosí.[35]

What mostly caught Meade's ire during the Mexican War was not individual correspondents or false news reports, but fellow soldiers who took to writing letters replete with exaggerated praise of their battlefield exploits, a behavior to which junior officers seemed the most susceptible.[36] In a letter written on December 3, 1846, he addressed at length the embellished narratives portrayed in newspapers, particularly concerning individual heroism during the fight at Monterrey. Two junior officers from Maryland's 1st Company of Baltimore Volunteers merited mention. According to newspaper reports, Captain James Stewart and Lieutenant Benjamin Owens "did wonders in the way of killing Mexicans," Meade retorted, when in reality Stewart had taken cover in a quarry hole to avoid the incoming artillery fire, and only "harsh words" successfully extracted him from his protective lair. Owens, contrary to the published reports, did not participate in the fight at all but remained in camp to guard the baggage.[37]

A fellow engineer was among the most egregious offenders. Second Lieutenant John Pope arrived in Mexico in July 1846 and, after the victory at Monterrey, several "topogs," including Meade and Pope, moved into a palatial home once inhabited by a Mexican officer. There, Pope became Meade's messmate. Meade complained that the "letter-writers have created a great ferment in the camp." The news article that likely annoyed him appeared in Nashville's *Republican Banner* six weeks earlier and detailed the army's success at Monterrey. The correspondent described how Lieutenant Pope reconnoitered an enemy artillery position and came under severe cannon and musketry fire. On the morning of September 21, Pope led an infantry charge against a predetermined enemy position and, in the chaos of the fighting, rescued a wounded fellow officer, dragging him to safety "amidst a shower of balls that covered him in dust." As reported, "the gallantry of this young officer, now in his first battle, is spoken of in admiration by the Army."[38]

Meade was aghast at these exaggerations and proclaimed the paper a "scandal monger." Pope, he explained, did not perform with the courage as described in the articles, nor did he lead an infantry charge against the enemy position as reported. Of this alleged heroism, he added, "the army never knew it till after the letter so stating the fact came back in the papers." Pope performed his duty, Meade declared, but did "nothing more than all the rest of the army did." How did Pope manage to garner such a prominent role in the correspondent's reporting? Meade claimed that his fellow officer befriended the correspondents and assisted them in crafting their articles. Certainly, Meade was also an ambitious young officer and sought recognition for his deeds, a characteristic that became more pronounced during the Civil War, but did little to ingratiate himself with the journalists. "For this reason my extraordinary performances have not reached your ear through the public prints," he explained to Margaret.[39]

This brazen self-promotion had adverse consequences on the army. Most simply, these reports spread falsehoods, as Meade noted: "All that I have read have been a tissue of nonsense and falsehoods, so palpably absurd as to make me laugh, though others are greatly annoyed." At considerable length he explained the unfortunate disconnect between soldiers' battlefield exploits and their vainglorious portrayal in the newspapers. "Instances of individual valor which were never known before the letters came here in the papers, extraordinary feats performed by persons who were never near the reputed scene of action," he outlined, "and all kinds of lies and absurdities have been set forth."[40] Furthermore, such self-aggrandizement undoubtedly fostered an atmosphere of jealousy, intrigue, and competition. This undermined the army's professionalism and esprit de corps. Outlandish reporting of individual battlefield conduct amplified the existing "cliques, factions, and parties" evident within both the regular army and the volunteers.[41] "If there is anything I do dislike, it is newspaper notoriety," Meade proclaimed. "I think it is the curse of our country, and fear it is seriously injuring our little army."[42]

This would not be the last time that Meade resented Pope's bold maneuvering. From their service in Mexico, the young officers' careers continued on a parallel trajectory. During the secession winter, both men, now captains, were tasked with surveying work in the Great Lakes. Captain Meade anxiously watched as appointments and promotions were doled out to regular-army officers in the newly forming volunteer army and in his private correspondence lashed out at fellow officers who jockeyed their way into a commission. Again, Pope caught his ire. Pope did not hesitate to politick for advancement, and his efforts proved successful when he received a commission as a brigadier general in May 1861. Two months later Meade received his own commission.[43]

Meade's aversion to cultivating a more amicable relationship with newspaper correspondents proved detrimental to his reputation during the Civil War. During the first three days of July 1863, his Army of the Potomac fought—and won—the largest and deadliest battle of the Civil War. Initially elated by Meade's success at Gettysburg, northern newspapers lavished praise on the commanding general and his army. Three days after the repulse of Pickett's Charge, the *Philadelphia Inquirer* proclaimed "Victory! Waterloo Eclipsed!!"[44] Meade, consistently attuned to the portrayal of his reputation in the media, cautioned, "I see also that the papers are making a great deal too much fuss about me." He preferred that they wait "a little while to see what my career is to be before making any pretension."[45] These public accolades quickly turned toward criticisms when the general chose not to attack the entrenched Confederate position at Williamsport, Maryland; later that fall, when the Army of the Potomac failed to accomplish anything of operational significance, correspondents howled for Meade to be relieved of command. On November 30, 1863, when Meade decided not to attack the entrenched Confederate position at Mine Run, Virginia, and subsequently moved his army north across the Rapidan River, journalists penned a panoply of editorials deliberating the wisdom of his decision and speculated that the general would be relieved of command.[46]

General Meade's relationship with the press reached its nadir in 1864, first with the famed "Historicus" article and then with the Crapsey affair, two incidents well analyzed by historians. On March 12, 1864, the *New York Herald* published a lengthy article under the pseudonym Historicus in which the author presented a particularly critical—also inaccurate—interpretation of Meade's leadership during the Gettysburg Campaign. Historicus attributed Federal victory at Gettysburg in large part to Major General Daniel Sickles, the Third Corps's commander during the battle. Suspecting the author was Sickles, Meade requested an inquiry into the matter. General in Chief Henry W. Halleck advised him to avoid further escalations. Although Meade believed the "slanders" needed to be addressed, he dropped the issue.[47]

The dynamic with the northern press continued to deteriorate in the spring of 1864. Edward Crapsey, a prominent journalist for the *Philadelphia Inquirer,* penned an article intimating that Meade had favored a withdrawal across the Rapidan River after the Battle of the Wilderness.[48] When the general read the article, he flew into a rage, immediately summoned Crapsey to headquarters and demanded an explanation for the "base and wicked lie." Finding his answers unsatisfactory, Meade determined to make an example out of the journalist.[49] Mounted backward on a mule and with a placard draped around his neck reading "Libeler of the Press," Crapsey was paraded through camp and exiled from the Army of the Potomac by Meade's order.[50] No doubt the general handled the Craspey affair poorly, and thereafter war correspondents colluded to minimize reporting on Meade, a decision that unquestionably shaped his reputation and legacy.[51]

Consistent with Meade's philosophy in both the Mexican War and the Civil War was a strident, unwavering aversion to political interference in military affairs. On several occasions Meade found President Polk's management of the earlier war lacking, specifically concerning issues of supplying the army and the need to increase the presence of the regulars in Mexico.[52] He urged a "vigorous prosecution of the war" but lamented that this would not be the case "as long as generals are made in the counting-house and soldiers on the farms."[53] The young officer also observed important lessons about the nature of civil-military relations. He certainly understood the political nature that characterized America's execution of the war in Mexico and lamented Taylor's treatment by Washington.[54] Concerned with Taylor's increasing popularity, Polk selected Winfield Scott to lead the expedition against Mexico City. Taylor, a Whig, suspected that the president's decision to now relegate him to northern Mexico while operations shifted toward the enemy capital were politically motivated. Meade agreed. The young lieutenant favored a move to Vera Cruz but believed the effort to minimize Taylor to be nothing more than an emboldened political scheme. Writing from Tampico on February 8, 1847, an emotional Meade demanded, "Let us show a bold and united front, forget *party* for an instant; now that we are in the war, prosecute it with all possible vigor."[55] These sorts of lamentations continued during the Civil War, a conflict by its very nature rife with an infusion of politics. When Lincoln relieved Major General George B. McClellan of command in early November 1862, Meade lamented, "What we are coming to I cannot tell, but I must confess this interference by politicians with military men, and these personal intrigues and bickerings among military men, make me feel very sad and very doubtful of the future."[56]

It is impossible to say what campaigns or battles had the most lasting influence on the future Civil War, but in his nineteen months in Mexico,

Meade developed an eye for detail and planning as well as topography and logistics. His mapmaking abilities were invaluable, and at times he functioned as Taylor's chief topographical engineer. One of the lieutenant's maps was used to denote a point of attack during the Battle of Monterrey. Additionally, after the Mexican army withdrew, Meade was tasked with preparing detailed maps of the battle and drawing the town and surrounding area. Taylor included these maps with his official report to the War Department, some of which were viewed not only by Secretary of War William L. Marcy but also by President Polk.[57]

Perhaps, then, in one of his first significant orders as commander of the Army of the Potomac, Meade drew on his topographical experiences in Mexico when he instructed his engineers to scout a defensive position for the army to assume along Pipe Creek in Carroll County, Maryland. Although the noteworthy "Pipe Creek Circular" became a contentious part of Meade's leadership after Gettysburg, it was a sound operational plan, one ordered by a general who appreciated the value of terrain and contingency, lessons first observed in Mexico.[58] Indeed, Grant would later extoll Meade's keen eye for terrain, writing, "He saw clearly and distinctly the position of the enemy, and the topography of the country in front of his own position." He had learned these instrumental skills in Mexico.[59]

Meade also learned the value of planning and logistics. As the U.S. Army sat idle in camp opposite Matamoras in the spring of 1846, the young engineering officer had repeatedly impressed upon Taylor the need to construct bridges to facilitate the army's crossing of the Rio Grande, but the general demurred. When enemy forces were routed from Matamoras, the Americans had no way to cross the river. Taylor's army remained stagnant for nine days as soldiers scrambled to facilitate a crossing, accomplished only when they procured some abandoned Mexican boats. Lieutenant Meade characterized Taylor's negligence to the matter of logistics as a serious "defect."[60]

At Monterrey Meade observed important military and political consequences resulting from a battlefield victory. A rare example of urban combat in American history, Taylor's forces captured the city at a loss of roughly 8 percent of his army. Rather than make a final assault against Ampudia's army, however, on the morning of September 25, 1846, Taylor agreed to a generous armistice. This decision quickly caught the ire of President Polk.[61] After considering the conditions of the respective armies, Meade found that he agreed with the general's decision. It was not a military imperative, he explained, that led to the armistice, but Taylor's desire to open conversations for peace and to end the unnecessary loss of life among both soldiers and civilians.[62]

Now finding himself at odds with the Polk administration, Taylor on at least one occasion confided to Meade that he would be happy to be relieved of command. The lieutenant believed now that the general was being asked to "perform impossible things." Ruminating on the infusion of politics into Taylor's operational situation at Monterrey, Meade recorded, "The mighty engine of political influence, that curse of our country, . . . forces party politics into everything."[63] Perhaps the young lieutenant learned an unfortunate lesson in leadership from the disaffected Taylor in the fall of 1846. Years later, in response to what he considered unwarranted prodding from the Lincoln administration during the pursuit from Gettysburg, General Meade first offered his resignation on the afternoon of July 14, 1863, just after the Army of Northern Virginia "escaped" across the Potomac River. Over the next four months, he offered to resign three additional times.[64]

But the comparisons of Taylor's leadership at Monterrey and Meade's at Gettysburg end there. Scholar Kevin Dougherty incorrectly argues that after Gettysburg Meade was in "no mood to exploit his victory" and launched only a "half-hearted" pursuit of Lee. Likening his performance at Gettysburg to Taylor's at Monterrey, Dougherty unconvincingly postulated that in Mexico "Meade learned to play it safe." In other words, during the pursuit from Gettysburg, the Union commander was "just following the example he had seen in Mexico."[65] Although both Meade's contemporaries and generations of historians have criticized a seemingly lack of aggression in the two-week pursuit of the Army of Northern Virginia to the Potomac River, Dougherty's overgeneralizations ignore the logistical and operational constraints facing the Army of the Potomac.

Overall, Meade found much to admire in the leadership of "Old Rough and Ready." In the spring of 1864, a month after Lieutenant General Grant had made his headquarters with the Army of the Potomac, Meade likened the general in chief to Taylor. Writing of Grant, Meade offered: "He has natural qualities of a high order, and is a man whom, the more you see and know him, the better you like him. He puts me in mind of old Taylor."[66] Grant would have been pleased with the comparison.[67]

Meade's service in Mexico began to wind down in the early months of 1847, when he was transferred first to Major General Robert Patterson's and then to General Scott's staff. Scott had already assembled a collection of topographical engineers, including Meade's future adversary at Gettysburg, Captain Robert E. Lee. Meade regretted his separation from General Taylor and grumbled about his minimal role during the siege of Vera Cruz, writing that he was "pretty much a spectator." Finding his services no longer required and owed to his length of service in Mexico, in late March Scott ordered the lieutenant to return to Washington. On April 20, 1847, Meade arrived at Washington, his service in the Mexican War concluded.[68] The young officer had proven his competency in the Mexican War and received praise from his superiors, including Patterson, Taylor, and Brigadier General William Worth. Importantly, he had fulfilled his duty, a tenet fundamental to understanding George Meade, both as a young lieutenant and later as a general.[69]

Fourteen years later the United States would once again call on the services of George Meade, and while the general never explicitly stated as much, no doubt he reflected on his experiences in the Mexican War while leading Federal soldiers in America's most defining epoch. Characteristics central to his Civil War experience—namely, skepticism for the press and an unconditional disdain for political meddling—were apparent in Mexico. No doubt Meade's contempt for volunteers predated his service in Mexico, but his time there only amplified his scorn for citizen-soldiers, particularly for their wanton lack of discipline. With his own soldiers, Meade earned a reputation as a strict disciplinarian. But by the summer of 1862, owing to their courageous performance on the battlefields of Virginia and Maryland, the general's opinion of volunteers had improved remarkably. He did not need to lead troops into combat to learn valuable lessons in Mexico and to internalize lasting impressions not only about war but also about the civilians and soldiers who waged it. These experiences during Meade's nineteen months in Mexico proved formative and helped shaped the most successful commanding general of the Army of the Potomac.

NOTES

1. Edwin B. Coddington, *The Gettysburg Campaign: A Study in Command* (New York: Charles Scribner's Sons, 1968), 493, 497.

2. George Gordon Meade, *The Life and Letters of George Gordon Meade, Major General United States Army,* 2 vols. (New York: Charles Scribner's Sons, 1913), 106–7 (hereafter cited as *L&L*); Samuel P. Bates, *Battle of Gettysburg* (Philadelphia: T. H. Davis, 1875), 155;

James Biddle to Gertrude, July 10, 1863, Box 1, James Cornell Biddle Letters (Collection 1881), Historical Society of Pennsylvania, Philadelphia (hereafter cited as HSP); James Starr to (Colonel) Meade, Feb. 7, 1880, Folder 9, Box 3, George G. Meade Collection (Collection 410), ibid.

3. *L&L*, 106–7; Biddle to Gertrude, July 10, 1863; Meade to Bachelder, Dec. 4, 1869, Box 4, Robert L. Brake Collection, U.S. Army Heritage and Education Center, Carlisle, PA; Emlen Carpenter to (Colonel) Meade, Sept. 27, 1880, Folder 9, Box 3, Meade Collection, HSP.

4. George Gordon Meade to Margaretta Meade (hereafter GGM to MM), May 9, 1846, Meade Collection, HSP (hereafter cited as MC, HSP). Palo Alto was Meade's baptism of fire.

5. Felice Flanery Lewis, *Trailing Clouds of Glory: Zachary Taylor's Mexican War Campaign and His Emerging Civil War Leaders* (Tuscaloosa: University of Alabama Press, 2010), xiv; John G. Selby, *Meade: The Price of Command, 1863–1865* (Kent, OH: Kent State University Press, 2018), 3. The U.S. Army had two different engineering corps during the Mexican War: the Corps of Topographical Engineers (Meade's corps) and the Corps of Engineers (in which future Civil War commanders Robert E. Lee, P. G. T. Beauregard, and George B. McClellan each served).

6. Lewis, *Trailing Clouds of Glory*, xvi.

7. *L&L*, 17–18. A graduate of the West Point class of 1835, Meade received a commission in the Third Regiment of Artillery but temporarily had left the army only to return in May 1842 with the appointment to the Corps of Topographical Engineers.

8. GGM to MM, Oct. 11, 1845, Apr. 21, 1846, MC, HSP; *L&L*, 7. For an excellent discussion of Meade's experiences in Mexico within the contours of nineteenth-century masculinity, see Christopher S. Stowe, "George Gordon Meade and the Boundaries of Nineteenth-Century Military Masculinity," *Civil War History* 61, no. 4 (Dec. 2015): 362–99.

9. John S. D. Eisenhower, *So Far from God: The U.S. War with Mexico, 1846–1848* (New York: Random House, 1989; repr., Norman: University of Oklahoma Press, 2000), 30–34; K. Jack Bauer, *The Mexican War, 1846–1848* (Lincoln: University of Nebraska Press, 1974), 17–19.

10. GGM to MM, Sept. 18, 1845, May 28, Nov. 10, 1846, Feb. 8, 1847, MC, HSP; Freeman Cleaves, *Meade of Gettysburg* (Norman: University of Oklahoma Press, 1960), 16; Christopher S. Stowe, "A Philadelphia Gentleman: The Cultural, Institutional, and Political Socialization of George Gordon Meade" (Ph.D. diss., University of Toledo, 2005), 107, 116; Samuel J. Watson, *Peacekeepers and Conquerors: The Army Officer Corps on the American Frontier, 1821–1846* (Lawrence: University Press of Kansas, 2013), 388. On December 31, 1840, Meade married Margaretta Sergeant (called Margaret by her family), the daughter of John Sergeant, who was Henry Clay's vice-presidential running mate in the 1832 election. At Corpus Christi Meade also met Capt. George McCall, a fellow Pennsylvanian who would later be his division commander in the Pennsylvania Reserves.

11. Richard Bruce Winders, *Mr. Polk's Army: The American Military Experience in the Mexican War* (College Station: Texas A&M University Press, 1997), 21. The most definitive study on the engineer corps during the Mexican War is Adrian G. Traas, *From the Golden Gate to Mexico City: The U.S. Army Topographical Engineers in the Mexican War,*

1846–1848 (Washington, DC: Office of History, Corps of Engineers and Center of Military History, 1993).

12. Bauer, *Mexican War*, 68–69.

13. Winders, *Mr. Polk's Army*, 194–97.

14. Ibid., 13, 199–200.

15. Ibid., 199. Alexis de Tocqueville observed a duality within America's military as both a democratic army and an aristocratic army. The democratic army, rooted in the tradition of the citizen-soldier, privileged freedom and the citizen over the soldier. By contrast, the aristocratic army was rooted in the West Point officer cadre and retained strict adherence to discipline and professionalization.

16. *L&L*, 12–14; Cleaves, *Meade of Gettysburg*, 13–15; Stowe, "Philadelphia Gentleman," 84–87. Unfortunately, no letters from Meade survive from his service in Florida to provide specific insight into his impressions or opinions on that war or the men who fought it. He was assigned to Company C, 3rd Artillery and suffered from recurring fevers (likely malaria), being sent home in the spring of 1836. Relative to Meade's disdain for volunteers, Christopher Stowe argues that he had been "socialized to display genuine consideration toward those less fortunate than he, a character trait befitting the archetypical gentleman." Ibid.

17. William B. Skelton, *An American Profession of Arms: The Army Officer Corps, 1784–1861* (Lawrence: University Press of Kansas, 1992), 295; GGM to MM, May 27, July 9, 1846, MC, HSP.

18. GGM to MM, May 27, 1846, MC, HSP.

19. GGM to MM, May 28, 1846, ibid.

20. GGM to MM, Dec. 3, 1846, ibid.

21. GGM to MM, July 9, 1846, ibid.; Winders, *Mr. Polk's Army*, 12–13.

22. GGM to MM, May 27, June 12, 1846, MC, HSP.

23. GGM to MM, Sept. 22, Oct. 12, 1861, MC, HSP; *L&L*, 216–17.

24. GGM to MM, Nov. 24, 1861, Sept. 3, 18, 1862, MC, HSP.

25. John Burnett to Gould, Oct. 27, 1894, John Gould Papers, Library Archives and Manuscripts, Dartmouth University, Hanover, NH; Frank Holsinger, "How It Feels to Be under Fire," ed. Henry Steele Commager, in *The Blue and the Gray*, vol. 1 (Indianapolis: Bobbs-Merrill, 1973), 315; Steven Ramold, *Baring the Iron Hand: Discipline in the Union Army* (DeKalb: Northern Illinois University Press, 2009), 181–218.

26. GGM to MM, June 28, July 9, 1846, MC, HSP.

27. GGM to MM, June 28, Dec. 3, 1846, ibid.; Bauer, *Mexican War*, 83.

28. GGM to MM, June 28, July 9, Dec. 3, 1846, MC, HSP.

29. GGM to MM, Feb. 8, 1847, ibid.

30. Mark Grimsley, *The Hard Hand of War: Union Military Policy Toward Southern Civilians, 1861–1865* (Cambridge: Cambridge University Press, 1995), 7–46. Grimsley identifies three phases of Federal policy toward civilians: conciliation, pragmatism, and hard war.

31. Uzal W. Ent, *The Pennsylvania Reserves in the Civil War* (Jefferson, NC: McFarland, 2014), 30–31; George Bayard, "Report of Col. George D. Bayard, First Pennsylvania Cavalry,"

Nov. 27, 1861, *The War of the Rebellion: A Compilation of the Official Records of the Union and Confederate Armies,* 70 vols. in 128 pts. (Washington, DC: Government Printing Office, 1880–1901), ser. 1, 5:448–49 (hereafter cited as *OR,* all references to ser. 1 unless otherwise stated); GGM to MM, Oct. 14, 1861, MC, HSP; George McCall, "Report of Brig. Gen. George McCall, Expedition to Gunnell's Farm, near Dranesville, Va.," Dec. 6, 1861, *OR,* 5:455–56; GGM to MM, Dec. 8, 1861, MC, HSP; Josiah Sypher, *History of the Pennsylvania Reserves* (Lancaster, PA: Elias Barr, 1865), 128; "From Our Volunteers," *Ebensburg (PA) Alleghenian,* Dec. 19, 1861; E., "Two Foraging Expeditions, and Incidents Connected Therewith," ibid., Dec. 26, 1861; Joseph Gibbs, *Three Years in the Bloody Eleventh: The Campaigns of a Pennsylvania Reserves Regiment* (University Park: Pennsylvania State University Press, 2002), 64–65.

32. GGM to MM, Dec. 8, 1861, MC, HSP.

33. Alexander G. Lovelace, "Meade and the Media: Civil War Journalism and the New History of War Reporting," *Journal of Military History* 85, no.4 (Oct. 2021): 911.

34. GGM to MM, May 15, 1846, MC, HSP.

35. GGM to MM, Nov. 27, 1846, ibid.; Bauer, *Mexican War,* 101; Eisenhower, *So Far from God,* 151.

36. Selby, *Meade,* 4; Lovelace, "Meade and the Media," 913.

37. GGM to MM, Dec. 3, 1846, MC, HSP.

38. GGM to MM, Oct. 20, Dec. 3, 1846, ibid.; *Republican Banner* (Nashville, TN), Oct. 16, 1846. Meade boasted of their luxurious quarters in General Ortega's home, noting they each had several servants at their discretion.

39. GGM to MM, Dec. 3, 1846, MC, HSP.

40. GGM to MM, July 9, 1846, ibid.

41. GGM to MM, Dec. 3, 1846, ibid.

42. GGM to MM, July 9, 1846, ibid.

43. GGM to [illegible], Aug. 5, 1861, ibid; Thomas J. Goss, *The War within the Union High Command: Politics and Generalship during the Civil War* (Lawrence: University of Kansas Press, 2003), 54.

44. "Victory! Waterloo Eclipsed!!," *Philadelphia Inquirer,* July 6, 1863; *New York Herald,* July 10, 1863.

45. GGM to MM, July 8, 1863, MC, HSP.

46. For a sampling of the news articles, see "The Escape of Lee's Army," *New York Tribune,* July 18, 1863; "General Meade," *Detroit Free Press,* Dec. 20, 1863; *Pittsburgh Daily Commercial,* Dec. 9, 1863; *Weekly Herald and Tribune* (St. Joseph, MO), Dec. 10, 1863; and *Louisville (KY) Daily Journal,* Dec. 7, 1863.

47. Historicus, "The Battle of Gettysburg," *New York Tribune,* Mar. 12, 1864; Meade to Townsend, Mar. 15, 1864, MC, HSP; GGM to MM, Mar. 16, , Apr. 6, 1864, ibid.; James A. Hessler, *Sickles at Gettysburg* (New York: Savas Beatie, 2009), 285–88; Halleck to Meade, Mar. 20, 1864, *OR,* 27(1):137; Meade to Halleck, Mar. 22, 1864, *ibid.*; GGM to MM, Apr. 2, 1864, MC, HSP. Many historians believe that Sickles wrote the Historicus letter, although

other potential authors include Henry Tremain (Sickles's aide) and Daniel Butterfield. The most thorough assessment of the Meade-Sickles controversy is Richard A. Sauers, *Gettysburg: The Meade-Sickles Controversy* (Dulles, VA: Potomac Books, 2003).

48. "Meade's Position," *Philadelphia Inquirer*, June 2, 1864. Both Crapsey's contemporaries and multiple historians have incorrectly spelled the journalist's surname as "Cropsey," but the weight of the evidence, including contemporary accounts written by the man in question, reveals his name as "Crapsey."

49. GGM to MM, June 9, 1864, MC, HSP. Grant approved this punishment.

50. Ibid.; Meade, "Order," *OR*, 36(3):670; Sylvanus Cadwallader, *Three Years with Grant*, ed. Benjamin P. Thomas (Lincoln: University of Nebraska Press, 1995), 206–7; Marseana Rudolph Patrick, *Inside Lincoln's Army: The Diary of Marsena Rudolph Patrick, Provost Marshal General, Army of the Potomac*, ed. David S. Sparks (New York: A. S. Barnes, 1964), 381.

51. Cadwallader, *Three Years with Grant*, 208–9; 256–57; Selby, *Meade*, 210–11.

52. GGM to MM, May 27, June 12, July 9, 1846, MC, HSP.

53. GGM to MM, Oct. 27, Nov. 10, 1846, Feb. 3, 1847, ibid.

54. GGM to MM, Jan. 24, 1847, ibid.

55. Winders, *Mr. Polk's Army*, 33; Eisenhower, *So Far From God*, 161; GGM to MM, Feb. 8, 1847, MC, HSP. Scott was Taylor's immediate superior, and Polk disliked Scott, who was also a Whig.

56. GGM to MM, Nov. 13, 1862, MC, HSP.

57. Traas, *From the Golden Gate to Mexico City*, 134, 137. Maj. Joseph Mansfield used one of Meade's maps to prepare his attack on Monterrey. Mansfield would fall mortally wounded at the Battle of Antietam in 1862.

58. Meade, "Circular," July 1, 1863, *OR*, 27(3):458–59; Coddington, *Gettysburg Campaign*, 238–39. For two recent interpretations of the Pipe Creek Circular as evidence that Meade did not want to fight at Gettysburg, see Stephen W. Sears, *Lincoln's Lieutenants: The High Command of the Army of the Potomac* (Boston: Houghton Mifflin, 2017), 546–47; and Allen C. Guelzo, *Gettysburg: The Last Invasion* (New York: Vintage Books, 2013), 118–19.

59. Ulysses S. Grant, *The Personal Memoirs of Ulysses S. Grant: The Complete Annotated Edition*, ed. John F. Marszalek, David S. Nolen, and Louis P. Gallo (Cambridge, MA: Harvard University Press, 2017), 753.

60. GGM to MM, June 7, 1846, MC, HSP; Traas, *From the Golden Gate to Mexico City*, 128–29, 134. Taylor blamed this delay on the War Department for not sending an adequate number of pontoon boats.

61. Bauer, *Mexican War*, 99–101; Eisenhower, *So Far from God*, 147–50, 161, 164; Winders, *Mr. Polk's Army*, 33. Bauer argues that Taylor erred in the armistice, noting that although his army was in bad shape, Ampudia's was much worse off and Taylor should have exploited his advantage. Because Taylor's army was badly damaged, Eisenhower suggested that the U.S. commander made the correct decision.

62. GGM to MM, Sept. 27, Oct. 5, Nov. 10, 1846, MC, HSP.

63. GGM to MM, Nov. 10, 1846, ibid.

64. Meade to Halleck, July 14, 1863, *OR*, 27(1):93; Meade to Halleck, July 31, 1863, ibid., 108–9; GGM to MM, Sept. 22, 1863, MC, HSP; Meade to Halleck, Oct. 18, 1863, *OR*, 29(3):346.

65. Kevin Dougherty, *Civil War Leadership and the Mexican War Experience* (Jackson: University Press of Mississippi, 2007), 81–85, 185. Recent scholarship has probed the constraints facing the Army of the Potomac and offers a more nuanced analysis of the pursuit from Gettysburg while contextualizing the pursuit within Lincoln's unrealistic expectation of decisive battle. See Jennifer M. Murray, "'Your Golden Opportunity Is Gone': George Gordon Meade, the Expectations of Decisive Battle, and the Road to Williamsport," in *Upon the Fields of Battle: Essays on the Military History of America's Civil War*, ed. Andrew Bledsoe and Andrew Lang (Baton Rouge: Louisiana University Press, 2018), 71–91; and Kent Masterson Brown, *Meade at Gettysburg: A Study in Command* (Chapel Hill: University of North Carolina Press, 2021), 306–70.

66. GGM to MM, Apr. 24, 1864, MC, HSP.

67. Brooks D. Simpson, *Ulysses S. Grant: Triumph over Adversity, 1822–1865* (Boston: Houghton Mifflin, 2000), 45; Cleaves, *Meade of Gettysburg*, 42.

68. GGM to MM, Mar. 8, 25, Apr. 20, 1847, MC, HSP; Traas, *From the Golden Gate to Mexico City*, 177–78, 185–86; Cleaves, *Meade of Gettysburg*, 42–44. Meade received a brevet for his services at Monterrey. He had at least one occasion to interact with Captain Lee during the Mexican War. On March 6, 1847, Scott and several of his staff officers, Meade included, were aboard a steamer reconnoitering the enemy's positions at Vera Cruz when Mexican artillery fired upon their vessel. Meade recorded that the enemy guns fired at least eleven shells, mostly sailing overhead. He concluded, "This operation I considered very foolish; for, having on board all the general officers of the army, one shot, hitting the vessel and disabling it, would have left us a floating target to the enemy." In addition to Lee, other future Civil War officers on board included P. G. T. Beauregard and George McClellan.

69. GGM to MM, May 28, Sept. 11, 1846, MC, HSP; Richard Meade Bache, *Life of General George Gordon Meade: Commander of the Army of the Potomac* (Philadelphia: Henry T. Coates, 1897), 13.

WHEN A LITTLE SLOW MATTERED MOST

George H. Thomas in Mexico

BRIAN STEEL WILLS

The stillness of the early morning hours of May 3, 1846, suddenly convulsed with the sounds of war as Mexican artillery opened on the small American defensive work known for a time as "Fort Texas" on the Rio Grande opposite the town of Matamoros. For George Henry Thomas, this was the first military action of any significance he experienced in a dispute over borders that brought the United States and Mexico to hostilities. The West Point–trained native of Virginia occupied the post as a junior officer in Company E, 3rd Artillery, alongside men from the 7th Infantry, under the immediate command of Major Jacob Brown. The observant artillerist may or may not have noticed the ominous signs of bells tolling the previous evening across the way and the specter of local priests moving from one gun position to another to bless the tubes for the coming baptism of fire, but the start of the 5:00 a.m. bombardment ended all speculation and assured that hot work was now at hand.[1]

In future years Thomas would establish himself as one of the best of the U.S. general officers during the American Civil War. His role in that conflict became so significant that Ezra Warner, the compiler of two volumes of biographical sketches of Union and Confederate commanders, describes him as the "third of the triumvirate who won the war for the Union."[2] Although he graduated in 1840 from the U.S. Military Academy at West Point with a ranking of twelfth and went on to a broad and distinguished career in the "Old Army" and during the Civil War, Thomas also endured criticisms reflected in the nickname he acquired, "Old Slow-Trot."[3]

As with so many of his colleagues, Thomas's service and distinction in the Civil War occurred in the context of his education and his prior life experience in the field. By the time the guns sounded in 1846 at Fort Texas, the young officer's duties had taken him to numerous posts from New York and Florida to Maryland and South Carolina. A war with Mexico added to that background and provided additional learning opportunities on campaign for future application. A modern scholar has offered an overall perspective that includes Thomas when concluding, "Certainly the Mexican War was a training ground to some extent for all of its American participants, some eight hundred of whom would serve in Confederate or Union forces."[4]

For those who knew him well, Thomas provided the example of a thoughtful and intelligent individual whose focus on preparation over impetuosity was undeniable. Future comrade Oliver O. Howard observed that "he was naturally a thorough student" whose "singular industry" led to "his retention of what was once comprehended," aided by "an unusual power of memory."[5] An instructor from Thomas's days at West Point recalled, "He never allowed anything to escape a thorough examination, and left nothing behind that he did not fully comprehend."[6] Most of the individuals who assessed his capabilities noted that Thomas was more prone to the efficient implementation of principles than to the creation of them, but they did not consider this attribute a deficiency.[7]

In addition to these academic qualities, the young officer demonstrated a willingness and capability to take what was happening, process it, and draw upon it afterward. "I have educated myself not to feel," Thomas declared later when difficulties confronted him in his career, rather than allowing himself to become consumed by emotions, jealousies, or setbacks.[8] Likewise, his sense of personal involvement came from his lived experiences. "I cannot leave," he confided to a colleague later over the question of furloughs, for "something is sure to get out of order if I go away from my command. It was always so, even when I commanded a post. I had to stick by and attend to everything, or else affairs went wrong."[9] He expected to assert control as much as possible personally and take responsibility for his actions accordingly.

The ever-practical Thomas had once worried that the small size of the regular army and the rare opportunities for combat experience would prove detrimental to his professional progress, although the departure of others from a potential line of promotion could help offset such disadvantages to some extent. As the newly minted officer explained from his posting at Fort Columbus, New York, in 1840 to his brother John, "if that should be the case, I shall not be so much displeased as I shall be a little higher in the army list, and as I shall have to depend upon my sword for a living for some time at least if not always I shall not grumble a great deal."[10] Still, routine assignments would count little, except to expose a person to negative assessments if something went awry.

As if to confirm his concerns, while in Florida during one of the many clashes of U.S. forces with the Seminoles in that region, administrative detail initially kept Thomas from the field. When he had the opportunity to join an operation under Major Richard D. Wade in November 1841, it resulted in the capture of some seventy Seminoles. His participation resulted in Thomas receiving the first of several brevets bestowed on him in these earliest years of his service. This one, for "Gallantry and Good Conduct in the War against the Seminole Indians," elevated him to brevet first lieutenant.[11]

By now a veteran of many diverse fields and circumstances, George Thomas was off to Texas in response to developments there as friction mounted between the United States and Mexico. His command left Fort Moultrie, outside Charleston, South Carolina, on June 26, 1845, and arrived in the port city of New Orleans by midsummer. On July 24 the troops proceeded to Corpus Christi, reaching that location on the Texas coast by August 2.[12] The nature of the departure had required that the unit proceed without its animals, thus one of Thomas's initial tasks upon arrival was to obtain stock of sufficient number and quality to serve the battery. Once more the duty demanded that the lieutenant exercise his practical skills for ensuring that he and his comrades had the appropriate resources to function, and he rose to the task with a commendable sense of effectiveness.[13]

Thomas was part of a force gathering under Brigadier General Zachary Taylor, whom staffer George G. Meade described as "a plain, sensible old gentleman."[14] Occasional profanity and an utter lack of outward pretension rendered "Old Rough and Ready" winsome to the soldiery.[15] Yet popularity did not shield the commander from the many challenges in the period ahead, when volunteers swelled the ranks and impatient citizens balked at the requirements of military service. In the meantime, the professionals presented an impressive force. In the latter part of 1846, West Pointer John Sedgwick wrote home to say that he considered Taylor's army at that point in the campaign "better organized, has a greater proportion of artillery, and is better equipped than any army we have ever sent into the field; and no one fears the result with any numbers that the Mexicans can bring against them."[16]

A long winter gave way to the likelihood of movement in the spring. "I find everyone here in a state of excitement," Meade observed on March 2, 1846, "incident to our approaching march on the Rio Grande. It appears General Taylor has received positive orders from Washington to march, and he is to take up a position on the river, immediately opposite Matamoros."[17] That sense of anticipation grew in the next days. "Everything here is hurry-scurry, preparatory for the march," Meade noted hastily on the fifth.[18] Then, on the morning of March 11, the Third Brigade, under Colonel William Whistler and containing Braxton Bragg's battery, Company E of the 3rd Artillery, with George Thomas, set out to follow their comrades.[19] By the end of the month, the troops appeared before Matamoros and immediately worked to establish a fortification capable of supporting artillery in the bend of the river opposite that town.[20]

For much of April, both sides watched each other suspiciously and worked diligently to improve their positions.[21] At the same time, ongoing internal debates and disputes at higher levels between generals and politicians plagued the combatant forces, but these were less likely to concern a junior officer like Thomas as much as the conditions on the ground. When Mexican general Pedro de Ampudia reached Matamoros on the eleventh and forwarded an ultimatum to General Taylor declaring that the Americans had twenty-four hours to withdraw to the Nueces River, matters took on a new urgency for all.

Increasingly, Taylor felt the necessity of connecting with and protecting his supply depot at Port Isabel and decided to take much of his force in that direction. Paring down the garrison at Fort Texas opened an opportunity for the Mexicans to attack the post.[22] Even so, Meade was not convinced that the enemy would succeed in Taylor's absence. "Our position was very strong, but the necessity of coming here for provisions obliged the General to leave with his whole force, except the garrison of the fort."[23] Certainly, the position was in good hands. According to historian Felice Flannery Lewis, these forces contained "fifteen future Civil War general officers—in addition to Bragg, [and] his lieutenants George Thomas and John Reynolds."[24]

Meade characterized the bombardment that inaugurated the clash on May 3 as a "vigorous and continuous fire during the whole day."[25] Although

Thomas's smaller 6-pounder tubes were not able to do much more than add to the general effect, heavier American pieces dismounted two Mexican cannon and bought the defenders a brief respite. In response, the attackers brought up additional guns, including a mortar, which allowed them to maintain their rate of fire. John Reynolds insisted in retrospect: "Of one thing I am certain. I can never again, I don't think, be placed in a more uncomfortable situation than the one we just got out of. I had rather be on ten battle fields than take another week's bombardment, such as we had in 'Fort Brown.'"[26] Another of the fort's defenders remarked similarly, maintaining that he "would rather have fought twenty battles" than undergo the steady and relentless shelling, short rations, and lack of sleep the Americans endured.[27]

Because Thomas's pieces were unlikely to be useful unless Mexican ground forces attempted to assault Fort Texas directly, the artillerist had occasion to witness the bombardments that the combatants traded with each other. Noting him sitting calmly during one exchange, a comrade asked for his assessment. Thomas described the American firepower and accuracy in largely positive terms but offered an important practical point as well. "Excellent, but I'm thinking that we'll need, after a while, the ammunition you're throwing away."[28] The comment demonstrates his aversion toward wastefulness and an understanding of the need for controlling the expenditure of vital resources that might be difficult to replenish via a long and tenuous supply chain. Various biographers and historians have suggested that Thomas learned from this situation an important lesson concerning the problem of overextended supply lines, but the soldier's practical bent focused more toward husbanding the supplies on hand.[29]

When Taylor found the road back to Fort Texas obstructed, his men fought at Palo Alto on May 8 and Resaca De La Palma on May 9 to break through. The two engagements allowed him to relieve the Fort Texas defenders, although the death there of Major Brown only a few days earlier tempered the successes. Renaming Fort Texas as Fort Brown in honor of the fallen officer, not to mention the ability of the U.S. forces to occupy Matamoros when the Mexicans evacuated the town, offered a degree of solace.[30]

The American commander then began planning his next operation. One soldier noted, "Upon receipt of the order to proceed to Reynosa, [Henry] Wilson's battalion recrossed to Matamoros, and on the morning of June 6, along with Lieutenant George Thomas, commanding the selected section of Bragg's battery, and a company of mounted Texans, followed the river northward." These troops arrived at Reynosa at noon on June 10.[31]

By the next month, Taylor was ready to probe farther into the Mexican interior with forces that included Thomas's artillery detachment.[32] The Americans left Reynosa on July 13 and reached Camargo three days later.[33] Daniel Harvey Hill recalled that the town "was captured without firing a gun," although to be in position to respond to any potential resistance, the occupying force contained "two field pieces under the command of Lt. Thomas, 3d Artillery."[34] As one modern scholar has explained, Thomas's section "had been the first to reach Camargo," with others following as Taylor ordered them up.[35]

The conditions in the town proved miserable, with heat and dust the most common element.[36] Thomas had already learned to adapt to circumstances in various settings, although he was not oblivious to any benefits or luxuries when they came his way. One new arrival recalled being shown to the regimental campsite "in the plaza," where he dined the following day "with Thomas and fared well. They had a most excellent dish that I never saw before, though it is an exceedingly simple one, viz: fried peaches. Thomas told me there were plenty of fine peaches in town just ripening."[37]

General Taylor was anxious to position his troops in the most advantageous manner, often moving and reassigning elements of his Army of Occupation to suit the occasion. He shifted an irascible Captain Thomas W. Sherman to a quartermaster post that left Lieutenant Thomas, as senior officer in Company E, 3rd Artillery, temporarily in command.[38] Yet Camargo was only meant as a stop on the road leading from the Rio Grande to the city of Monterrey. In this interim period the Virginian had learned firsthand the degree to which logistics and morale dictated the capacity of armed forces to fulfill their missions. The approximately 6,000 American troops finally lurched forward in September.

Their opponents at Monterrey enjoyed benefits in addition to protecting their native soil. The Mexicans had assembled a force of 7,303 men and at least forty pieces of artillery to control strongpoints for defending the city. A massive fortification known as the Citadel overlooked Monterrey, aided by a collection of earthworks and converted structures, including a tanyard on the outskirts that lent its name to a set of works known as La Tenería.

Lack of heavy ordnance and American impatience worked against any notions of siege operations. Despite their numerical limitations, Taylor planned to overwhelm the defenders through a concerted and coordinated effort that would require them to meet threats from several sectors at the same time. He planned to use David E. Twiggs's First Division to feint in one direction, while William J. Worth advanced his Second Division on the other side of the Citadel. Twiggs could always convert his diversionary action into a more comprehensive effort if the opportunity presented.[39]

At the outset, as planning turned into operation, factors seemed to conspire against the chances for success for the U.S. forces. An ill Twiggs was unable to lead his men into action personally. Lieutenant Colonel John Garland thus assumed temporary command of the division, with Taylor boldly instructing him "take any of them little forts down there with the bayonet." But the attack quickly lost its focus. One account labeled the operation "an ill-starred movement," as the diversionary effort turned into a full-blown engagement.[40]

Sustained Mexican artillery fire pummeled the men as they struggled forward. The American artillery meant to provide support for these troops had to confront the same gauntlet of fire. General Taylor had assigned John Pope the task of assisting the "advanced troops [in] entering, or trying to enter, the place." The men lost precious time and suffered from exposure to enemy shells while "tearing away with a small body of pioneers, the rough abatis which lined the face of the town, so as to admit more easy passage of troops, especially of artillery." Thomas watched the drama unfold before he sent one of his own men forward to help, "with a lighted port-fire to set fire to the dry branches and brush of the abatis." Pope, who had described his comrade from Virginia "as always, tall and stalwart" with an "impassive, unmoved countenance," surely appreciated the assistance.[41]

Unfortunately, as the artillery teams attempted to navigate the narrow streets, they became subjected to heavy fire and were only able to clear the tubes momentarily through raw manpower. Smoke from the firing and clouds of debris from the shattered adobe houses limited the effectiveness of weapons that required sighting to be accurate. Flailing horses compounded the confusion of the battle.[42] Soldiers attacking the defenders of the Tenería offered the best hope for the battered cannoneers when they overran the Mexican position, giving the artillerists and their immediate infantry support an opportunity to regather and consolidate their positions. Yet for all the dramatic elements of the First Division's advance, not much else appeared to have been accomplished on its front. The town's defenses re-

mained largely intact, and it was difficult to determine the success or failure of American arms elsewhere. Thomas's contribution for the moment
became, of necessity, more defensive than offensive in nature.

As night closed on the town, the Mexican forces decided to pull back
to positions around the plaza deemed more defensible. They had added
makeshift barricades of debris and stone supported by all the firepower they
could bring to bear on the approaches. Aside from the strength of the works
they had erected to make a stand, the nature of the surrounding structures
aided the defense. One participant explained, "The dwelling houses all had
flat roofs, surrounded by walls three feet high forming so many small for-
tresses."[43]

Still, Mississippian Jefferson Davis reported that his men adapted to
the situation. "We continued to advance and drive the enemy by passing
through courts, gardens and houses, taking every favorable position to fire
from the house tops; which from their style of architecture furnishes a good
defense against musketry."[44] Subsequently, General Taylor reported, "The
streets were at different and well chosen points, barricaded by heavy masonry walls, with embrasures for one or more guns." He recognized that
challenging work lay ahead. "These arrangements of defences gave to our
operations at this moment a complicated character, demanding much care
and precaution."[45] As the Americans closed in on their final objective, Davis
noted, "near the Plaza . . . we found all the streets barricaded and swept by
a fire so severe that to advance from our last position it became necessary
to construct a defence across the street."[46]

Taylor wisely understood the fruitlessness of frontal assaults to achieve
a breakthrough. Lieutenants Thomas and Samuel G. French became responsible for the placement of an artillery piece at a strategic location from
which the Mexican barricades could be tested and potentially breached.
The nature of the urban road system was such that all of the work would
have to be done out in the open, although French recalled employing a
technique he had learned from an incident in street fighting in Philadelphia in which the gun crew used ropes and the gun's recoil to reload while
remaining relatively unexposed.[47] As Reynolds's biographer observed, "'By
the left wheel' made some sense on the flat terrain of the drill ground, but
the manual was silent on the handling of guns jammed up against house
walls in mere alleyways."[48]

During this phase of the fighting, Thomas and French were required to work in tandem, with smoke from the fire of one screening the movement of the other. Even so, little headway seemed possible, and the lack of knowledge as to how the other division under Worth was faring complicated matters for Taylor. Consequently, he ordered the effort in this quarter discontinued, requiring Thomas to disengage from his exposed position.[49]

General Twiggs highlighted the work of the artillerists, who he felt deserved "the highest praise, for their skill and good conduct under the heaviest fire of the enemy, which, when an opportunity offered, was concentrated against them."[50] Major General J. Pinckney Henderson complimented "Lieutenant Thomas, of the artillery, and his brave men, for the bold advance and effective management of the gun under his charge." Then he added dramatically of the officer, "When ordered to retire, he reloaded his piece, fired a farewell shot at the foe, and returned (we hope without loss) under a shower of bullets."[51]

As things turned out, Worth's command had succeeded in pushing its way into the city and reached a point from which it could bring the plaza defenders under fire. Given such circumstances, the Mexican commander opened negotiations for ending the fighting. The Americans understandably rejected General Ampudia's request for permission to march out of the city without restrictions, but the battered combatants chose to surrender rather than continue fighting. The cost for Taylor's victory at Monterrey stood at 120 killed, 368 wounded, and 43 missing. Ampudia's casualties in the battle were 367 killed and wounded.[52]

Both sides required a period of recuperation before further military operations occurred. In the meantime, reports and plaudits flowed for the participants. Although circumstances had limited his engagement, Thomas received a promotion to brevet captain for his performance, having demonstrated "gallant conduct in the several conflicts of Monterrey, Mex."[53]

Unlike Fort Texas/Brown, where the situation had necessitated more distant firing, Monterrey had required Thomas and his compatriots to bring their combat skills to bear in an urban setting. The special circumstances of street fighting for flexibility and creativity taxed and refined their capabilities. In the process the officers and their men gained valuable experience as to what such conditions required from them and their abilities to meet those demands.

Subsequently, Bragg's promotion and reassignment left Thomas in charge of the company temporarily after November 21, 1846. Lieutenant Cadmus M. Wilcox recalled, "Near the Third Infantry was Bragg's battery, and with it were George H. Thomas and John F. Reynolds." Describing Thomas as exhibiting a "tall spare form" with "large, black eyes and heavy brows, [and a] nervous, tremulous voice, [that] attracted notice," Wilcox also recognized his fellow officer's "industry, attention to duty, and strict regard for discipline."[54]

Unfortunately, in the course of these assignments, the young officer had a brief but disagreeable personal confrontation with General Twiggs, who had ordered Thomas to supply a mule team for his use. A stickler for procedure, the Virginian deferred while he sought instruction on the matter from someone higher in the chain of command. This act struck Twiggs as rank insubordination and disobedience of orders, which became even more galling when Thomas's actions won him approval.[55]

A new year brought additional prospects for Thomas but found him in ill health for a brief period. Daniel H. Hill recorded in early January 1847 that, in addition to having "most of my days, spent in idleness and folly," he had made contact with "Lt. Thomas, 3d Artillery, who was left sick at Monterey [but since] came up. He represents Monterey to be exceedingly sickly."[56] The continued advance of Taylor's command would be a welcome development for the recovering soldier.

On February 19 a number of these troops proceeded by water as part of the transfer. "We were carried out in the steamer *De Rosset* to the ship *Henry*," Hill recalled, "crowded, four hundred of us, on a vessel scarcely calculated to take half that number." The next day when "a Norther came up," matters became worse. "I was exceedingly sick all day," Hill confessed. "Some stalls were put up for the officers about three feet wide. In one of these I slept or attempted to sleep with Lt. Thomas, 3d Artillery, dividing my bed with him as he had lost his in the unutterable confusion with which our baggage had been thrown together."[57] Thomas left no record of the experience or the appalling conditions he and his temporary bunkmate endured, but it surely tested his well-developed sense of order and efficiency. Certainly, he learned for himself what the transportation of larger bodies of troops for campaigning at the discretion of their superiors entailed.

Thomas also watched as other imperatives, military and political, altered the nature of the command to which he was attached. Detachments of forces for operations with Major General Winfield Scott in Central Mexico diminished Taylor's army and separated Thomas from other comrades. Regardless of the conditions, the relative quiet of the period could not last indefinitely—nor would Thomas's greater level of command responsibility. Captain Sherman's return put the Virginian once more in his place in Company E's chain of command alongside Reynolds and French. As for the army, by moving to Saltillo, its lines of communications and supply operated under greater strain than ever. Much like with Camargo, Taylor meant Saltillo to serve primarily as a staging ground for his next major advance.

Thus, when several of the principal American commanders rode out of the town to examine the terrain and discuss viable options, Brigadier General John Wool thought that the likeliest choice lay on ground near a hacienda called Buena Vista ("Beautiful View"). A narrowing of the road passage at Angostura Pass suggested substantial advantages. To one of the accompanying dragoons, Wool explained, "this is the very spot of all others I have yet seen in Mexico, which I should select for battle, were I obliged with a small army to fight a large one."[58] Even so, the nature of the ground presented dangers as well from the numerous gullies and deeper ravines cutting through the landscape.

At the same time, multiple challenges appeared in the form of internal squabbling in the officer ranks, shortages of supplies for enlisted personnel, and the behavior of the numerous volunteers who had joined the command. Arguments over the appropriate tactical deployment continued to complicate matters over whether to defend a position at Agua Nueva or to pull back to the ground Wool had noticed near Buena Vista.[59] A further unwelcome situation occurred when a dispatch rider with a copy of the American plan of instruction fell into the hands of the overall Mexican commander, Antonio López de Santa Anna. Learning more about the conditions under which Taylor and his forces were operating, Santa Anna elected to strike quickly. A smashing victory here would allow him to concentrate against other threats from Scott and deal a blow to the entire U.S. war effort.

While Santa Anna pressed his men relentlessly, some of Taylor's 4,500 Americans concentrated near Buena Vista. Wool, who was responsible for establishing a defensive line, tried to use the topography of the area to his best advantage. He secured the road leading north to Saltillo with artillery and infantry and positioned troops on the heights to the east. Taylor approved of Wool's disposition of troops before returning to Saltillo, a mile and a half away, to oversee the defense of his supplies.[60] Lieutenant Wilcox noted that in the center of the U.S. line, "six companies of the Second Illinois" under Colonel William H. Bissell "were posted on the plateau opposite the head of the ravine; in their left and a little retired was a 12-pound howitzer, under Lieut. S. G. French, Third Artillery, and in like position a 6-pounder, under Lieut. George H. Thomas, Third Artillery. To the right and rear of Thomas were two companies of the First Dragoons, under Capt. Enoch Steen, and to their right and near the head of the ravine was [Ben] McCulloch's company of mounted Texans."[61] The Americans were as prepared as they were going to be to receive the shock of the expected Mexican blows.

Meanwhile, Santa Anna's army of approximately 16,000 men, now having lost the element of surprise, spent most of the day on the twenty-second deploying for action. The sounds of music, occasional cheering, and clouds of dust filled the air and heightened the anticipation for the combatants, adding to the colorful pageantry and intimidating nature of the exhibition. Once he was satisfied with his arrangements, Santa Anna sent a demand for surrender to his counterpart, which Taylor declined.

A single artillery round opened the Battle of Buena Vista at 3:00 p.m. on February 22, 1847. Mexican attacks exposed Taylor's weak left flank, but despite the pressure, the Americans held their positions as night fell across the field. That evening brought a brief serenade from Santa Anna's personal band and speeches to stiffen his troops' morale for renewed fighting, but the weather turned inhospitable for the men on both sides. Artillerist French asserted, "I cannot recall a night when I came so near perishing from cold."[62]

At daybreak, Santa Anna resumed the engagement with three heavy attacking columns. Thomas' guns worked feverishly to stymie the advance, and Lieutenant French, his comrades in the 3rd Artillery, recalled that they "used canister as rapidly as men (so well trained as ours were) could serve the guns." Captain Sherman observed in his report that Thomas's section was positioned on the plateau so to "support . . . the right of a brigade of infantry," and as the fighting intensified, the company's "reserve section was ordered up and took position on the right of Lieut. Thomas' pieces." The combined "sharp fire of cannister and shells" from these guns held the enemy in check briefly. Sherman recalled, "I joined Lt. Thomas who had been constantly engaged during the forenoon in the preservation of that important position and whom I found closely engaged with the enemy and that time in a very advanced position."[63]

Troops under Generals Francisco Pacheco and Francisco Pérez pressed the American left and center almost to the breaking point. In conjunction with the 2nd Illinois Artillery, Thomas and French fired at close range and, according to Wilcox, "literally strewed the ground with the enemy's killed and wounded." Yet with their superior numbers, Mexican troops were able to push beyond the American left, which Wilcox later recalled subjected Thomas's and French's guns to a dangerous fire on their left and in front.[64]

This threat caused some of the American forces to break and head for a deep ravine, hoping for cover or an avenue of escape. Instead, they found themselves trapped under heavy Mexican fire and virtually surrounded by enemy lancers. "They are most miserable shots," William H. L. Wallace observed with palpable relief, "or they would have killed every one of us huddled as we were in the [most] utter confusion."[65]

In the ensuing chaos, a round struck French in the leg while he was attempting to mount his horse. Robert S. Garnett, a cousin of Thomas's West Point classmate Richard, took French's place when the latter left the field for treatment. Suddenly, the personnel serving the guns began running in short supply. Sherman and Reynolds came up from the reserve as the available tubes shifted from point to point to meet emergencies.[66]

The American left began to bend back, which placed Thomas and the other artillerists in the center in an increasingly vulnerable situation. Captain James H. Carleton remembered that the retrograde movement "left on the plateau Lieutenant [John Paul Jones] O'Brien with two pieces, and Lieutenants Thomas and Garnett each with one."[67] Although they served their guns valiantly, the sheer weight of numbers was proving too much for the limited firepower that remained. Taylor had little choice but to divert these four guns to the threatened sector, where they "fired successively upon the enemy in front, on the heavy guns near the foot of the mountains, then on the masses threatening the left and rear."[68] One account described Thomas's and the other guns, which "played upon the Mexican troops as they passed and repassed," and the "skill and rapidity" with which they fired on enemy positions. It was a decisive moment that halted the enemy attack. Once the Mexican advance receded, other guns fired against the Mexican batteries while "Thomas and O'Brien swept the line of retreat."[69]

Taylor had committed everything he had, and as Thomas and O'Brien fed as much canister as they could bring to bear, their opponents finally gave way. But the American line remained tenuous, and when Santa Anna

sent in his reserves, the fortunes of war threatened to shift again.[70] Again
it was the three guns of Lieutenants Thomas and O'Brien that helped keep
the enemy in check. Wilcox identified this as "the crisis, the issue to be decided in a few minutes." Taylor's presence and influence remained, despite
the fact that for this moment, "there was nothing" between the general and
the enemy "but O'Brien and Thomas, the one with two, the other with one
gun."[71] A contemporary account of the fighting underscored the vital role
these artillerists played in helping secure the American victory, noting that
they maneuvered and fired their guns in whichever direction was warranted
by enemy pressure "and always with marked effect."[72]

Employing a tactic that used the recoil of the tubes from each shot to
reposition the pieces, the artillerists gave ground grudgingly.[73] Thomas held
on grimly. O'Brien was not so fortunate, as Mexican troops swarmed his
pieces and captured them. One contemporary concluded: "It never occurred
to O'Brien to save his pieces; there was too much at stake. To delay the enemy, to hold him in check, was his determination, even if he lost his guns
and life, for the plateau held, the battle was won."[74] Of course, the choice to
save any tubes for future use exhibited no less courage and conviction on
the part of officers like Thomas.

A steady stream of fire was the only hope for salvation. Wilcox explained
that even with "no time being lost in aiming, . . . the enemy could not fail
to receive the full effects of each discharge, the distance being so short and
their columns covering so much of the plateau." The bursts of these rounds
left the ground over which these formations advanced "strewn with their
dead and wounded." Yet the Mexican fire punished the Americans as well.
"O'Brien's little squad was also falling; two horses had been killed under
him and this third bleeding, he himself wounded, and nearly every horse
of his two pieces killed or wounded; the horses of Thomas had been equally
unfortunate."[75]

The ebb and flow of fighting at Buena Vista provided Thomas with additional tests of his fortitude and determination as well as the opportunity
to showcase and develop those characteristics. Although Braxton Bragg
emerged with a colorful reputation after General Taylor had purportedly
ordered him, "Double shot your guns and give 'em hell, Bragg," the exigency
of these moments required much the same of all of them.[76] Thomas would
remember the moment in his compelling and concise style: "I was under
fire from 6 o.c. a.m. until 4 p.m."[77]

Subsequently, doctor and correspondent Josiah Gregg toured the ground of the Mexican advance and repulse, bearing witness to the gruesome effects of the American cannon fire on the opposing columns. "With regard to the destruction of Mexicans on the field, I observed that our artillery had made great havoc among them." Gregg described the graphic scenes he witnessed: "In one row I saw seven that had been mowed down by a single cannonball! In another five, and in many places, three and four!" Many of the Mexican survivors he encountered insisted that they were conscripted into duty, with some impressed into service at the last minute from rear-echelon positions. Still, the U.S. artillery, including Thomas's piece, had executed its work upon veteran soldier and unwilling recruit alike with deadly effect.[78]

Santa Anna determined to disengage his weary and battered army. The engagement had not been one sided or with U.S. victory assured. Taylor's Army of Occupation survived the desperate fighting at Buena Vista at a cost of 272 killed, 387 wounded, and 6 missing of his 4,000 troops. Some twenty officers and men from the 3rd Artillery were among the casualties.[79] By contrast, Santa Anna set his own losses at 591 killed, 1,048 wounded, and 1,894 missing.[80]

In the aftermath of this bloody contest, Taylor recognized and expressed his appreciation for the role of his cannoneers. His official report, sent from Agua Nueva and dated March 6, 1847, offered considerable praise for the men who had prevailed at Buena Vista. The commander's observations were especially positive toward his artillery branch. "The services of the light artillery, always conspicuous, were more than usually distinguished. Moving rapidly over the roughest ground, it was always in action at the right place and the right time, and its well-directed fire dealt destruction in the masses of the enemy." Taylor was careful not only to highlight the commanding officers but also their subordinates. "I deem it no more than just to mention all the subaltern officers," he wrote. "They were nearly all detached at different times, and in every situation exhibited conspicuous skill and gallantry." Lieutenants Thomas, Reynolds, and French all found their names in the report, the last identified as having been wounded "severely."[81] Taylor concluded, "Our artillery did more than wonders."[82]

Brigadier General Wool was equally effusive. From "Head-Quarters Camp Taylor, Agua Nueva," he recorded his appreciation to the artillery commands, "to whose service at this point, and in every other part of the field, I think it but just to say, we are mainly indebted for the great victory so successfully achieved by our arms over the great Army opposed to us." Realizing the tenuous nature of the bitter fighting at its height, he explained simply, "Without our artillery we could not have maintained our position for a single hour."[83]

Captain Sherman also lavished praise on his subordinates. "Lieuts. Thomas and Reynolds behaved nobly throughout the action and their coolness and firmness contributed not a little to the success of the day." He identified the Virginian with particular attention for his skill and expertise. "Lieut. Thomas more than sustained the reputation he has long enjoyed in his regiment as an accurate and scientific artillerist."[84] This focus on the young officer's skill and determination on the battlefield demonstrates a recognition of the qualities that this conflict allowed Thomas to display and develop under the extreme conditions of combat.

Such notices were essential elements for promotion and morale for those who received them. As a biographer of Reynolds has observed, "To be cited favorably in official battle reports is lifeblood for professional soldiers."[85] George Meade observed: "When you reflect that of nearly two hundred officers only some twenty-five were mentioned, you must certainly acknowledge it a compliment. And the very fact of its being brought to your notice by so many persons proves that it was a compliment of no small value."[86]

The execution of his duty in the cauldron of battle brought the Virginian additional rewards. Another brevet for "gallant and meritorious conduct in the battle of Buena Vista, Mex." elevated Thomas to the rank of major.[87] Biographer Francis McKinney concludes, "Three brevets in seven years marked Thomas as one of the outstanding junior officers in the army."[88] Henry Coppée notes simply that the soldier had become, in a positive sense, "a marked man."[89]

In the period after Buena Vista, Thomas paused to communicate with a former comrade then serving with Scott in Central Mexico. In his letter to James Duncan, the Virginian demonstrated his awareness of the importance of local intelligence, a healthy skepticism for its accuracy, and an appreciation of the larger strategic picture of the war. The return of numerous residents to Saltillo in the aftermath of "our Great Battle which you have no doubt heard of" elicited from them "all manner of protestations of their inocence [sic] in the affair." But those same individuals also provided significant information concerning the state of Santa Anna's army and the nature of his actions in the volatile atmosphere that had prevailed since

Buena Vista. "I give you this as the information secured from the people here," Thomas noted, "not that we believe *them* at all." He understood that even a victory of the scope the Americans had achieved, "where the opposing troops have run[,] whipped at this place at least four to one[,] the disaster will produce but little effect upon the nation because we have not been able to follow up our victory." For Duncan, as part of Scott's campaign, the prospects promised to be much greater. "But the taking of Vera Cruz and their other seaports will cut them off from all support and they will then begin to appreciate their situation." Together, the operations stood the best chance of bringing Mexican forces "to unconditional terms" and thus ending the war favorably for American interests.[90]

Thomas's Southampton County neighbors were less concerned with such matters. They were understandably proud of their native son and sought to honor his service and recognize his success. The desire to find an appropriate way to express their gratitude came in the form of a specially crafted ceremonial sword that lauded the officer for his contribution to American arms. Local farmer Daniel William Cobb took special notice of the plans in his diary in an entry on July 19, 1847, "Lutenanat Thomas was [to be] presented with a sourd price $2 or 300." The gesture impressed him to the point that several days later he elaborated, "On Munday our last Cort day the people noticed our neighbour Loutenant Thomas who has been so suckscessfull in the Flordia war and also Texas war was in several engagements and won the prise." The farmer was especially proud that Thomas "never has been defeated in no battle what ever he has been engaged in." Cobb recorded: "The people of Southampton his oald friends and neighbours . . . want hm to [k]now we feel much regoiced at his keen and suond management of the gun he had in command and the successful manner [in which] he managed his men[.] That we have purched a soward of the amt of value of $3 or 400 and seluted him with it or may be said presented to him in be half of his sucksess and Bravery."[91]

The citizen's meeting the farmer had referenced produced a glowing resolution. The pronouncement reflected the ways in which the citizens of Southampton linked their local acquaintance with the greater effort represented by American arms in the conflict: "*Resolved,* That whilst we glory in the unfailing fame which our heroic army in Mexico has acquired for herself and country, our attention has been expressly drawn to the military skill, bravery, and noble deportment of our fellow countryman, George H.

Thomas, exhibited in the campaign of Florida, at Fort Brown, Monterey, and Buena Vista, in which he has given ample proof of the best requisites of a soldier—patience, fortitude, firmness, and daring intrepidity." They affirmed Thomas's "character as a citizen and a soldier" by forming a committee with the obligation "to collect by subscription a sum sufficient for the purpose and [then] cause to be fabricated a sword to be presented to the said George H. Thomas through the hands of his noble and heroic commander Maj. Genl. Zachary Taylor."[92]

The communications between the local leaders and the Thomas family expressed the same high level of appreciation they had for the officer. They believed that his achievements reflected well on the community as well as the soldier himself. As "chairman of [the] meeting," James Maget informed Thomas's sister Judith of the unanimous resolution and presentation sword, with both serving as a "token of their regard" for "Lieut. George H. Thomas (Capt. By Brevet) of the Artillery, and now with the army in Mexico, for galantry, skill and noble daring displayed by him, in the various battles in which he has been engaged." The sword including the details in which "your distinguished brother participated and their dates, as well as in Florida as Texas & Mexico."[93]

It was not until early in the following month that the Southampton official communicated with Elizabeth Thomas about the planned recognition. "I herewith present you with the subjoined proceedings at a meeting of the Citizens of the county," which had occurred on February 4, "held more particularly in compliment to our distinguished fellow citizen your gallant son Capt. George H. Thomas 3d Artillery[,] he in whose heroic fame we all glory and which redounds to his mother & sisters." Glowingly, Maget asserted, "Inestimably honoured is she who add[s] a jewell to the briliant escutheon of old Virginia."[94]

The recipient of these honors responded to the gesture from Buena Vista, the site of his most dramatic exploits. "Your letter of the 8th February transmitting the Resolution of the citizens of Southampton at a meeting in their Court House on the 19th July 1847 was received by the last mail," he reported. "In accepting the Sword presented me by my fellow countrymen, and in acknowledging the very high compliment paid me in those resolutions, I beg you to present to the committee, and through them, to my old friends of Southampton my sincere and heartfelt thanks." The officer's natural modesty, coupled with a shyness that caused him to shun public displays and a belief that his actions provided sufficient evidence of his accomplishments, caused him to diminish his record. "Aware that the little service that I have been able to render my country, although performed with cheerfulness, and to the utmost of my ability does not in the least entitle me to this very high compliment of kindness of heart and a friendliness of feeling on their part, which renders their obligation doubly grateful, and as such will ever be a proud recollection to the last hour of my life."[95]

These traits remained part of his character, as did his reticence at having to speak at public events. To his brother John he exposed the extent of his feelings from his posting at Fort Brazos. "I have thought of it a great deal," he noted of the planned occasion, "[and] at first I was determined not to go to the County for one or two years, but upon reflection I had concluded to go as soon as I could get a leave and have the thing off my mind, before I received your letter." John must have prevailed upon his brother to accept the plaudits, but George could not divest himself of his desire to postpone the uncomfortable moment as long as possible. "I hope they will not enact the absurd ceremony of presenting me with the sword for in truth it has already been presented and accepted by letter some months since." In any case, he lamented, "if I could get off with a dinner only I should have great cause to congratulate myself."[96]

As the fulfillment of his duties in Mexico demonstrated, Thomas was a soldier first, but his sensitivities remained as well. In his reply regarding the recognition by his Southampton neighbors, he further observed, "Next to consciousness of having done his duty the Sympathy of friends is the highest reward of the Soldier."[97] Whatever his thoughts concerning the public aspects associated with the honor, Thomas appreciated the gesture and valued the context out of which it arose. On every level of his career and in his life, examples of duty, obligation, patriotism, and loyalty were an important part of his Mexican War service and legacy.

Of Thomas's participation in the conflict, biographer Richard O'Connor insists, "it is doubtful, on the face of their records," that among future Civil War generals on either side "any learned their lessons in battle more thoroughly than George H. Thomas."[98] Scholar Kevin Dougherty believes that this experience accounted for the future general's greater appreciation for "secure lines of supply" after his own "close brush with disaster under Zachary Taylor," his development of "a dogged persistence," and the employment of "well-placed artillery" to enhance his "ability to stand fast" on a battlefield.[99] Thomas's combat tenacity was no better illustrated than on September 20, 1863, when he earned the nickname "the Rock of Chickamauga." Biographer Christopher Einholf has determined that Thomas's service in Mexico "certainly" established that conflict "as a training ground" for him and included "the importance of drill, discipline, supply, and morale in making good soldiers" among the vital pieces of wisdom he obtained.[100] Of course, while Thomas benefited from the lessons of this period as a rising professional developing a sense of his capabilities under the pressures of active campaigning, they built upon the officer's preexisting qualities and character.

In any event, Thomas never forgot the degree to which his service in those early days shaped his subsequent career. Critics who chose to do so emphasized the reputation he had acquired for deliberateness. Yet if the Virginian harbored a sensitivity to such remarks, he deflected them with a dry sense of humor and pride in his accomplishments. As a comrade in the Civil War recalled, "General Thomas once told me himself, that he had always been called slow, but he added with a grim smile: I saved my section of Bragg's battery at Buena Vista by being a little slow."[101] Those who knew him from those earliest years bestowed the understandable sobriquet "Old Reliable" on the man who had proven that stubbornness and determination were admirable qualities on any battlefield.[102]

The artillerist in Thomas never subsided. Biographer O'Connor concludes that the "Buena Vista [experiences] he was never to forget, and they were to insure [sic] Federal victories on more than one battlefield," which reflected the general's continuing appreciation for the artillery arm and its capabilities on the battlefield.[103] His personal role in placing batteries where they could be most effective remained important to him as well. A dramatic example of this tendency occurred at Peachtree Creek on July 20, 1864, when the general personally positioned several batteries and directed their fire upon Confederate attackers.[104] With a nod to the reputation for slowness, O. O. Howard thought his comrade "could move quickly enough when duty demanded it" in "turning his attention and resources to best effect."[105]

George Henry Thomas's education in the streets and fields of Mexico advanced his skills and practical knowledge as well as nurtured a calm and cool persona under fire that demonstrated he was more than a capable administrative officer and garrison commander or a classroom student. He could absorb and adapt the information he received and the experiences he lived. The lessons he learned in 1846–47 remained with him through the rest of his military career and informed his exemplary service in the American Civil War. Perhaps most fittingly, when the stresses of combat exerted themselves most dramatically, Thomas illustrated that being slow to withdraw from his position mattered most and allowed him to render significant service in the face of a determined foe.

NOTES

1. John S. D. Eisenhower, *So Far from God: The U.S. War with Mexico, 1846–1848* (New York: Random House, 1989), 75.

2. Ezra Warner, *Generals in Blue: The Lives of Union Commanders* (Baton Rouge: Louisiana State University Press, 1964), 500.

3. For Thomas, see Brian Steel Wills, *George Henry Thomas: As True as Steel* (Lawrence: University Press of Kansas, 2012).

4. Felice Flanery Lewis, *Trailing Clouds of Glory: Zachary Taylor's Mexican War Campaign and His Emerging Civil War Leaders* (Tuscaloosa: University of Alabama Press, 2010), xvi.

5. Oliver Otis Howard, "Sketch of General George H. Thomas," in *Personal Recollections of the War of the Rebellion: Addresses Delivered before the New York Commandery of the Loyal Legion of the United States, 1883–1891,* ed. James Grant Wilson and Titus Munson Coan (New York: Published by the Commandery, 1891), 288–89.

6. Quoted in Francis F. McKinney, *Education in Violence: The Life of George H. Thomas and the History of the Army of the Cumberland* (Detroit: Wayne State University Press, 1961), 15.

7. See, for example, William F. G. Shanks, *Personal Recollections of Distinguished Generals* (New York: Harper and Brothers, 1866), 77–78.

8. Ibid., 72; Richard W. Johnson, *Memoir of Maj.-Gen. Thomas* (Philadelphia: J. B. Lippincott, 1881), 236.

9. Oliver Otis Howard, *Autobiography of Oliver Otis Howard, Major General United States Army,* 2 vols. (New York: Baker and Taylor, 1908), 1:495.

10. George H. Thomas to Dear Brother, Fort Columbus Sept. 27, 1840, Thomas Papers, Virginia Historical Society, Richmond (hereafter cited as VHS).

11. George W. Cullum, *Biographical Register of the Officers and Graduates of the U.S. Military Academy at West Point, N.Y. from Its Establishment, in 1802 and 1890, with the Early History of the United States Military Academy,* 2 vols. (Boston: Houghton, Mifflin, 1891), 2:33.

12. Ibid.; Thomas B. Van Horne, *The Life of Major-General George H. Thomas* (New York: Charles Scribner's Sons), 5.

13. McKinney, *Education in Violence,* 31.

14. "Camp at Corpus Christi, Texas, September 18, 1845," Meade, *Life and Letters,* 26.

15. Doctor and Correspondent Josiah Gregg was one of many who employed the nickname. See, for example, "Mon. 22 [1847]," "Thurs. 27, [1847]," and "My Dear Bigelow, Saltillo, Mexico, March 13, 1848," Josiah Gregg, *Diary & Letters of Josiah Gregg: Excursions in Mexico & California 1847–1850,* ed. Maurice Garland Fulton (Norman: University of Oklahoma Press, 1944), 47, 136–37, 211.

16. "Reynosa, Mexico, September 10, 1846," John Sedgwick, *Correspondence of John Sedgwick, Major General,* ed. Henry Sedgwick, 2 vols. (New York: De Vinne, 1902–3), 1:18.

17. "Camp at Corpus Christi, Texas, March 2, 1846," George Meade, *The Life and Letters of George Gordon Meade Major-General United States Army* (New York: Charles Scribner's Sons, 1913), 49–50.

18. "March 5," ibid., 51.

19. Lewis, *Trailing Clouds of Glory,* 42.

20. "Report of Captain Mansfield, Fort opposite Matamoros, Texas, May 12, 1846," *Niles National Register,* June 20, 1846, 254.

21. "My Dear M—, Camp opposite Matamoros April 14, 1846," and "My Dear Sister, Camp opposite Matamoros April 23, 1846," George A. McCall, *Letters from the Frontiers: Written during a Period of Thirty Years' Service in the Army of the United States* (Philadelphia: J. B. Lippincott, 1868), 441 and 443; R. S. Ripley, *The War with Mexico,* 2 vols. (New York: Burt Franklin, 1849), 1:165.

22. Eisenhower, *So Far from God,* 62–63.

23. "Camp at the Frontone, Point Isabel, May 2, 1846," Meade, *Life and Letters,* 74.

24. Lewis, *Trailing Clouds of Glory,* 68.

25. "Camp at the Frontone, Point Isabel, May 2, 1846," Meade, *Life and Letters,* 75.

26. Quoted in Edward J. Nichols, *Toward Gettysburg: A Biography of General John F. Reynolds* (University Park: Pennsylvania State University Press, 1958), 25.

27. Quoted in "Camp at the Frontone, Point Isabel, May 2, 1846," Meade, *Life and Letters,* 75.

28. Quoted in Lloyd Lewis, *Captain Sam Grant* (Boston: Little, Brown, 1950), 152. A slight variation appears in Donn Piatt and Henry V. Boynton, *General George H. Thomas: A Critical Biography* (Cincinnati: Robert Clarke, 1893), 67.

29. On lessons concerning overextension of supply lines, see Wilbur Thomas, *General George H. Thomas: The Indomitable Warrior* (New York: Exposition, 1964), 84; and Frank A. Palumbo, *George Henry Thomas Major General, U.S.A.: The Dependable General* (Dayton, OH: Morningside House, 1983), 23–24.

30. Eisenhower, *So Far from God,* 84.

31. Lewis, *Trailing Clouds of Glory,* 95.

32. Ibid., 101.

33. Freeman Cleaves, *Rock of Chickamauga: The Life of General George Henry Thomas* (Norman: University of Oklahoma Press, 1948), 29.

34. Daniel Harvey Hill, *A Fighter from Way Back: The Mexican War Diary of Lt. Daniel Harvey Hill, 4th Artillery, USA,* ed. Nathaniel Cheairs Hughes Jr. and Timothy D. Johnson (Kent, OH: Kent State University Press, 2002), 5.

35. Lewis, *Trailing Clouds of Glory*, 103.

36. Thomas B. Buell, *The Warrior Generals: Combat Leadership in the Civil War* (New York: Crown, 1997), 18.

37. Philip Norbourne Barbour, *Journals of the Late Brevet Major Philip Norbourne Barbour . . .*, ed. Rhoda van Bibber Tanner Doubleday (New York: G. P. Putnam's Sons, 1936), 95.

38. Lewis, *Trailing Clouds of Glory*, 179.

39. K. Jack Bauer, *The Mexican War, 1846–1848* (New York: Macmillan, 1974), 93.

40. McKinney, *Education in Violence*, 36.

41. John Pope, *The Military Memoirs of General John Pope*, ed. Peter Cozzens and Robert I. Girardi (Chapel Hill: University of North Carolina Press, 1998), 94.

42. Samuel G. French, *Two Wars: An Autobiography of Gen. Samuel G. French (Nashville: Confederate Veteran, 1901)*, 62.

43. Ibid., 65–66.

44. Jefferson Davis to J. A. Quitman, Sept. 26, 1846, Letters Received, Adjutant General's Office (hereafter AGO), M567, National Archives, Washington, DC (hereafter cited as NA), Roll 361.

45. Zachary Taylor Report, Camp before Monterey, Sept. 23, 1846, ibid.

46. Jefferson Davis to J. A. Quitman, Sept. 26, 1846, ibid.

47. French, *Two Wars*, 66.

48. Nichols, *Toward Gettysburg*, 33.

49. French, *Two Wars*, 66–67.

50. D. E. Twiggs report, Headquarters 1st Division, Army of Occupation, Camp near Monterey, Mexico, Sept. 29, 1846, Letters Received, AGO, M567, NA, Roll 361.

51. J. Pinkney Henderson report, Headquarters Texas Forces, Monterey, Oct. 1, 1846, ibid., 98. See also Donn Piatt, *Memories of the Men Who Saved the Union* (New York: Belford, Clarke,1887) 184; and Piatt and Boynton, *General George H. Thomas*, 67.

52. Bauer, *Mexican War*, 100.

53. Cullum, *Biographical Register*, 2:33.

54. Cadmus M. Wilcox, *History of the Mexican War* (Washington, DC: Church News, 1892), 118.

55. Jeanne Twiggs Heidler, "The Military Career of David Emanuel Twiggs" (Ph.D. diss., Auburn University, 1988), 178–79; Thomas, *General George Thomas*, 101.

56. Hill, *Fighter from Way Back*, 54–55 (Jan. 1, 4, 1847).

57. Ibid., 65–66 (Feb. 19, 20, 1847).

58. Quoted in Harwood P. Hinton and Jerry Thompson, *Courage above All Things: General John Ellis Wool and the U.S. Military, 1812–1863* (Norman: University of Oklahoma Press, 2020), 123.

59. Ibid., 130. Harwood Hinton and Jerry Thompson insist that Wool forced Taylor into accepting this choice by announcing he was moving his troops there on his own authority.

60. David Lavender, *Climax at Buena Vista: The Decisive Battle of the Mexican-American War* (Philadelphia: University of Pennsylvania Press, 2003), 176–78.

61. Wilcox, *History of the Mexican War,* 219.

62. French, *Two Wars,* 78.

63. Thomas W. Sherman's report, Mar. 2, 1847, Letters Received, AGO, M567, NA, Roll 362.

64. Wilcox, *History of the Mexican War,* 222.

65. W. H. L. Wallace to Dear George, Camp Taylor, 20 miles south of Saltillo, Mex., Mar. 1, 1847, in Isabel Wallace, *Life and Letters of General W. H. L. Wallace* (Chicago: R. R. Donnelley, 1909), 48.

66. French, *Two Wars,* 80.

67. James Henry Carleton, *The Battle of Buena Vista, with the Operations of the "Army of Occupation," for One Month* (New York: Harper and Brothers, 1848), 85.

68. Wilcox, *History of the Mexican War,* 226.

69. Ripley, *War with Mexico,* 1:412–14.

70. Bauer, *Mexican War,* 216.

71. Wilcox, *History of the Mexican War,* 231–32.

72. Carleton, *Battle of Buena Vista,* 85.

73. Ripley, *War with Mexico,* 1:418.

74. Wilcox, *History of the Mexican War,* 233.

75. Ibid.

76. McKinney, *Education in Violence,* 44; Bauer, *Mexican War,* 216; Robert Selph Henry, *Story of the Mexican War* (New York: Da Capo, 1961), 252–53; Grady McWhiney, *Braxton Bragg and Confederate Defeat, vol. 1* (New York: Columbia University Press, 1969), 90–92.

77. [Thomas to] Captain, Camp Cooper, TX, Sept. 21, 1859, Thomas Papers, Huntington Library, San Marino, CA.

78. "Tues. 23 [1847]," Gregg, *Diary & Letters,* 56.

79. Carleton, *Battle of Buena Vista,* 191–92.

80. Bauer, *Mexican War,* 217.

81. "Zachary Taylor Report. Head-Quarters, Army of Occupation, Agua Nueva, March 6, 1847," *Report of the Secretary of War, 1847,* in *Message from the President . . . at the Commencement of the First Session of the Thirtieth Congress, S. Exec. Doc. 1,* 30th Cong., 1st sess. (1847), 101, 138, online via Hathi Trust, https://catalog.hathitrust.org/Record/009025291.

82. "Gen. Taylor's Letter," *Niles National Register,* May 1, 1847, 135.

83. "John E. Wool Report, Head-Quarters Camp Taylor, Agua Nueva, 20 miles north of Saltillo, Mexico, March 4, 1847," *Report of the Secretary of War, 1847,* in *Message from the President,* 150, online via Hathi Trust, https://catalog.hathitrust.org/Record/009025291. See also Henry, *Story of the Mexican War,* 253.

84. Letters Received, AGO, M567, Roll No. 362, NA; "T. W. Sherman Report, Agua Nueva, March 2, 1847," *Report of the Secretary of War, 1847,* in *Message from the President,* 205, online via Hathi Trust, https://catalog.hathitrust.org/Record/009025291.

85. Nichols, *Toward Gettysburg,* 33.

86. "Matamoros, July 9, 1846," in Meade, *Life and Letters,* 113.

87. Cullum, *Biographical Register*, 2:33.

88. McKinney, *Education in Violence*, 45.

89. Henry Coppée, *General Thomas* (New York: D. Appleton, 1893), 18.

90. Thomas to Dr. Duncan, Buena Vista, Mex. Mar. 18, 1847, Ms. 658, Cullum File, Manuscript Collections, U.S. Military Academy Archives, West Point, NY.

91. "Munday, 19 July," Daniel William Cobb 1847 Diary, Cobb Papers, Virginia Historical Society; Daniel William Cobb, *Cobb's Ordeal: The Diaries of a Virginia Farmer, 1842-1872*, ed. Daniel W. Croft (Athens: University of Georgia Press, 1997), 58–59.

92. Quoted in Piatt and Boynton, *General George H. Thomas*, 67–68.

93. James Maget to Dear Miss Judith, Southampton, VA, July 20, 1847, Thomas Papers, VHS. According to historian Daniel W. Crofts, Capt. James Maget was "an active Democrat and prosperous lower-county member of the county court." Crofts, *Old Southampton: Politics and Society in a Virginia County, 1834-1869* (Charlottesville: University Press of Virginia, 1992), 187.

94. James Maget to Dear Madam, Southampton County, Feb. 8, 1848, Thomas Papers, VHS. Another letter went to Thomas's brother William. See James Maget to Dear Sir, Thomas Papers, VHS.

95. Thomas to Dear Sir, Buena Vista, Mex., Mar. 31, 1848, Thomas Papers, VHS.

96. Thomas to Dear Brother, Brazos Island, TX, Oct. 25, 1848, Thomas Papers, VHS.

97. Thomas to Dear Sir, Buena Vista, Mex., Mar. 31, 1848, Thomas Papers, VHS. The sword and scabbard are in the Virginia Historical Society.

98. Richard O'Connor, *Thomas: Rock of Chickamauga* (New York: Prentice-Hall, 1948), 79.

99. Kevin Dougherty, *Civil War Leadership and Mexican War Experience* (Jackson: University Press of Mississippi, 2007), 110.

100. Christopher J. Einholf, *George Thomas: Virginian for the Union* (Norman: University of Oklahoma Press, 2007), 97.

101. Thomas M. Anderson, *General George H. Thomas: His Place in History, a Paper Read before Oregon Commandery of the Military Order of the Loyal Legion of the United States, March 7, 1894* (Portland, OR: A. Anderson, 1894), 11–12.

102. Shanks, *Personal Recollections of Distinguished Generals*, 79; Cleaves, *Rock of Chickamauga*, 34.

103. O'Connor, *Thomas*, 79.

104. See Wills, *George Henry Thomas*, 269; and Henry Stone, "The Siege and Capture of Atlanta, July 9 to September 8, 1864," in *The Atlanta Papers*, no. 3 (Dayton, OH: Morningside Bookshop, 1980), 112.

105. Howard, *Autobiography*, 1:619.

LEARNING FROM THE BEST AND WORST OF WINFIELD SCOTT'S EXAMPLE

Robert E. Lee in the Mexican-American War

JOSEPH T. GLATTHAAR

Seconds ticked by like minutes; minutes lapsed as if they were hours. Amid the April heat and humidity of the Mexican coastal lowlands, Captain Robert E. Lee hid under a huge log. On a reconnaissance mission, he dove beneath it to avoid discovery when Mexican soldiers approached. Some enemy troops sat on the log while others gathered around it in conversation. There Lee lay, sweat dripping from him and insects crawling over his body. The same individual who graduated from West Point without a single demerit tapped all that discipline to remain motionless, hour after hour, concealing his presence.

Major General Winfield Scott's army had seized the port city of Vera Cruz, but it now confronted not only a well-positioned Mexican army but also impending disease. Yellow fever and malaria season were almost upon the Americans, and it was imperative that Scott's men reached a higher altitude quickly to escape the devastating sicknesses, yet the Mexican army blocked the road. A frontal assault likely would result in severe losses, something the small invasion force of under 9,000 could not endure. Scott had to find a way around the Mexican position.

On April 15 he sent Lee to discover a route around the enemy left flank. Lee, along with his guide, John Fitzwalter, followed an old trail that led them into the Mexican rear, where Lee had to conceal himself beneath the log. Finally, as night began to fall, the Mexican soldiers arose and returned to their camp. Lee climbed from underneath the fallen tree, rejoined his comrade, and retraced the difficult route back to camp, where the captain reported his discovery to Scott. The next day the general sent him back out with a work party to improve the route. On April 17 Scott feinted a direct attack while Lee guided Brigadier General David Twiggs's division on a flanking movement. In fighting that lasted over two days, Twiggs relied heavily on Lee to guide and position his forces for attacks that helped rout the Mexican army and seize the critical road to Jalapa and higher altitude.[1]

This was not the first time Lee had conducted a dangerous reconnaissance. Just weeks earlier he had scouted the Mexican defenses of Vera Cruz, coming so close that he heard dogs barking and the voices of defenders. But this time the reaction to his bravery and resourcefulness was overwhelming. Colonel Bennet Riley, whose brigade led the flank attack, wrote is his battle report, "I cannot refrain from bearing testimony to the intrepid coolness and gallantry exhibited by Captain Lee, United States engineers, when conducting the advance of my brigade under the heavy flank fire of the enemy." Twiggs echoed Riley's statement, lauding Lee for "the invaluable services which he rendered me," elaborating: "I consulted him with confidence, and adopted his suggestions with entire assurance. His gallantry and good conduct on both days deserve the highest praise." Even the army commander, Scott, made "special mention" of Lee's exploits in his report. "This officer, greatly distinguished at the siege of Vera Cruz, was again indefatigable during these operations, in reconnaissance as daring as laborious, and of the utmost value. Nor was he less conspicuous in planting batteries, and in conducting columns to their stations under the heavy fire of the enemy." In two short months a junior officer who had never seen combat emerged as one of the most acclaimed officers in the U.S. Army, exhibiting just a few of the qualities that would make him a renowned army commander during the Civil War. He received a brevet promotion to major for his impressive service.[2]

Before the Mexican War, Lee had an honorable yet undistinguished career. The son of Revolutionary War hero "Light Horse" Harry Lee and Ann Hill Carter, who was the daughter of one of the wealthiest men in all of Virginia, Robert grew up among affluent relatives and a declining immediate-family fortune, largely due to his father's profligate habits. He attended the U.S. Military Academy at West Point, serving as a model cadet and graduating second in his class. The new, young officer then entered the Army Corps of Engineers, where he performed a range of duties admirably but never witnessed hostile gunfire. Although Lee missed the initial campaigns in the north against the Mexican army, he joined Brigadier General John W. Wool's command in late September 1846. There he functioned alongside a captain who was seven years his junior but had received his captain's commission on the same day as Lee. The two worked on relatively mundane matters and saw no combat. From Lee's perspective, it seemed like a dead-end job.

Fortunately, he soon received orders to join Scott's staff for the major campaign against Mexico City. Doubtless, the general knew of Lee. As a fellow Virginian, the U.S. Army's commanding general surely was aware of the Revolutionary War reputation of Lee's father and probably knew that the younger man had married the great granddaughter of Martha Custis Washington, the initial first lady of the United States. Yet it seems more likely that Colonel Joseph Totten, chief of the Corps of Engineers, suggested that Scott assign Lee to his staff. The captain had worked as Totten's assistant in Washington and had accomplished valuable work on the New York fortifications so that by the mid-1840s, he had earned the colonel's high regard.

It did not take Scott long to recognize Lee's talents. With each assignment that he fulfilled, Scott's estimation of him and his ability increased. In no time Lee became one of four officers who constituted the commander's "little cabinet," analyzing situations, formulating plans, and discussing military matters in general. Scott was a towering man in physique, intellect, and ego, and Lee quickly learned how to tender his opinions with great deference. To Scott's credit, the commanding general carefully weighed suggestions from subordinates whom he respected.[3]

Lee's first exposure to gunfire was on a shipboard reconnaissance, with Mexican shells falling well astray of the vessel. His second experience was a narrow escape from friendly fire. After scouting the enemy, Lee and Lieutenant P. G. T. Beauregard encountered a twitchy sentry who shot without discriminating between friend and foe. The ball zipped under Lee's arm and nearly struck his chest, singeing his jacket.

In the attack on Vera Cruz, Lee played an important role. He positioned artillery guns, and when Scott sought greater firepower, he directed Lee to plant six navy guns—32-pounders and 8-inch shell guns. Once again Lee selected the ground and fortified the position with skill, shielding cannons, the working parties, and the gun crews. He even won a grudging concession from the navy captain who provided the guns and crew but then opposed throwing up works for protection. "I reckon you were right," he conceded afterward.[4]

After the victory at Cerro Gordo, Scott's army pressed on to Jalapa and eventually to Puebla, where it awaited reinforcements to replace soldiers whose one-year enlistment was about to expire. During those months, Lee broadened his knowledge of military affairs as Scott discussed and resolved campaign issues and other military matters with senior officers. Lee observed how a first-class military mind worked through myriad problems.

He also labored in conjunction with the chief topographical engineer, Major William Turnbull, to draft an accurate map of the approaches to Mexico City for upcoming operations. They drew upon a wide range of information and even interviewed Mexican travelers. The maps proved extremely accurate and useful for the upcoming campaign.[5]

With some 10,000 troops, Scott began the advance on Mexico City, cutting loose from his supply line and living off the land. Still, he could not afford to suffer heavy losses. The Mexicans had fortified defenses east of the capital city on the road from Puebla, so he feinted a direct advance and swung to the south around Lake Chalco to approach Mexico City from the south.

From this new position, Scott sent Lee to reconnoiter the area west of the lake and over to the town of San Agustín, which he found open. The problem that confronted the general, though, was that the Mexican forces had detected the shift southward and were preparing defenses along the road south of Mexico City both at a hacienda called San Antonio and several miles farther north at Churubusco. To make matters worse, just north of San Agustín and west of San Antonio was a huge, treacherous dried lava bed called the Pedregal. Scott ordered a contingent to reconnoiter north to San Antonio, which they found well fortified, while Lee guided infantry and cavalry across the edge of the Pedregal to bypass the hacienda completely. The forces with Lee encountered some Mexican cavalrymen who occupied a strong position in the Pedregal. After both sides exchanged gunfire, the Mexican horsemen retreated westward. Lee then scaled some high ground from which he discovered two valuable pieces of information. He observed Mexican troops in force along the road west of the Pedregal. He also realized that if the Mexicans had crossed a portion of the Pedregal to attack the Americans, then U.S. troops could cover the same route, which he perceived as an opportunity to turn the enemy position. Lee's presentation to a council of war ultimately convinced Scott to approach the defenses along the road west of the Pedregal.

On August 19 Lee undertook his first in a series of assignments that would occupy his time and attention for thirty-six consecutive hours. He began by directing 500 soldiers in building a road through the Pedregal for artillery and wagons. As they neared the fortified Mexican position, the Americans came under heavy fire. Lee quickly positioned two batteries, but enemy fire compelled the troops to advance through the Pedregal and turn the Mexican left flank, thereby blocking the road northward and preventing the defending troops from retreating toward Mexico City. Yet that placed the Americans between two elements of the Mexican army. Lee and Brigadier Generals Persifor Smith and George Cadwalader discussed the situation, and the generals determined to launch an attack on the forces to the south early the next morning. Despite heavy rain, Lee agreed to cross the Pedregal that night to alert Scott of their plan and to seek reinforcements to shield the American attackers from enemy forces to the north. With several men, Lee drew on his uncanny sense of direction and recollection of terrain, along with occasional illumination from bolts of lightning, to link with U.S. reinforcements. There he learned that Scott had returned to San Agustín, and the captain, drenched and exhausted, trudged three more miles to brief Scott. He then piloted Twiggs back to his command and pushed on to Brigadier General Franklin Pierce's brigade to position troops by dawn for the feint attack. He stood alongside Pierce's men as they endured heavy gunfire while the other American forces struck southward and routed the Mexican command at Contreras. The enemy troops to the north then retreated, with the Americans winning an impressive victory, due in part to Lee's heroics and stamina.

Lee briefly visited the captured position to the south, where he consoled his old friend Joseph E. Johnston on the loss of his nephew, and then embarked on a search for the commanding general for new orders. Scott, sensing a major victory, attacked the Mexican forces who held the bridgehead over the Churubusco River at the town of Churubusco. Meanwhile, he had Lee guide Brigadier General Shields's brigade north of the river in an effort to turn and capture a large part of the defenders. Mexican troops reacted to Shields's movement and extended their line up the road toward Mexico City. Lee went back to Scott and procured reinforcements, but the Americans still could not outflank the enemy forces. With no alternative,

Shields attacked in the front while Brigadier General William Worth's command struck northward, carrying the bridgehead and rolling up the Mexican flank, driving those forces back to the outskirts of the capital.

In his exhausted state Lee rested, but his exploits earned the kudos of five different generals plus the commanding general for his herculean efforts at the Battles of Contreras and Churubusco. Generals Smith, Twiggs, Gideon J. Pillow, Shields, and Pierce all sang the captain's praises. Scott, however, reserved the highest plaudits for Lee. He described him "as distinguished for felicitous execution as for science and daring." Under oath in testimony, he lauded Lee's service at the Pedregal as "the greatest feat of physical and moral courage performed by an individual, in my knowledge, pending the campaign."[6]

The American army now closed in on its prize, Mexico City. Before Scott could follow up on the victories at Contreras and Churubusco, however, the opposing armies entered into a negotiation about surrender. After two weeks the truce expired with no progress on bringing the war to an end. At Scott's direction Lee and a small number of officers began reconnoitering to determine the best route into the city. The general ultimately concluded to swing part of his command westward and assault a foundry called Molino del Rey, then deploy converging columns to strike the military academy Chapultepec.[7]

Lee played no role in the battle at Molino del Rey, but his scouting provided vital information. For the attack on Chapultepec, he labored for two consecutive days and nights leading up to and throughout the battle. He positioned batteries, consulted with Scott about possible avenues of attack, and conveyed orders from the commanding general to various division and brigade commanders. In the course of the fight, he sustained a minor wound. Once American attackers overwhelmed the bastion, they pursued the fleeing defenders to the gates of the city. Rather than join the soldiers, Lee returned to seek fresh orders from Scott. As they rode through Worth's victorious troops, Lee suddenly fainted from exhaustion and loss of blood. Fifty-six hours without rest had taken its toll. That night Mexican troops evacuated the capital city, and before dawn the next morning, Lee was back in the saddle, once again delivering Scott's orders.[8]

With the victory in hand, Lee returned to his mapmaking duties and devised routes of travel for occupation troops in the surrounding communities. He also watched as victory unraveled any sense of mutual appreciation among senior officers and politicians. Scott, Worth, and Pillow quarreled over responsibility for the victorious campaign, while Secretary of War William Marcy and President James K. Polk, a Democrat who had exhibited open hostility toward the Whig Scott, removed the commanding general and recalled him home to appear before a court of inquiry. Always antagonistic toward Scott, Polk assigned him as commander of the expedition only because his reputation as a great military mind transcended his politics and egotism. But in this instance Polk believed his Tennessee friend, Pillow, over his victorious commanding general. Privately, Lee found Polk's behavior outrageous. To his brother he wrote, "The great cause of our success was in our leader," Scott. Had the general "abused his trust and authority," he should have been held accountable. "But to decide the matter an ex-parte statement of favorites; to suspend a successful general in command of an army in the heart of an enemy's country; to try the judge in place of the accused, is to upset all discipline; to jeopardize the safety of the army and the honor of the country, and to violate justice." Twice Lee stood by Scott in the political battles and testified truthfully under oath: once in a case that Pillow brought against Lee when someone in the Engineer Bureau published his update letter illegally and without his knowledge, and again in the inquiry against Pillow. Scott was fully appreciative. Before he left for Washington, the general made sure that Lee attended a dinner party that a wealthy Englishman threw for Scott. When the general headed back to the United States, he handed the key to his wine closet to Ethan Allen Hitchcock and told him to distribute the contents to a doctor, Lee, and other friends.[9]

After overseeing the shipment of materiel and personnel, Lee headed back to the United States, arriving at Arlington, Virginia, his home, on June 29, 1848. Although he gained little notoriety among the American public, no officer other than Scott emerged from the war with a better reputation in the U.S. Army than Lee. He received three brevet promotions to colonel and one commissioned promotion to major. The highest praise, though, came from the commanding general. In 1857 Scott referred to Lee in an official letter as "the very best soldier I ever saw in the field," a truly impressive compliment.[10]

Lee returned to the Corps of Engineers, working in Baltimore. In 1852 President Millard Fillmore appointed him as superintendent of West Point. Secretary of War Jefferson Davis, who served in that office from 1853 to 1857, convinced Congress to expand the army by four regiments and promoted exclusively on merit to fill their officer billets. Among those who received a prized advancement in rank was Lee, who became a lieutenant colonel in the 2nd U.S. Cavalry, Lee's first combat command. Stationed in Texas, he battled with Apaches and Comanches and struggled with settlers. While on leave at Arlington in 1859, he led a contingent of marines who put down John Brown's insurrection at Harpers Ferry. Seventeen months later, in March 1861 and just weeks before he resigned from the army, Lee was promoted to colonel and command of the 1st U.S. Cavalry. General in Chief Scott hoped that Lee would assume command of the combat forces in the U.S. Army.

Despite claims that Lee agonized over the decision to leave the U.S. Army and return to Virginia, he had made up his mind some time before Lincoln took office. Governor John Letcher of Virginia promptly appointed Lee as commander of the Virginia Forces, and when the state turned those troops over to the Confederacy, Lee became the principal military advisor to Jefferson Davis, at the time the provisional president of the Confederacy. Lee's first field command was in 1861 in western Virginia, where he attempted to coordinate three separate commands under poor leadership in an attack. The plan was complicated, too complicated for two inexperienced political generals and a barely competent professional officer. When it failed, Lee's reputation with the public plummeted.[11]

Yet Lee, who proved to be the most accomplished Confederate general, persevered. Davis sent him to head the Department of South Carolina, Georgia, and Florida, where he earned kudos for his work in placing Charleston's defenses in proper order. In March 1862 Davis recalled Lee to Richmond for the spring campaign as head of "military operations of armies of the Confederacy." Even the anti-Davis newspaper the *Charleston Mercury* praised the appointment. When the commander of the Confederate army in the Department of Northern Virginia, Joe Johnston, suffered a severe wound on May 31, 1862, Davis tapped Lee to replace him. In time Lee won the hearts, souls, and minds of the soldiers in the Army of Northern Virginia through his campaign successes, and he and that command became emblematic of the independent Confederacy. In the eyes of the southern people, this army represented the viability of the Confederate States of America. It was the one truly successful institution in the South.[12]

Not surprisingly, Lee drew on his service during the Mexican War for most of his strengths as an army commander. Within the old army, he emerged from the war with an outstanding reputation, but few politicians knew him. With Scott as the commanding general, his mentor informed everyone of importance how highly he regarded Lee and ensured that the rising officer received choice assignments that showcased his protégé's ability. Lee learned at the feet of Scott, a truly accomplished field commander. Yet the lessons that he mastered were not always positive experiences for Scott. Lee learned from both the commanding general's successes and his problems.

Scott, as Lee quickly realized, was an exceedingly smart and well-read individual. Lee's insights from studying Napoleon Bonaparte's campaigns, combined with his experiences observing and participating in a central role during the Mexican campaigns, taught him how to command on the operational level of war—the use of military forces to attain strategic goals in a theater of war through the conduct of campaigns and major operations.

Scholars often compartmentalize Thomas J. Jackson's Shenandoah Valley Campaign, the Seven Days' Battles around Richmond, the turning movement and Second Battle of Manassas, and the raid into Maryland in 1862 into separate operations. But Lee weaved these seemingly disparate elements into a larger campaign to liberate Virginia from enemy presence and to take the war to the North. President Davis established the military strategy of the Confederacy as one in which forces concentrated rapidly to strike powerful blows against the enemy as close to the border as possible in hopes of convincing the United States that the price for reunion was far too high and probably impossible to achieve. He also supported movements into the Union states with the prospect of affecting politicians, demoralizing people on the home front, and consuming valuable resources there. Lee fulfilled that strategy better than any other Confederate general. He guided Jackson's liberation of the Shenandoah Valley, the army's breadbasket; cleared Federal troops from Virginia; and captured the last major element of Yankees at Harpers Ferry (the largest surrender of U.S. troops until World War II). Lee then crossed into Maryland to influence the upcoming congressional and state elections in the United States; to live off Maryland and perhaps Pennsylvania farmers for as long as possible, which reduced the burden on Virginia growers; and to recruit Marylanders to his banner. The campaign failed after the bloodbath at Antietam, but Lee did not give up on the concept. In 1863 he planned to defeat the Federal invasion in the spring, which he did at Chancellorsville, and again to head northward to raid the United States, with a plan to consume foodstuffs from locals and deflate morale in those states. Unfortunately for Lee, the Battle of Gettysburg was not a fight of his choosing, and heavy losses brought the campaign to an end. A third time, in 1864, in an effort to relieve the Siege of Petersburg, Lee sent Lieutenant General Jubal A. Early with troops to liberate the Shenandoah Valley and threaten Washington, DC, in hopes that it would compel the Federals to withdraw from the Petersburg area to protect the U.S. capital. The fall of Washington would likely convince many northerners that three and a half years of bloodshed had achieved little, and that failure would severely damage the 1864 presidential reelection bid of Abraham Lincoln. That gamble almost succeeded.[13]

During the Mexico City Campaign, Scott cut loose from his base of supplies and drew from the Mexican countryside for food and fodder. He was careful to instruct his officers and men to treat civilians with respect and to pay for anything they took, fearing that the invading army would antagonize the Mexican population even more and instigate a widespread civilian uprising. Lee, too, had to live off the land. While he refused to confiscate foodstuffs from Confederate civilians, fearing that the army would alienate the civilians from the cause of independence, he did not hesitate to do so on his raids into the North. Like his mentor, he instructed officers to pay northerners for goods. Those who refused to sell had their property confiscated and were given receipts in return. In three different years—1862, 1863, and 1864—Lee followed the practices of Scott and drew on northerners for food.[14]

From Scott, Bonaparte, and his father's Revolutionary War experiences, Lee also learned the value of audacity in combat. In most instances he fought an enemy army that was larger and better supplied than his own. To compensate, he had to rely on boldness, power at the point of attack, and surprise. Lee knew that the Confederate people believed their society produced superior soldiers and expected their general officers to fight aggressively to utilize this strength. Like his sources of insight, Lee cut loose from his supply base and fed his troops off the locals in Maryland and Pennsylvania. He employed exceptional flanking maneuvers, often at great risk, to engage with more power at the critical points of attack. During the Seven Days' Battles, he left a third of his army in the trenches to shield Richmond while he hurled 60,000 men against the Federal flank. Had George B. McClellan stormed the Confederate defenses with his superior numbers, he might have shattered Lee's scheme and pried open the door to Richmond. Yet Lee gambled that he read McClellan correctly and that the U.S. army commander would retreat rather than attack. Lee also detached Early's Corps from the Confederate works around Petersburg and Richmond in 1864 in a daring effort to draw the Federal army northward. During that same campaign, Lee explained his thinking about generalship to acting corps commander Richard Anderson. "I think in all cases it is the best to employ all our available force without reference to the weakness of the enemy," he counseled. This approach compensated for inferior numbers, a concept that Lee's father and Scott knew all too well.[15]

Among the many skills that Lee learned in Mexico, mapmaking aided his ability to envision various possible operations and to direct campaigns accordingly. He demonstrated a rare knack for blending his map-reading talents with his ability to grasp his opposing leader's mindset. By careful study of maps, he could perceive ways of getting at the enemy forces and then execute operations to strike boldly at them. And as he studied the reaction of his opponents to his movements, he gained valuable insights into their thought processes, skills, and fears. Lee then designed operations based on the maps and his knowledge of the enemy to exploit both to his advantage.[16]

As Davis's military adviser, Lee studied the map and communicated with Jackson in 1862, laying out various scenarios and offering options for his operations in the Shenandoah Valley. Lee gained great insight into President Lincoln by gauging his reaction to Jackson's failed attack at Kernstown, Virginia, in March 1862, which alerted Lincoln that McClellan had left far fewer troops to defend Washington than he had claimed. Lee realized that he had an opportunity to delay vital reinforcements to McClellan's army around Yorktown with Jackson's troops in the Valley. Union forces in the region were divided, and by combining Jackson's force with Major General Richard S. Ewell's small command, they could strike powerfully against the Federals. He laid out his preference for the target but left that choice to Jackson. Lee counseled, "The blow, wherever struck, must be successful, be sudden and heavy." He also suggested that "the troops used must be efficient and light." Yet he refused to direct Jackson from afar, pointing out that Jackson, not himself, was on the scene and needed to make the decision. Jackson knew his troops, the road conditions, the weather, and the best time to attack. The result was the Valley Campaign in 1862, one of the most successful operations of the Civil War.

Lee viewed high-quality maps as a critical tool for himself and his subordinate commanders. Confederate maps, even those of the state of Virginia, were poor. As commander of the Army of Northern Virginia for barely a week, he directed the head of the Commission of Engineers and Draughtsmen to prepare maps of Virginia that showed "the R.Rds. [railroads] Stage Farm Rds, Water Courses, Woods Clearings, farm houses, Ponds, Marshes & Commanding Elevations." Lee used a number of these maps throughout the war.[17]

During the Mexican War, Lee met and worked with a number of individuals with whom he got to know reasonably well. One of those was George McClellan. He observed McClellan's actions in Mexico, confronted him years later in western Virginia, and then studied his command decisions in northern Virginia and during the Peninsula Campaign. The insights that Lee gained then enabled him to launch an audacious attack against McClellan's army around Richmond without the Federals striking his trenches protecting the Confederate capital. His attack drove Union forces back twenty miles despite the inability of Lee's senior commanders to execute effectively.

On the Confederate side, Lee also knew many principal commanders personally or by reputation. Like Lee, Jackson earned a superb record during the war in Mexico, and Lee quickly learned to work well with him. The same was true with his old and dear friend Joe Johnston and James "Pete" Longstreet. Another great beneficiary of Lee's experiences in Mexico was P. G. T. Beauregard. Beauregard had served well at the First Battle of Manassas and the Battle of Shiloh, but his impertinent behavior ran him afoul with President Davis. Lee resurrected Beauregard and helped secure for him command of the Department of North Carolina and Cape Fear, which included southern Virginia up to the Petersburg area. His faith was not misguided. Beauregard played a critical role in blocking Major General Benjamin Butler's advance on Petersburg in the spring of 1864 and then checking Meade's attack on Petersburg that June before Lee's army could arrive.

From experience in the Mexican War, Lee learned the value of personal reconnaissance. Much to the dismay of his troops and President Davis, Lee scouted beyond his own line and several times narrowly escaped getting shot. At Malvern Hill Federal sharpshooters fired upon him, and at Second Manassas a Federal bullet creased his cheek, prompting him to make a joke out of it. In February 1863 Lee suffered what was most likely a heart attack, and after that he was too unwell to attempt personal reconnaissance at Chancellorsville or Gettysburg. Just days after the repulse at Gettysburg, Lee wrote Davis that the president needed a more fit officer in command the army, believing that it was essential to have a commanding general with vigor to handle the myriad essential tasks, including personal reconnaissance. Davis would hear none of it and informed Lee to find someone more suitable that he was to "demand an impossibility." Lee remained in command, yet later in the year, he could no longer resist the temptation and once again came under fire, this time by artillery. In the 1864 campaigns he continued to expose himself on occasion.[18]

Lee's reconnaissance efforts and subsequent examination in Mexico also taught him the value of entrenchments. Scott had his engineers oversee the emplacement of and fortifications for infantry and artillery at Vera Cruz, and Lee employed the practice in other battles during the campaign near Mexico City. He realized that shielding his gunners and infantrymen from enemy fire ensured their safety and enhanced their combat effectiveness. Once he became the commander of the Army of Northern Virginia, Lee ordered his soldiers to dig trenches for their own protection. As he explained to Davis, "There is nothing so military as labour, & nothing so important to our army as to Save the lives of its soldiers." He used those trenches as the springboard to his attack by reducing his defending troop strength in the fieldworks and using the freed-up manpower to augment the attacking force on the U.S. flank during the Seven Days. At the Battle of Fredericksburg, Longstreet's Corps fortified its position, and throughout most of the 1864–65 campaigns, Confederates fought behind defensive works, once again enhancing the combat power of the defenders by shielding life and limb.[19]

Perhaps the greatest lesson that Lee extracted from his service during the Mexican War was the issue of civil-military relations. Although Scott was not the Whig nominee for president in 1844, his name was bandied about until the party united behind Henry Clay. The Democratic Party nominated Polk, who won the presidency handily. As a loyal Democrat, Polk looked upon Scott as a political rival and loathed the idea of giving any Whig an opportunity to become a military hero in the war. The initial field command thus went to Zachary Taylor, who had neither voted nor declared for a political party, and the Polk-Scott relationship continued to sour until they deeply disliked one another. For the major overland campaign against Mexico City, Polk passed on Taylor, who had come out as a Whig and was sure to get the party nomination for president in 1848. He then attempted to find an alternative to Scott, but even his own party balked over his choice of the inexperienced Thomas Hart Benton. Polk acquiesced, grudgingly selecting Scott to lead the expedition. Nonetheless, the president saddled him with a number of political generals, including his old friend Pillow. Throughout the campaign, Scott encountered problems that he blamed on Polk or his secretary of war, William Marcy. Thus, when Scott and various high-ranking individuals, including Pillow, filed charges against each other, Polk removed the commanding general and recalled him to face an inquiry.

The Polk-Scott fiasco ingrained in Lee's mind that as a soldier, he took orders from the political leaders. During the Civil War, President Davis was commander in chief, and Lee had to report to and obey the president's directives. As Lee viewed the situation, it was his job to make sure that he communicated and cooperated effectively with Davis.

In fact, Davis and Lee got along well. Even though Davis detested Scott, he respected the general's military judgment, and Scott considered Lee the best soldier in the army. When Lee resigned from the U.S. Army and the Confederacy took over the Virginia forces, Davis appointed him as his military advisor. Later, he gave Lee a reprieve from the sharp criticism from newspapermen, military personnel, and the public by sending him away from the Richmond fishbowl to South Carolina, Georgia, and Florida. When his relationship with Joe Johnston, the commander of the Confederate Army of the Potomac in Virginia, began to sour, Davis brought Lee back to Richmond to be in charge of "military operations in the armies of the Confederacy." Lee often served as a buffer between Davis and Johnston, but even then Johnston was far too sensitive of his prerogatives as an army commander.

Lee understood the military strategy that Davis sought and did his best to execute it. He grasped the strengths and limitations of the Confederacy and adopted a nationalist perspective. When Johnston went down with a severe wound, the president chose Lee to assume command not because he was the closest individual available, but because in Davis's opinion he was the best person for the job.[20]

Once Lee took the command, he implemented Davis's policies. The day after Lee's appointment to army command, the president requested, "please keep me advised as frequently as your engagements will permit of what is passing before and around you." Lee did just that. He wrote regularly and with important information. Johnston claimed that he did not write Davis

because if the president recommended a course of action, then he felt compelled to execute it. By contrast, Lee frequently solicited Davis for his opinion on matters. Since they communicated regularly and Davis understood
fully what Lee was doing, the president did not feel compelled to interfere;
he merely extended his views. Even when Lee tackled policies with which he
disagreed, such as Davis's request that he consolidate regiments into state
brigades, he responded that he had qualms and stated them but concluded
that he would do it because Davis wanted it done. Lee then pledged that
all new brigades would be formed by state and the older brigades would
swap regiments, but he warned Davis that it would take some time because
they were in the presence of the enemy. Always, Lee communicated to the
president with respect, deference, and sensitivity to Davis's position and
problems, much like he had done with Scott.[21]

Lee also handled political appointees with skill. He knew that Davis
needed to award generalships to individuals from all of the Confederate
states, and these appointees might not have much military experience.
They did, however, carry considerable political clout in their home state
and sometimes the entire Confederacy, and their support for southern independence bolstered the cause. Lee respected these individuals and what
they brought to the war effort. Nonetheless, he placed great faith in West
Point graduates and allocated the most important ranks to them.

At times, individuals without that West Point pedigree became frustrated. Wade Hampton of South Carolina, one of the wealthiest men in all
of the South, grumbled frequently over Virginia appointees and thought he
should be in charge of cavalry, not J. E. B. Stuart, who was a first-rate officer.
Yet Lee's status as the great Confederate general tended to suppress much
criticism of the way he handled problems and promoted individuals. And,
ultimately, Lee did elevate a number of non–West Pointers to positions of
great authority. Robert E. Rodes, a graduate of Virginia Military Institute,
became the first non–West Point graduate to earn a division command.
At the time of his death in September 1864, he was probably the best division commander in the Army of Northern Virginia. Wealthy Georgian
John B. Gordon served under Rodes early in the war and rose to command
a corps, having sustained numerous wounds in battle. Even Hampton took
command of Lee's cavalry after Stuart's death instead of Fitz Lee, a West
Point graduate and the commanding general's nephew, indicating that Lee
rewarded those who commanded skillfully.

Just how successful Lee would have been if he had not served on Scott's staff is a matter of pure speculation. Anyone examining Lee as a field commander cannot divorce the lessons that he learned from his service in Mexico alongside Scott. Certainly, he possessed the innate qualities of an outstanding combat commander. Lee was extremely smart, planned carefully, and fought audaciously. He possessed the ability to anticipate the movements of his opposing commander and utilized this to his advantage. And he inspired his troops like no other commander in the Civil War and probably better than anyone in American military history due mainly to his extraordinary victories against superior numbers and resources. Yet he also learned valuable lessons from Scott's triumphs and difficulties. From Scott as well as from extensive readings, Lee learned to think and execute on the operational level, to live off the land, to conceptualize plans through the use of maps, to scout personally, and to utilize flanking movements whenever possible. He also learned lessons that Scott struggled to grasp or accept. Lee fully understood that the president was commander in chief and that he must accommodate his wishes as fully as possible. That included accepting general officers who received their appointments not because they were skilled officers, but because they contributed in important political ways to the cause of Confederate independence.

Robert E. Lee was one of the most talented commanders in American history, and he learned from another one of the best in Winfield Scott.

NOTES

1. Winfield Scott, *Memoirs of Lieut.-General Scott Written by Himself,* 2 vols. (New York: Sheldon, 1864), 2:432–33, 444–45.

2. Ibid., 450.

3. Ibid., 423.

4. J. William Jones, *Life and Letters of Robert Edward Lee, Soldier and Man* (New York: Neale, 1906), 45–46.

5. See Douglas Southall Freeman, *R. E. Lee,* 4 vols. (New York: Charles Scribner's Sons, 1934), 1:250–51; Ethan Allen Hitchcock, *Fifty Years in Camp and Field: Diary of Major-General Ethan Allen Hitchcock, U.S.A.,* ed. W. A. Croffut (New York: G. P. Putnam's Sons, 1909; repr., Legacy Reprint Series, 2010), 256 (May 15, [1847]).

6. Freeman, *R. E. Lee,* 1:271–72.

7. P. G. T. Beauregard recommended this, although Scott most likely had already decided to adopt that course of action.

8. Scott, *Memoirs,* 2:533–34.

9. Freeman, *R. E. Lee*, 1:289–92; Hitchcock, *Fifty Years*, 320, 328.

10. J. William Jones, *Personal Reminiscences, Anecdotes, and Letters of Gen. Robert E. Lee* (New York: D. Appleton, 1875), 58; Fitzhugh Lee, *General Lee* (New York: S. Appleton, 1897), 42; Freeman, *R. E. Lee*, 1:294.

11. See Joseph T. Glatthaar, *General Lee's Army: From Victory to Collapse* (New York: Free Press, 2008), 125–26.

12. Ibid., 126.

13. For an insightful exploration into the subject, see Jay Luvaas, "Lee and the Operational Art: The Right Place, the Right Time," *Parameters* (Autumn 1992): 2–18.

14. See Glatthaar, *General Lee's Army*, 270–71. Confederate soldiers did plunder their own people, despite Lee's directives against it.

15. Lee to Anderson, Aug. 29, 1864, R. E. Lee Papers, Gilder-Lehrman Collection, Morgan Library (now at New-York Historical Society), New York. See also Gary W. Gallagher, *The Confederate War: How Popular Will, Nationalism, and Military Strategy Could Not Stave Off Defeat* (Cambridge, MA: Harvard University Press, 1997), 113–53.

16. Detailed pen-and-ink drawing of routes from Mexico City to Zacaticas [*sic*], Mexico, 1847, compiled by Lee as captain in the U.S. Army Corps of Engineers, Robert E. Lee Papers, #00422, Southern Historical Collection, University Libraries, University of North Carolina at Chapel Hill.

17. Lee to Jackson, Apr. 25, 1862, *The War of the Rebellion: A Compilation of the Official Records of the Union and Confederate Armies* , 70 vols. in 128 pts. (Washington, DC: Government Printing Office, 1880–1901), ser. 1, 12(3):865–66 (hereafter cited as *OR*, all references to ser. 1 unless otherwise stated); Stevens to Campbell, June 9, 1862, in Richard W. Stephenson, "General Lee's Forgotten Mapmaker: Major Albert H. Campbell and the Department of Northern Virginia's Topographical Department," *North & South* 8, no. 2 (Mar. 2005): 66, 69. See also Joseph T. Glatthaar, *Partners in Command: The Relationships between Leaders in the Civil War* (New York: Free Press, 1994), 21–8. Jackson also benefited from a great mapmaker, Jedediah Hotchkiss, during his Valley Campaign.

18. Chas. S. Venable diary, July 4, 1862, Charles Scott Venable Papers, University of South Carolina, Columbia; Charles S. Venable journal, Aug. 29, 1862; and Venable, "Personal Reminiscences of the Confederate War," 55–56, Charles S. Venable Papers, University of Virginia, Charlottesville (thanks to Robert K. Krick for his help on this); C.E.D. to Brother, Dec. 4, 1862, Denoon Family Papers, Library of Virginia, Richmond; Lee to Davis, Aug. 8, 1863, in *Wartime Papers of R. E. Lee*, ed. Clifford Dowdey and Louis H. Manarin (Boston: Little, Brown, 1961), 589–90; Lynda Lasswell Crist, Mary Seaton Dix, and Kenneth H. Williams, eds., *Papers of Jefferson Davis: January to September 1863*, vol. 9 (Baton Rouge: Louisiana State University Press, 1997), 337–38; W. J. Seymour journal, Nov. 26, 1863, Schoff Collection, Clements Library, University of Michigan, Ann Arbor. See also Glatthaar, *General Lee's Army*, 337–38.

19. Lee to Davis, June 5, 1862, R. E. Lee Papers, U.S. Military Academy, West Point, NY; General Orders No. 62, HQ, Dept. of Northern Va., June 4, 1862, Folio 167, General and

Special Orders and Circulars Issued, Army of Northern Virginia, Record Group 109, M921, National Archives, Washington, DC, Reel 1.

20. General Orders No. 14, War Department, Adjutant and Inspector General's Office, Mar. 13, 1862, *OR*, 5:1099; Davis to Lee, Mar. 2, 1862, ibid., 400.

21. Davis to Lee, June 2, 1862, *OR*, 11(3):569; Davis to Varina, June 19, 1862, War Department Collection of Confederate Records: Confederate Papers Relating to Citizens or Business Firms ("Citizens File"): Davis, Jefferson, Box 20681, Record Group 109, National Archives; William C. Davis, "Lee and Jefferson Davis," in *Lee the Soldier*, ed. Gary W. Gallagher (Lincoln: University of Nebraska Press, 1996), 293–95.

THE QUEST FOR RECOGNITION AND GLORY

P. G. T. Beauregard in Mexico

SEAN MICHAEL CHICK

Lieutenant Pierre Gustav Toutant Beauregard was among a handful of officers who emerged from the Mexican-American War with a significantly enhanced reputation. Of those, few were less like a prototypical American than Beauregard. In a society dominated by Protestants of Anglo-Saxon extraction, his heritage as a Catholic Louisiana Creole made him unique.[1]

Unlike many at the U.S. Military Academy at West Point, Beauregard also had military preparation. As a child he took an interest in warfare and grew up with tales of Andrew Jackson's victory at New Orleans. His tenth birthday saw him gifted a musket from that battle. The turning point came when he attended the Frères Peugnet School in New York. It was run by a pair of officers who served under Napoleon, who in turn became Beauregard's hero and military ideal. He studied Bonaparte and decided to attend West Point.[2]

Beauregard excelled at West Point, graduating second in his 1838 class. Dennis Hart Mahan, who taught military theory, earmarked him as a future general in the army. While he received prestigious posts, including to his native Louisiana, promotion was slow and his career seemed to stall. There were also personal frustrations; Beauregard almost fought a duel with Lieutenant John C. Henshaw. Also, on the eve of war with Mexico, Colonel Joseph Gilbert Totten, head of the Engineering Corps, offered Beauregard promotion but did not follow through. Additionally, Beauregard missed Brigadier General Zachary Taylor's opening battles, instead being assigned to oversee the fortification of Tampico.[3]

The chance for glory came when Beauregard was posted to Major General Winfield Scott's Engineer Company. The company doubled as Scott's staff and did much of the scouting. The general had not attended West Point, nor had most of the high-ranking officers. But many of the junior officers had, and Scott leaned on their expertise and knowledge. The company numbered several future Civil War generals, including Captain Robert E. Lee and Lieutenants Gustavus W. Smith, George B. McClellan, John G. Foster, Zealous B. Tower, and Isaac Stevens. They were overseen by Major John L. Smith and Captain James L. Mason, although neither of them fought during the Civil War. With these men, Beauregard saw action from the Siege of Vera Cruz to the fall of Mexico City.[4]

West Point faced its first great trial in the war with Mexico, and Beauregard was in the thick of the Siege of Vera Cruz and three of the five major battles that followed. In 1852 he wrote an account of his extensive service in Mexico. A few copies were made and circulated among friends, most notably John A. Quitman, a Mississippi politician and division commander in Mexico. Titled "Personal Reminiscences of an Engineer Officer during the Campaign in Mexico under General Winfield Scott in 1847–8," Beauregard offered a colorful but peevish account of the conflict. He was bitter that Scott and Totten had not given him more credit for his services. Indeed, he nearly left the army in 1856 and even made a run for mayor of New Orleans in 1858. While writing his memoirs, Beauregard supported Franklin Pierce in his 1852 run against Scott for president, an unusual action for an officer who longed for promotion and recognition. In addition, while Beauregard lauded Scott, he was obviously hurt that he did not receive more praise and, on more than one occasion, leveled his own criticisms against his commanding officer.[5]

This account remained unpublished until 1956, when it was edited by historian T. Harry Williams, who found it while writing his biography of Beauregard. Published under the title *With Beauregard in Mexico: The Mexican War Reminiscences of P. G. T. Beauregard*, it is among the most valuable works for understanding the course of the Mexico City Campaign, in particular how the Battles of Cerro Gordo, Contreras, and Chapultepec were planned and fought. It also offers a window into Beauregard's military mind, which was highly developed by 1852. By then, he could not only rely on his extensive knowledge of military history and theory but also his firsthand impressions of war. In Mexico he was engaged in engineering, scouting, planning, and fighting, giving him a more diverse experience than most of his fellow Civil War generals.[6]

Beauregard's account begins with the Siege of Vera Cruz, which took place in March 1847. West Point was a military engineering school, and this operation was perfect for its graduates. It was not an exciting event for Beauregard though. While he calls the landing "one of the finest spectacles I ever witnessed," his description of it is brief. Writing for posterity and the general reader, Beauregard notes that the details of the siege would interest an engineer, but for others it "would but render this narration rather too voluminous." Beauregard took pride in helping establish some of the artillery positions set up for the bombardment. Vera Cruz fell, but the lieutenant felt that his efforts went unacknowledged by Scott. Indeed, Beauregard was annoyed that equal praise was given to others when he felt himself, as well as Lee and McClellan, were owed a greater share. In his memoir Beauregard writes pleadingly of his disappointment: "have I not the right, if not to complain, at any rate to feel surprised and pained?" Recalling that Napoleon first gained fame for sighting cannon at the 1792 Siege of Toulon, he proclaims, "the establishment of a battery stamped a young officer of artillery as a very promising one in the eyes of his superiors!" Beauregard obviously felt he did not get his due, a trait that stayed with him until his death.[7]

The next great test came when Brigadier General David Twiggs found his division facing Antonio López de Santa Anna's army in a strong position at Cerro Gordo on April 12. Twiggs sent some of his officers to reconnoiter the Mexican left, with Beauregard taking part in the effort. Along with Lieutenant William T. H. Brooks, another future Civil War general, Beauregard found a path that would allow Twiggs to get around the left. Armed with this intelligence, the general decided to attack both Santa Anna's front and flank. Beauregard and Brigadier General Robert Patterson, commanding another division, concluded that more of the column should be moved to the enemy's left, with merely a feint aimed at their front. Beauregard advised Twiggs of his proposed attack plan without mentioning Patterson's involvement. Twiggs decided to attack but then seemed to have second thoughts, at which Patterson rose from his sickbed to rescind the order.[8]

Scott arrived and authorized further reconnaissance by Beauregard and Lee to find a way not just to outflank Santa Anna but also to seize the road in the Mexican rear. Beauregard, however, fell ill, and much of the work was done by Lee, who gained most of the credit for Scott's subsequent April 18 victory. While the campaign was far from won, Santa Anna never again fielded an army as large as he did there, and his losses were appalling; The Mexican commander judged it the turning point of the war. It also might have been a turning point in Beauregard's estimation of Scott. He felt that precious time was wasted in having Lee do further reconnaissance and in the placement of artillery that "did more noise than execution." It was bold for Beauregard to criticize what is often considered Scott's most skillfully executed and decisive battle.[9]

The Battle of Cerro Gordo showed Beauregard as an enterprising officer who could be lavish with praise and show more tact than is sometimes recognized. Despite his peevishness, he did not direct his petulance at men he considered deserving of credit. Of Brooks he graciously writes, "there is not a better or more gallant officer in the service." He even praises Twiggs, who was generally unpopular. Beauregard cunningly did not tell Twiggs it was Patterson's idea to make the flank attack the primary effort. The generals did not like each other, and Twiggs would have dismissed Patterson for interfering with his plan had he known.[10]

After Cerro Gordo, Scott stopped at Jalapa and then at Puebla. There he gathered his forces, awaited reinforcements, and scouted the approaches to Mexico City. The army remained in Puebla until August 7; Beauregard has little to say about the weeks of inactivity. While as a commander he rarely neglected details, Beauregard's conception of war was still that of great events such as sieges and battles. He also knew a motionless army held few interests for readers, and his account has a notable flair for the dramatic. Indeed, Scott shared this assessment, and in his own memoirs declares, "Waiting for reinforcements, the halt, at Puebla, was protracted and irksome." Yet Beauregard's Mexican War memoir stands in some contrast to *The Military Operations of General Beauregard in the War between the States, 1861 to 1865* (1883). Published in two volumes and written with Alfred Roman (the sole official author), the account is detailed and in places mundane. But by the 1880s, an elderly Beauregard had scores to settle, while in 1852 he wanted to tell a good story and gain recognition. He was then still an officer on the make.[11]

When the American offensive resumed, Santa Anna was well positioned at El Peñon due east of Mexico City. Scott resorted to a flank move, and his engineers did extensive scouting. For Beauregard it was frustrating work.

He felt that battle reports gave Colonel James Duncan undue credit for the flank movement. The lieutenant also favored a direct attack on Mexicalcingo to the southwest, which was naturally strong but weakly held and isolated. Beauregard thought striking that position would draw Santa Anna out into a battle where he could be decisively beaten. He compared it to Napoleon's great victory at Arcola but thought it "would not by any means have presented the same difficulties." To Beauregard, Napoleon was the model, and his fellow officers, whatever their abilities, were not his equal, particularly when given a supposedly easier task than what the master had faced.[12]

Soon Beauregard got his wish for a climactic battle. On August 15 Scott outflanked El Peñon by marching south, where he hoped to occupy San Agustín and threaten Mexico City. But Santa Anna shifted to a good position at San Antonio just north of San Agustín, blocking the way to the capital.[13]

Scott sent two parties of engineers to scout ahead, with Lee and Beauregard in one group. The pair went west and found an abandoned path along the southern edge of the Pedregal, a huge dried lava bed adjacent to San Antonio. The Mexicans had used rocks and felled trees to further obstruct the unused path, but the two engineers thought it could be improved and made passable for American troops. Furthermore, creating a makeshift road would allow Scott's army to continue its flank march around Mexico City without having to work its way through the Pedregal, which was impenetrable for horses and artillery. The Americans did just that, Beauregard noting they likely only faced one division near Contreras "and as we felt confident we could defeat the whole army, the result in our minds could not have been doubtful one moment." Work on the road had to be halted as Mexican soldiers gamely skirmished with Scott's soldiers. Major General Gideon J. Pillow's division also became scattered.[14]

The Americans advanced on the Mexican position, which was on the southwestern side of the Pedregal, and found it was stronger than anticipated, Beauregard thinking they presented "a most imposing and beautiful appearance." Brigadier General George Cadwalader sent Beauregard back for help. The lieutenant reluctantly followed orders, fearing that he would miss the coming battle, but on the way back he ran into Brigadier General Persifor Smith, who ordered him to come along with him. Smith, Cadwalader, Beauregard, and Lee scouted the enemy positions, hearing Mexican military music and spying Santa Anna riding amid his men, although this was likely General of Division Gabriel Valencia, the commander in the area.[15]

Smith wanted to make a dusk attack. Beauregard disagreed but held Smith in high regard and did not want to openly dispute a superior officer. Yet he tried to enlist the aid of other officers, notable Lee and Lieutenant Colonel Joseph E. Johnston, to talk to Smith but to no avail. Thankfully, darkness prevented the attack. A scouting party that included Brooks and Tower found a path into the rear of the Mexican position, and during the night, American troops repositioned for a surprise attack. Beauregard, along with Gustavus W. Smith and McClellan, helped place part of Persifor Smith's force in position. At dawn on August 20, the Americans routed the Mexicans posted there. In the fighting Beauregard received the swords of two Mexican colonels.[16]

Ordered to carry the news of the victory to the commanding general, Beauregard delivered the message to an exuberant Scott, who proclaimed, "Young man, if I were not on horseback, I would embrace you." Beauregard, hungry for praise, later noted that with those "few words," Scott had repaid "all our toils and dangers!" That same day the Americans stormed Churubusco after hours of heavy fighting. It was a costly and mismanaged battle, but regardless, they had won two victories in a single day. Beauregard took great pride in his role at Contreras. He helped in the scouting and planning, even leading one of the attacking columns into position. The young officer continued to add to his laurels. During the pursuit, he discovered a band of Mexican soldiers led by General José Mariano Salas. Weeks before, Salas had ordered his men "to prosecute against the infamous Yankees a war of extermination, a war to the knife, granting or accepting no quarter." The general did not live up to his words and offered no resistance, but Beauregard believed it better not to force his surrender. Instead, he left this to General Smith after telling him of *"the kind of a bird he had in his cage."*[17]

After the twin victories of Contreras and Churubusco, Santa Anna asked for a truce and Scott agreed. During that time, no reconnaissance or other military activity was permitted, but Beauregard later fumed, "it was a notorious fact, that the enemy was violating it day and night." He was correct. Santa Anna replenished his forces and strengthened the defenses during the truce. Regardless, Mexico City would be hard for the Americans to take. It was surrounded by marshes to the south while to the west stood the fortress of Chapultepec.[18]

On September 6 the truce ended, and engineers resumed scouting the approaches to the capital. Beauregard's first mission was a dangerous one. He was to reconnoiter the southern approaches at night, doing so at General Pillow's request and with Scott's acquiescence. With a platoon close enough to provide support, the lieutenant and a local guide ventured forward and probed the roads south of the city. During their mission, the two were questioned by a Mexican sentry. The trembling guide was so nervous he could not respond, so Beauregard answered in his best Spanish, then ordered the nearby platoon to attack. The sentry raised his musket and fired as the pair turned and fled. Beauregard reported that his guide jumped into a canal while the platoon appeared ready to run. Striking a defiant pose, the officer dramatically tried to rally the men with oratory borrowed from Julius Caesar: "Where are you going to, you are mistaken, the enemy is here and not there!" The men reformed and attacked, but with the Mexicans now on alert, nothing more could be learned.[19]

Beauregard did not participate in the assault at Molino del Rey on September 8, but he offered his thoughts on the action. He considered it possibly Scott's worst battle, thinking the enemy position should have been either reduced by artillery or stormed with the bayonet alone. Scott tried to do both, so that "a sort of mixed attack was adopted which resulted almost in a disaster." Beauregard was not alone in his condemnation. Lieutenant Colonel Ethan Allen Hitchcock thought, "a few more such victories and this army would be destroyed." Most historians agree that Molino del Rey was Scott's worst-conducted battle, although still a victory.[20]

After Molino del Rey the engineers were busy but short staffed. Foster had been wounded, and while Stevens was ill, he did assist at times. McClellan and Gustavus W. Smith oversaw the sappers. Meanwhile, starting on the afternoon of September 8, Beauregard, Lee, and Tower reconnoitered Mexico City. The engineers advised Pillow to occupy Piedad, a mile south of the city, which he did. They also concluded that Santa Anna had more men, the ground for an approach was unfavorable, and Mexico City was daily being further fortified. Taking the capital would be difficult.[21]

On September 11 Scott met with his generals and the engineers. He believed "a heavy and last blow" must be landed to win the war and wanted the advice of others on where to make that strike. Scott made clear that no matter what, he would attack after the meeting; this was no council of war meant to provide an excuse for retreat. He wanted to strike from the west at the fortress of Chapultepec, near Molino del Rey. Pillow disagreed, wanting to hit from the south. Nearly all the generals agreed with Pillow, along with most of the engineers, including Lee, Stevens, and Tower. Twiggs supported Scott, but he also cited his general ignorance of the terrain and defenses. Brigadier General Bennett Riley, one of Twiggs's brigade commanders, asked which alternative would require more time for setting up artillery. When told that would be the southern approach, he bluntly said, "Well, I go in for less work and more fighting." Riley was at this point the only one who fully supported Scott's plan. During this debate, Beauregard stayed quiet (although he did not explain why in his 1852 narrative). He disagreed with his fellow engineers but did not want his views known if a defeat occurred, believing his words might cause jealousy among his fellow officers in that event. The lieutenant also still harbored some bitterness over the lack of recognition for his services at Vera Cruz.[22]

Scott noticed that Beauregard refused to speak, despite the entreaties of others. He asked pointedly, "You, young man, in that corner, what have you got to say for yourself?" Beauregard made an eloquent argument in favor of an attack on Chapultepec. He surmised it would surprise the Mexicans, who expected the attack from the south favored by Pillow. The lieutenant used military theory and his knowledge of the terrain to argue that the southern approach would be harder than the attack at Churubusco. Scott next asked if anyone else had thoughts, and Brigadier General Pierce changed his views to support an attack on Chapultepec. After some silence, Scott declared, "Gentleman, we will attack by the Western gates!"[23]

The next night the army commander met with his subordinates and gave orders in a "clear and precise style which could seldom be misunderstood." They would be needed, as many doubted if a victory was possible. Major General William Worth, perhaps still despondent over the bloodbath at Molino del Rey, believed, "We shall be defeated." Hitchcock thought, "if we fail or suffer great loss, there is no telling the consequences." Beauregard was detailed to aid Pillow, who was told by Scott, "*Spare my Engineer officers.*" Beauregard did not regret this order, but as it turned out, he would be in the thick of the fight.[24]

On September 13 the Americans struck. Beauregard briefly commanded a cannon and then accompanied Johnston's Voltigeurs. He recalled the Mexican lines were "one continued sheet of flame." The Voltigeurs were under constant fire, Beauregard comparing it to "a tempest at sea with the wind howling, hissing and whizzing through the cordage." Johnston encouraged his men as Beauregard pitched in. Knowing that dramatic gestures could be quite effective, he grabbed a rifle; looked at Johnston, a noted sharpshooter; and asked, "colonel, what will you bet on this shot?" Johnston replied with either, "A picayune, payable in the City of Mexico," or "Drinks in the City of Mexico." Beauregard felt his heroics encouraged the men, and soon the Mexican artillery on the southern side of Chapultepec was silenced by the Voltigeurs and the nearby regular infantry.[25]

Beauregard hoped to be the first American in Chapultepec and to take down the Mexican flag. He was certainly one of the first. In the confused melee the lieutenant saved the life of a Mexican engineer who was nearly run through. In storming the citadel he found Mexican soldiers praying for mercy, Beauregard musing they little deserved it after how they treated American wounded at Molino del Rey. He believed his delay in dallying with prisoners allowed Captain John G. Barnard to have the honor to take down the Mexican flag, causing Beauregard to muse "*L'homme propose et Dieu dispose*" (man proposes and God disposes). Meanwhile, Santa Anna had his own words: "I believe if we are to plant our batteries in Hell the damned Yankees would take them from us." One of his officers quipped, "God is a Yankee."[26]

While that honor was denied, a wounded Beauregard took a leading role in storming the city. He found Brigadier General Quitman's division, helped lead it into place, and assisted as the troops breached the city walls that night. An exhausted Beauregard, who only had water and coffee that day, asked if he could be relieved. But with Stevens wounded, Lee hurt, and McClellan and Gustavus Smith needed with the sappers, he gamely stayed at the front and assisted.[27]

The Americans prepared to storm the city at dawn only to see a white flag emerge. Beauregard spoke Spanish fluently and accompanied by Lieutenant Mansfield Lovell, another future Confederate general, who accepted the capitulation of Belen Garita, one of the fortified city gates. When asked to give a receipt for surrendered items, Beauregard said such receipts were given "with the points of our swords!" He then accompanied a few regiments into the city, and at the Palace of the Montezumas, they hoisted the U.S. flag. Quitman then sent Beauregard to inform Scott of the situation. After traveling through the "death-like stillness" of the city, he found the commanding general and conveyed the news that Quitman had occupied the main plaza. The battle was over, and Beauregard had won his honors in the struggle. Naturally, he later ended one of the best accounts of Scott's incredible campaign with a quotation from Napoleon.[28]

The end of the war, followed by the U.S. Army's evacuation of Mexico in the summer of 1848, began a new chapter in Beauregard's life. In June he and other troops received a hero's welcome when they arrived in New Orleans. When Beauregard returned home to St. Bernard Parish, the community hosted a party, and his father honored him by renaming their plantation "Contreras" in commemoration of the battle. But this new phase also brought frustrations. In addition to the death of Beauregard's wife, Marie Laure Villeré, advancement in the army was slow. His 1858 bid for mayor of New Orleans was a failure. Yet his second marriage to Caroline Deslonde brought political connections and appointment as superintendent of the U.S. Military Academy at West Point. But he served at the academy a scant three days in 1861; Louisiana had seceded, and Beauregard was promptly removed from the post. Within a few months, he gained fame when he oversaw the bombardment of Fort Sumter.[29]

Despite his stellar service in Mexico, Beauregard is remembered as a Confederate general. Battles such as First Bull Run, Shiloh, and Petersburg overshadowed in scope, bloodshed, and fame the likes of Cerro Gordo, Contreras, and Chapultepec. His service in the American Civil War was influenced by his education at West Point, knowledge of military history and theory, understanding of Napoleon, and experiences in Mexico. The last gave him even more confidence in his abilities. Beauregard was highly intelligent and came from one of Louisiana's top-tier families; he was never modest. But Mexico confirmed many of his ideas on war. He would use these during the Civil War with conflicting results. He proved a capable military commander, marred mostly by personal deficiencies.

Beauregard was by training and profession an engineer. He used these skills to practical effect in Mexico, first at Vera Cruz. Beauregard was among the first commanders of the Civil War to order entrenchments, which he did before First Bull Run. He used defensive works to hold Corinth, Mississippi, for weeks longer than was otherwise possible. Finally, he used entrenchments to contain Major General Benjamin Butler's Army of the James at Bermuda Hundred, Virginia.[30] But his best talents in engineering were showcased in the defense of Charleston, South Carolina. Despite a major Union land and sea campaign, the city held, providing the Confederates with their only major strategic victory of 1863. Chancellorsville and Chickamauga were tactical victories, for when the Confederacy tried to capitalize on them, those ventures ended in defeat at Gettysburg and Chattanooga respectively. Major General Richard Taylor's victory at Brashear City in Louisiana netted him much needed supplies but did not save Port Hudson nor lead to the capture of New Orleans. Beauregard's finest hour, though, came at Petersburg. Lieutenant General Ulysses S. Grant, a compatriot of Scott's campaign, hoped to seize the city and thus checkmate Richmond before Lee could shift his army to block him. The battle opened on June 15, 1864, and on the following day, Beauregard wisely selected a defensive line in the rear and had it entrenched. This line was attacked on June 18 and held. He had the lines improved after the battle, which was one reason why the Crater attack on July 30 failed. In fact, the lines Beauregard's men constructed were never successfully stormed, not even when Grant launched his all-out assault on Petersburg's defenses on April 2, 1865.[31]

Beauregard also learned the use of bold leadership in Mexico. Few generals were as beloved by their men and wildly cheered throughout the war as him. At First Bull Run he was conspicuous rallying units and ordering attacks. The general was also popular in camp. At the 1864 battle of Drewry's Bluff, he spent the night before the fight chatting with the men and smoking a cigar.[32]

The ultimate test came at Shiloh in April 1862. With General Albert Sidney Johnston's death on the first day of battle, Beauregard found himself in command. By then, the South's chances of victory were diminishing. Major General Don Carlos Buell was on the way with over 20,000 fresh troops, which counterattacked on April 7 along with the rest of Grant's army. The second day's fight was a severe test of Beauregard's skill, but he succeeded in cobbling together a defense several times, even as the army frayed under constant pressure.[33]

In this maelstrom Beauregard took drastic action. Around 2:00 p.m. Colonel Thomas Jordan, his most trusted staff officer, asked: "General, do you not think our troops are very much in the condition of a lump of sugar thoroughly soaked with water, but yet preserving its original shape, though ready to dissolve? Would it not be judicious to get away with what we have?" Beauregard replied, "I intend to withdraw in a few moments." Yet he could not run just yet. Lieutenant Colonel Alfred Roman, then fighting with the 18th Louisiana, later concluded: "To indulge a hope of success with these fearful odds against him would have been to show a lack of judgment impossible to such a soldier as Beauregard. The die, however, was cast. There was no means of avoiding the issue." With that in mind, the general led a series of counterattacks. To the 18th Louisiana and Orleans Guard Battalion, Beauregard shouted, "Forward, fellow soldiers of Louisiana! One more effort and the day is ours!" After that advance failed, Beauregard grabbed the flag of the Orleans Guard, a unit he briefly served in and filled with friends and family. He shouted, *"Allons mes braves Louisianois en avant!"* When he was scolded by an officer for exposing himself, Beauregard replied, "The order must now be *follow,* not go!" These were not empty theatrics. Battlefield charisma and leadership made tactical sense, particularly in an emergency, and it bonded the men to their commander. Just as important, the attacks worked. The Federals paused, having encountered what Lieutenant Colonel Joseph B. Dodge of the 30th Indiana called "a terrible storm of musketry and artillery."[34]

Beauregard also learned the importance of giving credit when earned. His memoir of Mexico is filled with him weighing who deserved praise. Beauregard was arguably greedy for credit, but he was certainly not alone in that regard. In the small antebellum army, promotion was slow and officers jockeyed for laurels. What can be said of Beauregard was that he was more forthright. In addition, his desire for glory did not make him stingy with praise for his fellow officers. He doled it out in large portions, even praising Twiggs and Pierce, men sometimes maligned in accounts of the Mexico City Campaign. This trait also played out during the Civil War, where Beauregard freely praised and noticed success, from generals to privates. He was always willing to single out men and units. During the siege of Corinth, Beauregard ordered an attack at Farmington. Despite some success in driving back the Federals, the grander scheme of outflanking Major General John Pope's Army of the Mississippi was unsuccessful. Despite this, Beauregard told Brigadier General William Lewis Cabell, a former member of his staff, "I am proud of you and your Texans." Cabell boasted about that brief moment years later. After his victory at Drewry's Bluff in 1864, Beauregard told the members of the 6th Georgia they had played a large part in "the brilliant achievement won in the previous day's action." Such words played well with the men, although it helped that Company C of that unit had called themselves the "Beauregard Volunteers."[35]

Mexico taught Beauregard the value of a bold attack. The results of this were more mixed, however, during the Civil War. For one thing, the Mexican army, plagued by poor leadership and logistics, was inferior to the Union and Confederate forces. At First Bull Run Beauregard tried to seize Centreville, but coordination was poor and his staff was not up to the task. Shiloh itself was conceived as just such an attack, although the method of assault chosen by Beauregard and Jordan has come under criticism ever since. The Tennessee terrain, to be fair, was poor, but the plan was predicated on surprise and the fact that Grant had not fortified his camp. Once the battle started, Beauregard oversaw numerous assaults on April 6 and 7 until it was confirmed that Buell had arrived. Lastly, he ordered numerous attacks at Globe Tavern, fought south of Petersburg August 18–21, 1864. Two Confederate assaults heavily damaged the V Corps. The third, while carefully prepared, was easily defeated by an entrenched opponent.[36]

Beauregard won most of his Civil War battles, but his reputation has remained mixed. T. Harry Williams, supported by Charles Roland, argues that Beauregard was a by-the-book commander who was critical of Scott for taking chances that violated the principles of war. If Scott had faced a better opponent, goes the argument, he would have lost. Williams concludes, "There is no evidence that he [Beauregard] studied Scott's generalship in the Mexican campaign or learned anything from the general's strategy" and instead went into 1861 with a "rigid belief that certain rules of war must always be followed." Kevin Dougherty, by contrast, believes that Beauregard did learn from Mexico, but the lessons were more or less what not to do, concluding that Scott's wide turning movements only succeeded because they were executed against an inferior opponent. As such, "almost alone among the important Civil War generals, Beauregard would not typically employ the turning movement," at least on the tactical level.[37]

The Williams and Roland contention is unfair. It is true that Beauregard was a theoretician, but he showed flexibility. Much like Scott, on the level of strategy he believed in bold maneuvers and concentrated force. Tactically, Beauregard was not hidebound. At Petersburg he created a secondary defense line and then ordered a tactical retreat on the night of June 17–18, 1864. Night maneuvers were rare before the twentieth century, and when attempted were rarely so successful. Dougherty is wrong to see him as avoiding turning movements. In Mexico Beauregard recommended a turning movement at Cerro Gordo. Both his plans of attack at Corinth in 1862 relied on turning movements because Major General Henry W. Halleck's men were well fortified, thus any frontal assault would have been suicidal.

No doubt Beauregard could recall that the Mexicans did best when they were dug in, such as at Molino del Rey. His plans at Corinth failed due to the errors of Major General Earl Van Dorn. When not committing to a turning movement, he typically tried to turn the enemy's flank on the battlefield. At First Bull Run he tried to turn the Union left, and at Petersburg he recommended something similar to Lee on June 18, 1864.[38]

Roland has accused Beauregard of failing to finish off his opponent at First Bull Run and Shiloh and of failing to strike back when he defended Corinth. In reality, the general was an offensive-minded commander. Like Napoleon and Scott, he always considered how best to strike at the enemy when it was practical. At First Bull Run and Shiloh, it simply was not the case. Beauregard's forces were too disorganized and green at Bull Run and lacked cavalry. At dusk on April 6 at Shiloh, his men were tired, low on ammunition, scattered, facing rough terrain, and confronting a heavy line of cannon supported by gunboats. Time was needed to find a weakness, but the sun was setting. Instead, Beauregard could be faulted for being too quick to attack the following day. When Grant and Buell counterattacked at Shiloh, Beauregard's reaction was to strike back, even though he assumed Grant could be finished off and therefore should have questioned why he was instead attacking. The result was a series of disorganized assaults that wrecked the Confederate army and brought near-disaster by the afternoon of April 7. To be fair, Beauregard did not always seek the offensive. At Charleston in 1863 he stuck purely to defense and was successful. His "best battle of the war," according to Williams, was his defensive victory at Petersburg.[39]

Beauregard did not learn how to restrain his ambition. Of course, ambition is not wholly negative, and few generals are indifferent to accolades. Beauregard was more forthright with this trait, however, which grated on his superiors. He ached for praise. Much worse, he was not good at the game of politics, whether it be military or civilian. His 1852 account of the war with Mexico was written to gain notice, and in it he offered both praise and criticism of General Scott, his commander and America's most celebrated living soldier. Beauregard may not have received enough praise, but he was hardly punished by Scott during the war or after. In fact, he was rewarded with promotion in the U.S. Army, which occurred not only after the account was written but also after Beauregard publicly backed Pierce over Scott in the 1852 presidential race. It is not known if Scott ever knew of or saw the memoir, but he certainly knew that Beauregard was friends with Pierce and was supporting him openly. If Beauregard hoped to regain Scott's favor, such actions and writings were not the wisest course of action.[40]

After Beauregard wrote his work on Mexico, Quitman, Twiggs, Patterson, and Persifor Smith sent letters recommending him to William Walker, the most famous of the filibusters who had seized control of Nicaragua. Beauregard considered joining him. His memoir of Mexico was one means of gaining Walker's notice. Then a letter arrived from Scott. He called Beauregard "my gallant young friend" and warned, "If you go, abroad, you will give up that connection & also a high social position at some hazard." Smith also wanted to dissuade Beauregard, whom he considered Walker's superior as a soldier. As for Walker, Smith noted that he was "cold hearted & I think selfish, of contracted intellect," adding, "his caliber is too small for the events he is called upon to control." Events would prove Smith right about Walker. More importantly for Beauregard, Smith and Scott kept him in the ranks. For all the accusations that Scott was prickly and arrogant, with Beauregard he showed great tact and care. Robert E. Lee was his favorite, but clearly he considered Beauregard one of the best.[41]

Jefferson Davis, president of the Confederacy, was far less kindly toward Beauregard after First Bull Run than Scott was after 1852. Much of it was Beauregard's fault. The Confederate general carped, fumed, and made friends with the president's critics. Davis had seen Zachary Taylor undermined by politicians and subordinates back in Mexico and might have taken a page from that. The Mississippian was, for all his strengths, sensitive and given to grudges. By early 1862, Davis thought well of Beauregard the commander but not the man, and as such he sent him to help General Albert Sidney Johnson after the debacle at Mill Springs, Kentucky. By war's end, there were few southerners who hated each other as much as Davis and Beauregard. The animosity deepened after 1865 to the point that Beauregard refused a place of honor in Davis's massive New Orleans funeral in 1889. This failure at politics played out before and after the war with Beauregard's 1858 mayoral bid and his brief support for Louisiana's Unification Movement in 1873. The only success he enjoyed was his support for Pierce in 1852 and for racial moderates in Louisiana's 1876 elections. Beauregard's failure in the politics of command is all the more important, considering that Lee and Grant both cultivated good relationships with their political masters, a key reason both men had success.[42]

After the Civil War James Longstreet surmised that "Beauregard gave indications of a comprehensive military mind and reserve powers that might, with experience and thorough encouragement from the superior authorities, have developed him into eminence as a field-marshal." But it was not to be. As it was, General Scott showed Beauregard more regard than Louisiana's political masters in both parties, and his greatest foe turned out to be President Davis. Beauregard did not know it, but in 1852 he never again had such a good relationship with his superiors. He learned much from Scott and his experiences in Mexico. One wonders, though, if Beauregard might have learned to hold his tongue better then as well had Scott actually lived up to his sobriquet "Old Fuss and Feathers."[43]

NOTES

1. Sean Michael Chick, *Dreams of Victory: General P. G. T. Beauregard in the Civil War* (El Dorado Hills, CA: Savas Beatie, 2022), 1–3.

2. Ibid., 1–5; T. Harry Williams, *P. G. T. Beauregard: Napoleon in Gray* (Baton Rouge: Louisiana State University Press, 1955), 2–6.

3. Chick, *Dreams of Victory*, 7–10; Williams, *P. G. T. Beauregard*, 7, 13–14.

4. P. G. T. Beauregard. *With Beauregard in Mexico: The Mexican War Reminiscences of P. G. T. Beauregard*, ed. T. Harry Williams (Baton Rouge: Louisiana State University Press, 1956), 9; Chick, *Dreams of Victory*, 8–10.

5. Chick, *Dreams of Victory*, 16–19.

6. Beauregard, *With Beauregard in Mexico*, 3, 9.

7. Ibid., 25–31.

8. Ibid., 12–13, 36–37; Timothy D. Johnson, *A Gallant Little Army: The Mexico City Campaign* (Lawrence: University Press of Kansas, 2007), 80.

9. Beauregard, *With Beauregard in Mexico*, 13–14, 38–39; Johnson, *Gallant Little Army*, 96–97; Robert L. Scheina, *Santa Anna: A Curse upon Mexico* (Washington, DC: Brassey's, 2002), 64.

10. Beauregard, *With Beauregard in Mexico*, 33–37.

11. Ibid., 14; Winfield Scott, *Memoirs of Lieut.-General Scott*, 2 vols. (New York: Sheldon, 1864), 2:453; Williams, *P. G. T. Beauregard*, 304–18.

12. Beauregard, *With Beauregard in Mexico*, 15, 43–46; Justin H. Smith, *The War with Mexico*, 2 vols. (New York: Macmillan, 1919), 2:96–98.

13. Beauregard, *With Beauregard in Mexico*, 15, 47; Johnson, *Gallant Little Army*, 158–59; Smith, *War with Mexico*, 2:101–2.

14. Beauregard, *With Beauregard in Mexico*, 15–16, 47–48; Johnson, *Gallant Little Army*, 154, 160–61; Scott, *Memoirs*, 2:469.

15. Beauregard, *With Beauregard in Mexico*, 16–17, 49–51; Johnson, *Gallant Little Army*, 175–176; Scott, *Memoirs*, 2:480.

16. Beauregard, *With Beauregard in Mexico*, 16–17, 51–55, 57; Smith, *War with Mexico*, 2:108.

17. Beauregard, *With Beauregard in Mexico*, 17, 55–59; Smith, *War with Mexico*, 2:110–11.

18. Beauregard, *With Beauregard in Mexico*, 17–18; Smith, *War with Mexico*, 2:120–39.

19. Beauregard, *With Beauregard in Mexico*, 60–62.

20. K. Jack Bauer, *The Mexican War, 1846–1848* (Lincoln: University of Nebraska Press, 1992), 311; Beauregard, *With Beauregard in Mexico*, 64; Ethan Allen Hitchcock, *Fifty Years in Camp and Field: Diary of Major-General Ethan Allen Hitchcock, U.S.A*, ed. W. A. Croffut (New York: G. P. Putnam's Sons, 1909), 298; Johnson, *Gallant Little Army*, 208; Smith, *War with Mexico*, 2:147.

21. Beauregard, *With Beauregard in Mexico*, 64–67.

22. Ibid., 18, 68–70; Smith, *War with Mexico*, 2:149.

23. Beauregard, *With Beauregard in Mexico*, 70–72; John S. D. Eisenhower, *So Far from God: The U.S. War with Mexico, 1846–1848* (New York: Random House, 1989), 276–77, 337–38; Smith, *War with Mexico*, 2:149.

24. Beauregard, *With Beauregard in Mexico*, 75, 78; Hitchcock, *Fifty Years*, 301; Smith, *War with Mexico*, 2:153–54.

25. Beauregard, *With Beauregard in Mexico*, 79–81; Smith, *War with Mexico*, 2:156–58.

26. Bauer, *Mexican War*, 318; Beauregard, *With Beauregard in Mexico*, 81–83.

27. Beauregard, *With Beauregard in Mexico*, 20, 85–95; Smith, *War with Mexico*, 2:158–60.

28. Bauer, *Mexican War*, 321; Beauregard, *With Beauregard in Mexico*, 20, 97–102, 105; Smith, *War with Mexico*, 2:162–64.

29. Chick, *Dreams of Victory*, 15–30; Williams, *P. G. T. Beauregard*, 34–50.

30. The contention that Butler was "bottled up" inside Bermuda Hundred is not wholly accurate, but the Union entrenchments did limit his options. For more, see William Glenn Robertson, *Back Door to Richmond: The Bermuda Hundred Campaign, April–June 1864* (Newark, NJ: University of Delaware Press, 1987).

31. Chick, *Dreams of Victory*, 39, 67, 76–83; Alfred Roman, *The Military Operations of General Beauregard in the War between the States, 1861 to 1865*, 2 vols. (New York: Harper and Brothers, 1884), 1:222–23, 258–60, 270. For more on Beauregard's use of fortifications, see Sean Michael Chick, *The Battle of Petersburg, June 15–18, 1864* (Lincoln: Potomac Books, 2015); Earl J. Hess, *Field Armies and Fortifications in the Civil War: The Eastern Campaigns, 1861–1864* (Chapel Hill: University of North Carolina, 2006); Timothy B. Smith, *Corinth 1862: Siege, Battle, Occupation* (2012; repr., Lawrence: University Press of Kansas, 2016); and Stephen R. Wise, *Gate of Hell: Campaign for Charleston Harbor, 1863* (Columbia: University of South Carolina Press, 1994).

32. Chick, *Dreams of Victory*, 43–45, 90; Johnson Hagood, *Memoirs of the War of Secession* (Columbia, SC: State Company, 1910), 235; Ethan S. Rafuse, *A Single Grand Victory: The First Campaign and Battle of Manassas* (Lanham, MD: Rowman and Littlefield, 2002), 151.

33. Alexander R. Chisolm, "Gen. Beauregard at Shiloh," *Confederate Veteran* 10, no. 5 (May 1902): 213; Alfred Tyler Fielder, *The Civil War Diaries of Capt. Alfred Tyler Fielder, 12th Tennessee Regiment Infantry, Company B, 1861-1865* (Louisville: A. Y. Franklin, 1996), 44; Alexander Walker, "Narrative of the Battle of Shiloh, by Alex. Walker, of the N.O. Delta," in *Diary of the War for Separation*, comp. H. C. Clarke (Augusta, GA: Chronicle and Sentential, 1862), 155.

34. J. B. Dodge, "At Shiloh," *National Tribune*, Apr. 12, 1888; Journal of the Orleans Guard, n.d., Williams Research Center, Historic New Orleans Collection, New Orleans; Thomas Jordan, "Notes of a Confederate Staff Officer at Shiloh," in *Battles and Leaders of the Civil War*, ed. Robert Underwood Johnson and Clarence Clough Buel, vol. 1 (New York: Century, 1887), 603; Edmond Enoul Livaudais, *The Shiloh Diary of Edmond Enoul Livaudais*, ed. Stanly J. Guerin, Earl C. Woods, and Charles E. Nolan (New Orleans: Archdiocese of New Orleans, 1992), 32; Roman, *Military Operations*, 1:317-19; Walker, "Narrative," 158-59.

35. Chick, *Dreams of Victory*, 67; Wendell D. Croom, *The War History of Company "C" Beauregard Volunteers, Sixth Georgia Regiment Infantry* (Fort Valley, GA: Advertiser Office, 1879), 24.

36. Chisolm, "Beauregard at Shiloh," 213; Larry J. Daniel, *Shiloh: The Battle That Changed the Civil War* (New York: Simon and Schuster, 1997), 118-20; John Horn, *The Siege of Petersburg: The Battles for the Weldon Railroad 1864* (El Dorado Hills, CA: Savas Beatie, 2015), 171, 174, 178, 180, 183-84, 186; Timothy B. Smith, *Shiloh: Conquer or Perish* (Lawrence: University Press of Kansas, 2014), 41-47; Walker, "Narrative," 151-52; Williams, *P. G. T. Beauregard*, 78-83.

37. Kevin Dougherty, *Civil War Leadership and Mexican War Experience* (Jackson: University Press of Mississippi, 2007), 120-26; Charles Roland, "P. G. T. Beauregard," in *Leaders of the Lost Cause: New Perspectives on the Confederate High Command*, ed. Gary W. Gallagher and Joseph T. Glatthaar (Mechanicsburg, PA: Stackpole Books, 2004), 44-45; Williams, *P. G. T. Beauregard*, 33.

38. Thomas J. Howe, *The Petersburg Campaign: Wasted Valor, June 15-18, 1864* (Lynchburg, VA: H. E. Howard, 1988), 58, 106-7; Roman, *Military Operations*, 1:577; Smith, *Corinth 1862*, 36-38, 44-45, 77-78; Williams, *P. G. T. Beauregard*, 83-85.

39. Walker, "Narrative," 151-52; Chisolm, "Beauregard at Shiloh," 213; Giles B. Cooke Diary, Apr. 7, 1862, Giles B. Cooke Papers, Virginia Museum of Culture and History, Richmond; Rafuse, *Single Grand Victory*, 192-94, 202-3; Roland, "P. G. T. Beauregard," 47, 51-52; Smith, *Shiloh*, 232-33; Williams, *P. G. T. Beauregard*, 235.

40. Chick, *Dreams of Glory*, 17-18; Williams, *P. G. T. Beauregard*, 33, 38-40.

41. Beauregard, *With Beauregard in Mexico*, 107-12.

42. Chick, *Dreams of Victory*, 19, 45, 49-52, 55, 70-71, 124-25, 131-34.

43. James Longstreet, *From Manassas to Appomattox: Memoirs of the Civil War in America* (Philadelphia: J. P. Lippincott, 1895), 56.

SOUR GRAPES

Braxton Bragg and the Lessons of the War with Mexico

CECILY N. ZANDER

Braxton Bragg emerged from the Mexican-American War a household name. His fame derived from an apparent exclamation thundered by his commanding officer, Major General Zachary Taylor, amid the melee of the Battle of Buena Vista in February 1847. As then Captain Bragg aligned his artillery to fend off a desperate assault from Mexican troops under General Antonio López de Santa Anna, Taylor rode up to his subordinate and urged him to rush his battery of 6-pounders into a gap in the American line. When the captain queried his general as to how he was supposed to hold back the Mexican assault, Taylor replied, "A little more grape, Mr. Bragg." The story spread quickly in newspapers across the United States after Bragg's artillerymen and a late charge by Colonel Jefferson Davis's Mississippi volunteers held Santa Anna's men at bay.[1]

The story of Taylor's response—more than likely apocryphal—followed Bragg for the remainder of his life. It occasioned widespread comment in newspapers, periodicals, and even inspired a patriotic ballad.[2] As the secession winter of 1860–61 descended upon the United States and rumors of war turned from speculation to reality, many Americans recalled Bragg's heroics during the Mexican War. As a result, prognosticators on both sides speculated that the 1837 West Point graduate would be a force to contend with in the coming conflict. A pro-Union patriotic envelope from 1861 indicated that Bragg's military reputation struck fear in many in the North. The mail cover depicted the North Carolinian dead and hanging from a noose: "The BRAGG fruit of Palmetto *Tree*-son." War planners in the new Confederacy, meanwhile, hoped that Bragg would be a boon to their cause. The

Confederate Congress made him a major general in September 1861 and, following Albert Sidney Johnston's death at Shiloh in 1862, promoted Bragg to the rank of full general. At that time only four men ranked above him.[3]

Despite the high hopes of his Confederate countrymen, Bragg's tenure as an army commander during the Civil War did not feature a repeat performance of the military successes he achieved on the battlefields of northern Mexico. Though he commanded the second-most-important Confederate army for almost two full years, Bragg emerged from the war in 1865 counting only one victory to his name. That triumph, Chickamauga, owed more to the mistakes of U.S. major general William S. Rosecrans and the quick thinking of Bragg's subordinate Lieutenant General James Longstreet than it did from any strategizing or generalship on Bragg's part. Given the choice, he might have preferred that history remember him for his Mexican War gallantry rather than his Civil War failures.

Because Bragg's Civil War record could generously be described as abysmal, it is a challenge to assess whether the experience of the Mexican-American War directly influenced his later generalship. Even more frustrating is the fact that Bragg left behind no personal recollections of either conflict. And when his contemporaries wrote about him as a military officer, they often ignored his service in Mexico entirely. Accounts of Bragg gave his actions in that war little more than a passing mention because authors hoped to focus their ire on his Civil War service—admitting he had once proved to be a competent soldier would not bolster their argument. Bragg's contemporaries tended to treat the North Carolinian unkindly. Accounts often portrayed the general as unskilled at best and incompetent at worst. Postbellum writers rebuked his qualities as a leader and maligned his inability to get along with subordinates, to issue clear orders, and take responsibility for defeat.[4]

So, how can historians assess whether the Mexican War served as preparation for Braxton Bragg's Civil War leadership? Three points are worth emphasizing. One, his career in Mexico proved shorter than many of his contemporaries. Because of his contentious personality and penchant for criticizing other officers, only one of the two principle American commanders during that conflict employed him in their service. Two, Bragg demonstrated his commitment to properly training and drilling his troops. This habit carried over into the Civil War but often resulted in his being maligned as a martinet with a cruel streak. Third, Bragg's capable performance as an artillerist helped elevate the reputation of his branch. The strong showing of artillery throughout the Mexican conflict, in turn, made certain that the U.S. Army could no longer view the artillery arm as inessential or ineffective, ensuring that cannon shot and shell would play a similarly vital role during the Civil War.

On a personal level, Bragg did not emerge from the Mexican-American War with an improved ability to command soldiers. He had proved so argumentative and difficult to tolerate in the decade prior to that war that army leaders such as Major General Winfield Scott were unwilling to work with him. Throughout the 1840s, Bragg steadily alienated army leaders and some of his immediate superior officers. Thus, as a young captain he did not get to experience either the triumphs of Scott's army or his leadership firsthand because "Old Fuss and Feathers" did not order the transfer of Bragg's artillery company to his army at the outset of the march to Mexico City. The young North Carolinian's experience in the war was consequently shorter than many of his future Civil War colleagues. He was limited to experiencing only one command approach—that of Zachary Taylor.

The war that pitted the United States against Mexico featured three separate American armies. One, the Army of the West under Stephen Watts Kearny, is seldom featured in histories of the conflict.[5] This command marched first from Fort Leavenworth to Santa Fe and then to California. Zachary Taylor, a veteran officer who had overseen the final years of the bungled and costly effort to remove the Seminole Nation from Florida, commanded a force that occupied the disputed territory along the U.S.–Mexico border. After engaging Mexican forces along the Rio Grande in May 1846, it invaded northern Mexico and defeated enemy armies at Monterrey (September 1846) and Buena Vista before settling into occupation duties in the states of Coahuila, Nuevo León, and Tamaulipas. A final portion of the American army served under the command of Winfield Scott, a veteran general who led his troops on one of the most ambitious campaigns in the annals of American military history from Vera Cruz to Mexico City in 1847.

Bragg served as the captain of a light artillery company assigned to Taylor's army. The twenty-nine-year-old career army officer did not lack experience but, due to the slow rate of promotion in the antebellum regular army, had little rank to show for his years of service. Upon graduation from West Point in 1837, Bragg found himself a second lieutenant in Florida (where he would also begin his Civil War career) serving in the longest and costliest war against Native Americans in the nation's history. It was there that he contracted malaria, a disease from which he never fully recovered and that afflicted him with a series of physical ailments, which historians typically lump together as rheumatism but included boils, dyspepsia, and migraine headaches, for the remainder of his life.

A lifetime of near-constant physical pain did little to improve Bragg's naturally querulous temperament. Various recurring ailments also meant that he saw no combat service after taking medical leave from the army in 1838. Throughout the 1840s, most of his fighting took place in letters and editorials for army periodicals, where under the pseudonym "A Subaltern," he frequently and freely critiqued his fellow officers and army higher-ups for poor decision making and inefficiency. By the frequency with which one story of Bragg's argumentative tendencies appears in Civil War memoirs, there is little doubt that the officer had a reputation as a prickly character in army circles.

The tale deals with a period in which Bragg served as both a company commander and quartermaster at a western army post. As company officer he was supposed to have requisitioned supplies from the quartermaster; a request that he then, as quartermaster, turned down for being improperly filed. After one or two further rounds of requests and denials, Bragg forwarded the full set of paperwork to the post commander, who apparently declared, "My god Mr. Bragg you've quarreled with every man in this army and now you're quarrelling with yourself!"[6] Even if Bragg had not truly spent a fruitless afternoon refusing to sign orders that he himself had written while serving as both quartermaster and company commander at some far-flung western post, the idea that he would argue with himself suggests that the officer was constantly spoiling for a fight—his preferred weapons were simply rules and regulations rather than muskets and men.

Bragg's tendency to argue made enemies in high places. And in the antebellum army, having such enemies could mean the difference between opportunities for career advancement and a life spent as a second lieutenant in some military backwater in the West.[7] In Bragg's case, making an enemy of the army's commanding general, Winfield Scott, meant he had limited opportunities for service in the war with Mexico. His testy relationship with Scott began about 1840. That year Bragg had returned to Florida for his third service stint in the territory. Upon his arrival at Fort Marion near St. Agustín, the officer found the quarters occupied by his men seriously deficient. He wrote to the adjutant general of the army about receiving medicine or constructing a new barracks and received no reply. After waiting about five weeks, Bragg wrote again to Roger Jones, excoriating the longest-serving adjutant general in the army's history for risking the safety of his men and for ignoring his letters. Word of the exchange reached Scott, who scribbled a disapproving note on the back of Bragg's letter designating the entire batch of correspondence "improper."[8]

In the opening stages of the war with Mexico, however, Bragg's unwise choice to run afoul of Scott did not immediately threaten his opportunity to gain experience and battlefield glory. This was because President James K. Polk put Taylor, not Scott, in charge of the first U.S. force to invade Mexico. Polk's logic for this had its roots in the complicated relationship between party politics and the professional military. Throughout the early decades of the American Republic, professional soldiers were asked to avoid overt displays of political partisanship while serving their country. This stance was one of self-interest and self-preservation on the part of the regular army because the very existence of the institution stood at odds with the system of democratic government instituted by the founders: standing armies, historically, were viewed as a threat to liberty. The less political the army appeared, the more likely it would be preserved by the federal government.

Fearing that any man he selected could become a political rival, Polk agonized over who he should appoint to lead U.S. armies in Mexico, knowing well that soldiers could turn battlefield triumphs to victories at the hustings. As a protégé of Andrew Jackson, he certainly knew the type. In May 1846 Scott and Polk engaged in a skirmish over the president's proposal to appoint civilians to command the volunteer units that would compose most of the American forces in Mexico. The general speculated that the president would use the appointments to promote his Democratic allies, writing that "not a Whig would obtain a place under such proscriptive circumstances."[9] Scott's condemnation of the plan, cast in overtly political tones, convinced Polk that he could not send the Virginian to the front and risk increasing Scott's military fame (and the general's viability as a presidential candidate). Thus, he ordered Taylor to take charge of the war's opening campaign.

Polk's political logic was unimpeachable. Taylor had never engaged with politics, never even having voted in a presidential election. But after his early victories at Palo Alto, Resaca de la Palma, and Monterrey in 1846, Whig heads began to turn in Taylor's direction, and the national press began to whisper that the general would, if asked, run on the Whig ticket for the presidency in 1848.[10] By the war's midpoint, Polk's gambit had backfired, and the president felt that the only way to neuter the Taylor threat would be to send Scott into the field to conquer the Mexican capital—this would draw focus away from Taylor. To have the troops necessary to mount his campaign in central Mexico, Scott ordered the transfer of a large part of Taylor's army to his command. He took both regulars and volunteers but preferred the former over the latter, as would most American professional soldiers of the time.[11]

So long as Taylor remained in command of an army, Bragg had the opportunity to learn and ply his trade. His unwise choice to run afoul of Scott, however, meant the army's general in chief was unlikely to find a place for the North Carolinian in his army. Bragg's bad attitude, in other words, contributed to cutting his Mexican War participation short. As a result, he emerged from the conflict with less practical experience than many of his future colleagues and adversaries. When Polk did finally approve the plan to march from Vera Cruz to Mexico City, he authorized some 9,000 seasoned troops to be stripped from Taylor's army and transferred to Scott's command. A significant number of junior officers in Taylor's army received orders for Vera Cruz, among them Ulysses S. Grant, Joseph Hooker, James Longstreet, George B. McClellan, Pierre G. T. Beauregard, and Thomas J. Jackson (the future "Stonewall"). Though some of the 3rd Artillery Regiment was ordered south, Bragg's company was not among those selected to accompany Scott to the halls of the Montezumas.

A march to Mexico City lay far in the future, however, when Polk ordered Taylor to cross the Nueces River in 1845 and claim the Rio Grande as the southern border of Texas. This move indicated to most observers of the brewing border troubles that little hope remained for avoiding armed conflict between the United States and Mexico. When Mexican troops retaliated and shed "American blood on American soil," all eyes turned to General Taylor and his 3,550 soldiers. Almost all of these troops were drawn from the small professional army of the 1840s. Many of the junior officers, Bragg included, were West Point products, making the coming war one of the first in which the graduates of the national military academy would fill most officer roles.[12] On June 18, 1845, Bragg received orders to transfer his company of artillery from Fort Moultrie in Georgia to Corpus Christi, Texas, where he and multiple future Civil War officers would link up with their new commander. His light battery consisted of some of the army's best weaponry: two smoothbore brass M1841 6-pounder cannons—maximum range 1,532 yards (just under a mile)—and two M1841 12-pounder howitzers. They were the finest cannons in the service and the most technologically advanced.

Bragg excelled as a drillmaster and teacher. As Taylor and his staff went about readying the army to march and fight while the troops mustered at Corpus Christi, Bragg drilled his battery. No matter the weather, without any breaks, he made certain his men were able to execute all of the French and British tactical maneuvers that had been codified by Americans Samuel Ringgold and Robert Anderson as the science of artillery after the Napoleonic Wars.[13] This new "flying artillery" contained the potential to finally convince U.S. military leaders that cannons and cannoneers could have as much value as marching infantrymen or dashing cavalrymen. The new artillery science emphasized speed and rapid movement, incorporating the use of horses to move weapons and their operators. Smaller "flying" units proved their worth in the war with Mexico, as they were able to respond to acute crises on the battlefield in quick time. The new science required new training, and Bragg embraced the challenge of instruction. And his men, one observer wrote, "seemed to understand their business perfectly." After watching the captain train his cannoneers on the plains of Mexico, Luther Giddings was convinced that artillery would prove "the most formidable auxiliaries science has ever given to war."[14]

When he took command of Confederate troops at Pensacola, Florida, in 1861, Bragg maintained his commitment to rigorous preparation. One soldier who served under the general there and throughout the Civil War believed that he created a "solid army" despite the "arduous and ungrateful returns incident to the organization and disciplining [of] an army."[15] The troops Bragg trained on Florida's Gulf coast were considered some of the best in the Confederacy at a time when officers North and South were struggling to teach thousands of inexperienced men to wheel right, march on the double quick, and quickly reload their muskets while remaining in formation. Biographer Earl J. Hess has written that Bragg "excelled at the tedious process of turning raw troops into effective soldiers."[16]

Such exacting standards may have produced good soldiers, but they did not necessarily endear the commander to his troops. By the time of the Civil War, as Bragg proved unwilling to temper his high expectations, what had once been seen as one of his more admirable military qualities became a point of frequent criticism by soldiers and civilians alike. One Yankee soldier who opposed Bragg's small force at Pensacola in 1861 described the Confederate leader as having a "martinet soul."[17] Later historians echoed such descriptions; Bruce Catton has described Bragg as a "dour martinet."[18] Like many of his contemporaries, Bragg suffered from being a professional soldier tasked with training volunteers who chafed under the rigorous and constraining frameworks of army authority and military discipline. He faced a difficult challenge since "the American volunteer," as historian Peter S. Carmichael explains, "was not so easy to subdue."[19] Bragg occupied an unenviable position: He could enforce rigid discipline and produce troops who fought and marched as well as professional soldiers, but he would never therefore experience the adoration of the men he commanded.

During the war with Mexico, contemporaries exalted the results produced by Bragg's well-trained artillerists. His men were often noted for their refusal to retreat and their willingness to face down their opponents without breaking ranks, even when such actions came at a high personal cost. After the fighting at Monterrey in September 1846, journalists praised the artillerymen for their "coolness" while "frequently exposed to the enemy's fire."[20] During the Civil War, similar training methods did not yield similarly positive praise. Without battlefield successes to justify the hours of drilling and hardships imposed by Bragg, soldiers and civilians alike censured the Confederate commander. "If Gen. Bragg ever did anything right," one Texan proclaimed, "I never heard of it."[21] Though Bragg was committed to military rigor, his Mexican War experience did not repeat itself between 1861 and 1865.

The most lasting and influential element of Bragg's Mexican War service did not teach him any personal lesson so much as it influenced the course of American military science. His artillery service in Mexico helped elevate a previously underappreciated branch of the U.S. Army from occasionally supporting battlefield operations to being an integral component of most Civil War engagements. Bragg's skill in commanding his battery throughout the war also helped lend that arm credibility. Prior to the conflict in Mexico, many of the professional army's old guard looked askance at the notion of artillery as an essential fighting force. And one of the biggest old-army artillery skeptics was none other than Zachary Taylor. Taylor, historian Grady McWhiney writes, "had an infantryman's prejudice of artillery, which in his opinion had never done much in battle."[22]

The opening engagements of the war along the Rio Grande challenged both Taylor's opinion and army orthodoxy. In early May 1846 the general needed to move his army quickly to relieve an American force pinned down by a Mexican army at Fort Texas (present-day Brownsville). On May 8 and 9 his army's flying artillery proved its worth in battles at Palo Alto and Resaca de la Palma as Taylor fought his way to his beleaguered troops. But Bragg's men were minimally involved in these first few actions, their guns lacking the range to aid in the defense of the fort. Still, in a speech after the war, Bragg acknowledged the importance of the artillery in the earliest battles in Mexico, declaring that he "was indebted to the training of the lamented Ringgold and [Randolph] Ridgely, from whose hands he had received the corps in that full efficiency that enabled it to immortalize itself on the perilous and bloody field of Buena Vista."[23]

Indeed, it was at Buena Vista on February 23, 1847, that Bragg and his artillerymen would finally have their day. The intense two days of fighting south of present-day Saltillo, Mexico, featured Taylor's diminished army outnumbered more than three to one by Santa Anna's Mexican force. Aiming to push the invaders out of northern Mexico, Santa Anna's men trapped the Americans in a narrow valley near Hacienda San Juan de la Buena Vista in the twisting passages of the Sierra Madre. "The Buena Vista campaign represented Santa Anna's sole offensive of the whole war," K. Jack Bauer notes in his history of the conflict. The Mexican commander launched wave after wave of assaults on the American position over the course of the battle, hoping to find a weakness and exploit it.[24]

As Mexican soldiers charged his troopers, Taylor had no choice but to place his faith in his artillery, ordering Bragg to "double shot your guns and give 'em hell."[25] The gambit paid off, at least enough for the Americans to repel Santa Anna's final charges, forcing the Mexican army from the battlefield. Holding the field after two days, the Americans could claim a victory, even if only technically. But such technicalities were enough for many, prompting commentators across the United States to laud Taylor's small force. Most accounts not only celebrated Taylor's generalship but also praised Bragg and his cannoneers, claiming it was the American artillerists who had carried the day. "At the battle of Buena Vista," one North Carolina sheet exclaimed, "Bragg's 'grape,' like the incomparable charge of the iron-hearted Macdonald, at the bloody battle of Wagram, under Napoleon's eye, had crushed the enemy and won the day."[26]

The press made clear that battles such as Buena Vista had shown Americans what artillery could achieve when given the opportunity. From Charleston, South Carolina, one reporter proclaimed: "The fire of [Bragg's] artillery has written his name upon the walls of the temple of fame. . . . [T]he victory of Buena Vista is mainly attributed to him and the gallant few attached to his park of Flying Artillery."[27] One Maryland sheet said simply, "A 'little more grape' proved better than a thousand bayonets."[28] A newspaper from Bragg's home state of North Carolina positively linked the reputations of its native son and his chosen branch of service: "Buena Vista—perhaps altogether the greatest battle of America—was the scene of [Bragg's] most brilliant exploits. His battery . . . we have little doubt, was mainly instrumental in saving the day; and 'a little more grape Captain Bragg,' responded by Gen. Taylor . . . has become historical. It will yield an immortality ample enough for any man."[29]

Army leaders likewise recognized that Buena Vista represented a stellar example of artillery success. In his report of the battle, published by the *New York Herald*, Brigadier General John Wool singled out the artillery for praise. Wool noted that the country should consider itself "mainly indebted" to Bragg and the American artillerymen present at the battle, concluding, "without our artillery we should not have maintained our position a single hour."[30] An embedded reporter from Fayetteville, North Carolina, received similar testimony from prominent officers in Taylor's force. "Capt. Bragg is truly the hero of Buena Vista," the correspondent began. "I have conversed with Colonels [James L. D.] Morrison, [Humphrey] Marshall, and [Jefferson] Davis, who were in the arduous strife of blood for a whole day, and all of them concur in saying that Bragg was the ajax of that fight. Even the teamsters gathered around his big battery to witness its masterly management, and the deadly effect of his skill."[31]

After the war with Mexico proved their worth, American artillerists never again needed to worry about whether their branch would play a decisive role in the nation's military conflicts. Over the course of the Civil War, the U.S. government reported the following quantities of guns and ammunition supplied to its armies: 7,892 guns; 6,335,295 artillery projectiles; 2,862,177 rounds of fixed artillery ammunition; 45,258 tons of lead metal; and 13,320 tons of gunpowder.[32] Though he was not the only young artillery officer who achieved notoriety during the Mexican-American War, Bragg's success helped make certain that the Civil War would be as much an artillerist's war as it was one of an infantryman. Even if the guns were not always used to their fullest potential or usually decisive in the outcome of battles, very few engagements fought between 1861 and 1865 lacked the presence of artillery pieces.

In a stroke of irony, when it came to the Civil War, Bragg's supposedly superior understanding of artillery proved "to be his biggest weakness."[33] This was because Bragg had left the old army in 1856. In his own words he had grown tired of having to "chase Indians with six-pounders."[34] As Bragg turned his attention to the Louisiana sugar plantation he had purchased for his wife, Louisa, American artillery science left him behind. He never seemed to grasp that successful use of artillery in Tennessee or Kentucky would look vastly different than it had in Mexico. Because independently operating batteries had led to success in 1846, Bragg saw no need to mass his artillery strength in 1862, when a coordinated artillery bombardment might have helped his men claim a victory in Shiloh's Hornet's Nest. It was not until January 1863 that Bragg—under orders from Richmond—created a separate artillery arm in the Army of Tennessee.

The war with Mexico made Braxton Bragg's reputation as a capable young officer. Not even thirty years of age, he returned home from Mexico a hero whose name was associated with an essential victory for the American cause. His Mexican War reputation meant that by the time of the Civil War, Americans both North and South expected Bragg would play a critical role. And he did, though not in the way many expected. Bragg's spectacular failures as a Civil War commander are difficult to explain considering his earlier successes, and it is therefore a challenge to determine whether the Mexican-American War gave him any instruction for how to lead men and wage war when he found himself in command of the Army of Tennessee.

If anything, Bragg seems to have missed the most important lesson his service in Mexico offered: that flexibility was essential to battlefield success. The reason Zachary Taylor claimed victory at Monterrey and at Buena Vista was his willingness to move men during battle. He excelled at deploying (and redeploying) the light artillery of Bragg and his fellow cannoneers in response to the movements of his Mexican foe. Bragg's tenure as an army commander, by contrast, was defined by his rigidity. Once he drafted his battle plan, he seldom altered his course. At Chickamauga, for example, Bragg failed to adjust when one of his subordinates, the irascible Lieutenant General Leonidas Polk, opted to take time to eat a hearty breakfast before launching an attack that Bragg had ordered occur before dawn. Rather than move men to compensate for Polk's tardiness, he issued irate orders to hurry the fighting bishop along, though to no avail. The simple fact was that Bragg often failed to grasp the intricacies of military command. Fellow artillerist Edward Porter Alexander characterized him as "simply muddle headed." Bragg, Alexander explained, "never could understand a map, & that it was a spectacle to see him wrestle with one, with one finger painfully holding down his own position."[35]

Lack of coordination and the inability to adjust for the failures of his subordinates plagued Bragg throughout the Civil War. Though he was saddled with a veritable who's who of difficult personalities to work with, the general did little to mitigate the shortcomings of the men serving under him. Robert E. Lee faced a similar frustration at Gettysburg when Lieutenant General Richard S. Ewell interpreted an ambiguous order to attack Culp's Hill on July 1 as optional. As a result, the Confederates failed to reach the high ground that would soon anchor the Federal right flank. The lesson Lee derived from the failure was that he could not handle Ewell in the same way as he had his predecessor, Stonewall Jackson, who would likely have interpreted the order as a directive to attack and carry the position.[36] Lee adapted to Ewell after the latter's failure at Gettysburg, revising his expectations for what the corps commander might achieve in future engagements and issuing less ambiguous orders for him to execute. Such flexibility eluded Bragg in matters of both tactics and personnel.

Like his Civil War career, Bragg's tenure in Mexico is difficult to assess—especially without firsthand testimony from Bragg's own hand. It is fair to say that his contentious temperament was apparent even before that war and made him an object of Winfield Scott's disfavor, which limited his experiences during the conflict. In both wars Bragg demonstrated his commitment to preparation and improvement, a quality that even his biggest critics could admire. And while it did little to bolster his personal reputation, Bragg's service in Mexico had helped ensure that Americans took artillery seriously for the first time in the nation's military history.

NOTES

1. These "sententious expressions of Gen. Taylor," one periodical explained, "operated like magic." *Spirit of the Times: A Chronicle of the Turf, Agriculture, Field Sports, Literature, and the Stage,* May 22, 1847.

2. See William J. Lemon, *"A Little More Grape Captain Bragg": A National Song* (Philadelphia: Lee and Walker, 1847), accessed via Notated Music, Library of Congress, https://www.loc.gov/item/sm1847.430520/.

3. Francis B. Heitman, *Historical Register and Dictionary of the United States Army: From Its Organization, September 29, 1789, to March 2, 1903*, 2 vols. (Washington, DC: Government Printing Office, 1903), 1:142.

4. See, for example, the most famous memoir written by a common soldier in the western Confederates armies. Bragg, Sam Watkins wrote, "was the great autocrat. In the mind of the soldier, his word was law. He loved to crush the spirit of his men. The more of a hangdog look they had about them the better was General Bragg pleased. Not a single soldier in the whole army ever loved or respected him." Watkins, *Co. Aytch, Maury Grays, First Tennessee Regiment Subtitle; or, A Side Show of the Big Show* (Chattanooga, TN: Chattanooga Times, 1900), 39.

5. Kearny, a capable officer, had a Mexican War career that was less notable than his contributions to advancing the cavalry arm of the U.S. Army—shifting the institution away from dragoons (mounted soldiers who dismounted to fight) to fully mounted cavalrymen who fought on horseback. His reforms were so successful that most Civil War cavalry combat occurred between two mounted forces, though notable exceptions include the cavalry fight on July 3, 1863, during the Battle of Gettysburg.

6. Both Union general Ulysses S. Grant and Confederate general Edward Porter Alexander told a version of this story—thus, it appeared in two of the best and most widely read memoirs of the war. Alexander claimed the story originated with Richard Taylor, the son of Bragg's Mexican War commander, Zachary Taylor. See Edward Porter Alexander, *Fighting for the Confederacy: The Personal Recollections of General Edward Porter Alexander*, ed. Gary W. Gallagher (Chapel Hill: University of North Carolina Press, 1989), 307; and Ulysses S. Grant, *The Personal Memoirs of Ulysses S. Grant: The Complete Annotated Edition*, ed. John F. Marszalek, David F. Nolen, and Louie P. Gallo (Cambridge, MA: Harvard University Press, 2017), 450.

7. At least one historian has speculated that because the commanding general of the army, Winfield Scott, was among those who Bragg had irked during the first half of the 1840s, Scott assigned him to Taylor's command and chose not to utilize the artilleryman in his own army during the overland march from Vera Cruz to Mexico City. Grady McWhiney, *Braxton Bragg and Confederate Defeat*, vol. 1 (New York: Columbia University Press, 1969), 51.

8. Bragg to Jones, Dec. 12, 1840, Jan. 1, 1841, Letters Received, 1805–1889, Adjutant General's Office, Record Group 94, Records of the Adjutant General's Office, 1762–1984, National Archives and Records Administration, Washington, DC.

9. Scott quoted in K. Jack Bauer, *The Mexican War, 1846–1848* (New York: Macmillan, 1974), 74.

10. See Michael F. Holt, *The Rise and Fall of the American Whig Party: Jacksonian Politics and the Onset of the Civil War* (New York: Oxford University Press, 1999), 248–49.

11. Scott's choice is not surprising, especially in the context of his War of 1812 service. Volunteer militia in that earlier conflict had demonstrated that, especially when compared

to professional troops, they were untrustworthy, inefficient, and expensive while rarely helping achieve battlefield victories.

12. A total of 523 West Point graduates served in the Mexican War. John Crane and
James F. Kieley, *West Point* (New York: McGraw-Hill, 1947), 227.

13. In 1838 Secretary of War Joel Poinsett ordered Capt. Samuel Ringgold to mount
and equip one battery of light artillery to demonstrate the potential of the units to the army.
Along with Maj. Robert Anderson (the future defender of Fort Sumter), Ringgold prepared
flying artillery units for service. The battle in which he would lose his life, Palo Alto, demonstrated the effectiveness of artillery on the battlefields of Mexico. After that fight General
Taylor recorded that it was to the performance of Ringgold's artillerymen that "our success
is chiefly due." Boyd L. Dastrup, *King of Battle: A Branch History of the U.S. Army's Field
Artillery* (Fort Monroe, VA: Office of the Command Historian, 1992), 74.

14. Luther Giddings, *Sketches of The Campaign in Northern Mexico: In Eighteen Hundred Forty-Six and Seven* (New York: George P. Putnam, 1853), 76.

15. Maj. E. T. Sykes, "A Cursory Sketch of General Bragg's Campaigns," *Southern Historical Society Papers* 11 (1883): 305.

16. Earl J. Hess, *Braxton Bragg: Most Hated Man of the Confederacy* (Chapel Hill:
University of North Carolina Press, 2016), 21.

17. Gouverneur Morris, *The History of a Volunteer Regiment* (New York: Veteran Volunteer Publishing, 1891), 46.

18. Bruce Catton, *The Coming Fury* (New York: Doubleday, 1961), 275.

19. Peter S. Carmichael, *The War for the Common Soldier: How Men Thought, Fought,
and Survived in Civil War Armies* (Chapel Hill: University of North Carolina Press, 2018), 25.

20. *Richmond Enquirer*, Oct. 30, 1846.

21. John Douglas Cater, *As It Was: Reminiscences of a Soldier of the Third Texas Cavalry
and the Nineteenth Louisiana Infantry* (College Station, TX: State House, 1990), 236.

22. McWhiney, *Braxton Bragg*, 54.

23. *Charlotte (NC) Journal*, Oct. 6, 1848.

24. Bauer, *Mexican War*, 217.

25. K. Jack Bauer, *Zachary Taylor: Soldier, Planter, Statesman of the Old Southwest*
(Baton Rouge: Louisiana State University Press, 1985), 204–5.

26. *Wilmington (NC) Journal*, June 4, 1847.

27. *Charleston (SC) Courier*, June 2, 1847.

28. *Port Tobacco (MD) Times and Charles County Advertiser*, Apr. 6, 1848.

29. *Wilmington (NC) Journal*, Aug. 11, 1848.

30. *New York Herald*, June 1, 1847.

31. *North Carolinian* (Fayetteville), June 26, 1847.

32. David J. Eicher, *The Longest Night: A Military History of the Civil War* (New York:
Simon and Schuster, 2002), 250.

33. Larry J. Daniel, *Cannoneers in Gray: The Field Artillery of the Army of Tennessee*
(Tuscaloosa: University of Alabama Press, 2005), 85.

34. William Tecumseh Sherman, *Memoirs of General W. T. Sherman*, 2 vols. (New York: D. Appleton, 1889), 1:163.

35. Alexander, *Fighting for the Confederacy*, 307.

36. Gary W. Gallagher, "Confederate Corps Leadership on the First Day at Gettysburg: A. P. Hill and Richard S. Ewell in a Difficult Debut," in *The First Day at Gettysburg: Essays on Confederate and Union Leadership*, ed. Gary W. Gallagher (Kent, OH: Kent State University Press, 1992), 56.

THE TRAINING OF LEE'S FUTURE LIEUTENANT

Thomas J. Jackson's Mexican War

CHRISTIAN B. KELLER

It was probably a balmy day with highs in the mid-seventies when Second Lieutenant Thomas J. Jackson reached the peak of the Continental Divide on the National Road, which led from Puebla to Mexico City. Mid-August at that geographic location was cooler than many of the soldiers in Major General Winfield Scott's American expeditionary army expected. Jackson, as a junior officer in Company I, 1st U.S. Artillery under the direct command of Captain John B. Magruder, had remarked as early as April 1847 about the variable nature of Mexican weather, with the northern part of the country much dryer and hotter than that of the central plateau, which he and his comrades were about to leave. Initially assigned to Major General Zachary Taylor's northern army, the personnel of the 1st Artillery had gotten an unsavory taste of the arid climate around Monterrey and Saltillo before their transfer in February to Scott's forces in the vicinity of Vera Cruz, on Mexico's Gulf coast. There, participating in the siege of the coastal citadel in March and the ensuing movement inland, they experienced yet another climactic zone, the subtropical, as well as their first real combat. Now, several months and numerous engagements later, Jackson and his fellow artillerists gazed down from the heights into the great Valley of Mexico, replete with its many lakes, green fields, gardens, small villages, and, of course, the capital city. "Recovering from the sublime trance" that the view inspired, the young lieutenant, his men, and all the soldiers of Major General Gideon J. Pillow's division (to which Company I was assigned) began their descent toward their final military objective.[1]

If Jackson's previous experiences since landing at Vera Cruz were any indication, Mexico City would not fall without a bitter fight. He had served the batteries of the 1st Artillery in the investment of the former city's defenses and cheated death from a cannonball that "came in about five steps" of him. Cited by his superiors for "gallant and meritorious conduct," the recent West Point graduate from its famous class of 1846 received a formal promotion from brevet to full second lieutenant on March 3, 1847. It would be neither his last official commendation nor his final promotion: by the time the young Jackson retuned to the United States over a year later, he would hold the rank of brevet major, his name appearing in the official battle reports of all his commanders, including those of General Scott himself. One of the most rapidly promoted junior officers in the conflict, the Mexican War brought fame and public recognition to the nephew of a hardscrabble farmer from western Virginia. More significantly, it solidified certain personal traits that defined him later in the Civil War and awakened professional virtues that, cultivated further from 1861 to 1863, ensconced him as one of the most important and successful Confederate military leaders. For Jackson, the war with Mexico became both a training ground and a place of immense individual growth.[2]

Like most of the hundreds of future general officers who fought in what became known as "Mr. Polk's War," Tom Jackson left behind only a limited number of writings and other primary sources with which we can reconstruct his Mexican War career. His earliest biographers—John Esten Cooke, Robert Lewis Dabney, and G. F. R. Henderson—examined very few of them during their research and were much more interested in chronicling his exploits in the Civil War. Later historians, such as Lenoir Chambers, Frank Vandiver, and A. Wilson Greene, benefited from the donation of scores of early letters to major repositories in the twentieth century, especially those given to the archives of the Virginia Military Institute (VMI), the school where Jackson served as a professor in the years before secession. The 1916 publication of Thomas J. Arnold's edited collection of his uncle's letters to his mother, Laura Arnold, also illuminated more of Jackson's nearly two-year stay in Mexico and helped these later scholars better understand what he did there. Most recently, James I. Robertson and S. C. Gwynne, in their masterful biographies of the general, utilized not only these sources but also a few new ones subsequently brought to light thanks to the wonders of the internet. Still, despite this relative abundance of primary and secondary sources—especially compared to those available for other officers—only the highlights of Jackson's sojourn south of the Rio Grande are readily known. Even more challenging to discern is how, exactly, what happened in Mexico specifically affected him later during the Civil War. Yet the clues are there, and most emanate from his own words.[3]

Although he served as a junior officer of artillery from 1846 to 1848 rather than as an independent army or corps commander as he did later in 1862–63, and despite the obvious differences of age, emotional and intellectual maturity, and command responsibility between his two military stints, the young Jackson of Mexico foreshadowed the Stonewall of the Valley and the Army of Northern Virginia in many important ways. First, both the young lieutenant and the middle-age general demonstrated an unusual interest in health, religion, and intellectual advancement, as well as exhibiting a penchant for simple living and professional humility. These personal characteristics helped define the man as an individual and influenced how he performed professionally. Second, the younger Jackson revealed, through his letters home and in deeds reported by others, nascent military skills that would become hallmarks of his mature leadership later during the Civil War: a strict obedience to duty, physical courage, and an inherent grasp of the nature of war, its purpose, and the prerequisites for victory. Strengths in these areas, first developed through the experience of leading men in combat and observing senior leaders in Mexico, remained with Jackson during the thirteen years between the two wars and assisted in his rapid rise to senior command after Virginia's secession.[4]

As W. F. Bynum and Drew Gilpin Faust have reminded us, death was an omnipresent companion for Americans in the mid-nineteenth century. Women died in childbirth at alarming rates, industrial accidents were routine, and simple malnutrition created a much shorter life expectancy. Diseases with quaint-sounding names like consumption, dropsy, and the bloody flux were commonplace in an era before vaccines and an understanding of germ theory, and thus people evinced what we today might term a preoccupation with their health and that of their loved ones. Military leaders in both the Mexican War and the Civil War reflected this interest in the general population and furthermore recognized the serious damage diseases, such as yellow fever, could do to an army. General Scott, for instance, predicated much of his strategy on taking Vera Cruz quickly and advancing inland from the coast before the various subtropical fevers set in and attrited his numbers, while his opponent, Santa Anna, pinned some of his hopes on stalling the Americans in the low country for that very reason. Jackson was therefore not wildly eccentric when he wrote frequently about his health and inquired often about his sister's. Before even reaching Mexico, he penned her, "I am enjoying comparatively good health at present and I do not believe that I have the liver complaint." A year and a half later, in April 1848, he reported about an off-duty sightseeing trip to a local volcanic mountain some of his comrades arranged. "I should probably have gone my self [*sic*]," he claimed, "but as the temperature is so extremely low, resulting from the crest being capped with snow, I feared that my health might suffer." About six months earlier, he wrote Laura, "I can hardly open my eyes after entering a hospital, the atmosphere of which is generally so vitiated as to make the healthy sick." And in February 1848, still in Mexico City and alarmed by his sister's recent illness, he advised her "not to be deterred by any cause by saying to me plainly, 'that I am sick,' or 'I am unwell.'" Throughout his entire stay in Mexico, Jackson commented on health issues.[5]

That Jackson was more interested in his health than most other Civil War generals is probably true, and enough corroboration exists to confirm some of the stories about the lengths to which he would go to maintain it. But like his religious preferences, similarly lampooned and exaggerated by generations of storytellers, his attention to physical well-being existed on a spectrum upon which all Americans in his lifetime fell: he occupied a position a bit more extreme than most but certainly not off the charts. Health was simply a subject people thought and wrote about proportionately more at that time than in subsequent periods. Jackson's unusually strong attention to it, explains Robertson, probably originated during his years at West Point, but it makes sense that his service in Mexico expanded and enriched it, so that by the time he marched away from VMI at the head of a column of volunteers in 1861, he was, as Dabney Maury believed, borderline "hypochondriacal."[6]

The evidence supporting Mexico's profound influence on Jackson's religious development is even more concrete. It is arguable, in fact, that the young lieutenant's explorations of his personal beliefs were awakened by the example of his first company commander, Captain Francis Taylor, an ardent Christian who encouraged his new subaltern to read the Bible and think about the role of faith in his life as a soldier. One of Jackson's friends later thought that Taylor's influence "finally convinced [him] that it was a reasonable thing for him to do; and he made up his mind to do it." Letters home to his sister and other relatives during his time in Mexico, compared to those written before he left the United States, confirm that a spiritual change was underway in the young officer. On May 25, 1847, he wrote from Jalapa, where he had "the mortification of being left to garrison the town" while the rest of the 1st Artillery advanced with Scott's main body, that his fate was now in the hands of God. This is one of the very first known examples of Jackson's Christian providentialism, and by all standards of the day, it indicated he was already well on the road to what later became a hallmark of his personality as a Civil War general. "I throw myself into the hands of an all wise God and hope that it may yet be for the better. It may have been one of [his] means of diminishing my excessive ambition and after having accomplished his purpose whatever it may be[,] he then in his infinite wisdom may gratify my desire." Nine months later, while on occupation duty in Mexico City, he responded to a dire missive from Laura, predicting her imminent death, with language mimicking the type that peppered his personal and professional correspondence in 1861–63:

> I hope that these words imply nothing beyond what they literally state. To God this is the earnest prayer of your brother. But if he in his great wisdom has afflicted you with disease incurable then may he in his infinite goodness receive you into his heavenly abode where[,] though I should be deprived of you here in this world of care[,] yet I should hope to meet with you in a land where care and sorrow are unknown there with a mother[,] a brother[,] a sister[,] yourself[,] and I hope a father to live in a state of felicity uncontaminated by mortality.[7]

Most of Jackson's recent biographers believe that the flowering of his Christian faith, while initiated under Captain Taylor, was reinforced by the experiences of combat and its horrors as well as through a concerted and genuine inquiry into the belief structure of Roman Catholicism. What inspired the lieutenant's many conversations with Juan Manuel Irisarri, the archbishop of Mexico, is unclear; it is possible Jackson was seriously considering marriage to a particular señorita he vaguely referenced in a couple letters to Laura, who in turn wrote back quite concerned about that possibility. It is more likely that, as part of his personal religious growth, he wished to know more about a branch of Christianity to which he had previously had little exposure. Several earnest conversations occurred between the prince of the Mexican Church and the junior American officer in occupied Mexico City, but in the end, as his future second wife, Mary Anna, later declared, "his preference for a simpler form of faith and worship led him to wait until he could have the opportunity of learning more of other churches." Jackson did not wait long: shortly after his return to the United States, he was baptized on April 29, 1849, at St. John's Episcopal Church, across the street from his post at Fort Hamilton, New York. Captain Taylor was his cosponsor at this seminal event.[8]

The role of Jackson's Christian faith in his Civil War generalship is indisputable and very well documented by scores of authors. From avoiding battle or posting a letter on Sunday, to ascribing all victories to God in official dispatches, to underpinning his professional and personal relationship with General Robert E. Lee (another fervent Christian), Stonewall, now a Presbyterian, did almost nothing without deep religious reflection. He was intensely interested in the eternal salvation of his troops, as evidenced by his enthusiastic support of a revival in the camps after Sharpsburg that continued even after his death and the introduction of a bona fide corps chaplain, the Reverend Beverly Tucker Lacy, in the winter of 1862–63. A high percentage of his personal staff were ordained ministers, and nearly all were devoted men of faith. Jackson even anticipated his own departure from this world with an affirmation that he always wished to die on a Sunday. His religious devotion, in turn, helped inspire the Confederate people in their struggle for independence, becoming a symbol of the "righteousness" of the Rebel cause. The devastation felt across the South when he died was as much about what that event spiritually portended for the fate of the Confederacy as it represented a recognition that a great captain had fallen.[9]

Harbingers of other personal traits that influenced Jackson's character during the Civil War appeared while he campaigned in Mexico. Humility, nearly absent in most of his compatriots and adversaries fifteen years later, seemed less practiced in the lieutenant of 1846–48 but was still present. "That portion of praise which may be due to me must of course go to those above me or be included in the praise given to the army," he wrote Laura after the fall of Vera Cruz. A little over a year later, he explained his ardent desire to subjugate personal ambition to God's divine will. That hope apparently became reality by the time he earned his Stonewall moniker on the plains of Manassas; one searches in vain throughout his personal letters and wartime dispatches for even an inkling of self-congratulatory or egotistical rhetoric. Not only were all his successes the result of the Lord's providence, but when faced with the prospect of a return to independent command in the Shenandoah, Jackson fervently declined. Broaching the topic with Lee over the winter of 1862–63 while encamped outside of Fredericksburg, "Old Jack" clarified: "I would rather remain in a subordinate position as long as the war lasts; provided that my command is kept near my Commanding General. This is my real feeling." Once joined with Lee, he was content to serve as a subordinate, a sentiment in stark contrast to those harbored by other notable Mexican War veterans turned Civil War generals, such as James Longstreet and George B. McClellan.[10]

The Valley general's well-known preferences for unpretentious lodging, food, and dress possibly emanated from his experiences growing up in western Virginia under his uncle's watchful eye and were reinforced at West Point. Evidence from the Mexican War reveals those predilections remained and may well have been buttressed by the exigencies of serving as a junior officer in an army of invasion. In the same letter to his sister in which he humbly explained his disinterest in praise, he described his personal accommodations in a factual, nonchalant manner. "Even now I am using a box for a chair and my camp bedstead as a writing desk," he claimed, "and think myself comfortably situated." When Laura later chided him for purchasing a new horse during his stay in occupied Mexico City, young Tom expounded at length on the good deal he had negotiated and defended his overall thriftiness:

> You speak of my fine horse as in your opinion being rather extravagant but if an officer wishes to appear best he should appear well in everything. I bought the horse having plenty of money and need of [one] and have since been offered three hundred and fifty dollars for him, that is a hundred and seventy more than I gave and can at any time get more than I gave. My pay whilst with Capt. Magruder was one hundred and four dollars per month and I expect it will soon be the same here[,] but at present it is only about ninety so that I have plenty of money and am in the long run economical[,] although it would not appear to you so as here everything is dear and with you cheap. I dress as a gentleman should who wishes to be received as such. I do not gamble nor spend my money as I think foolishly.[11]

Spend money he did, however, both in Mexico and during the postwar years. The Jackson of Mexico was necessarily frugal, as these words attest, but he was willing to buy things that he found useful and helpful, such as a horse. This personal trait extended through the Civil War, revealing a man who, despite the folklore surrounding his spartan habits, thought carefully about how he used his money. That he wore essentially the same, threadbare uniform from Kernstown to Fredericksburg, for instance, signifies more about what he believed was important as an investment rather than sheer ignorance of or disdain for fashion. While actively campaigning, dressy clothes were an extravagant hindrance for him, but books, tithes to his church, and donations to various Christian organizations were not. While stationed at Fort Hamilton after Mexico, Jackson frequently ventured into New York City, where he haunted the bookstores and spent as he deemed appropriate for a man of faith. "My life is not one of privation, as you sometimes see among Christians," he wrote Laura in 1850, "but I enjoy the pleasures of the world, but endeavor to restrict them to the limits which Nature's God had assigned to them." His was a simplicity and parsimony borne of common sense and guided by religious principles. It was not the result of backwardness, aloofness, or indifference, as his closest friends in the Confederate army understood. Major General Jeb Stuart bought Stonewall a brand-new uniform in October 1862, following the bloodletting at Sharpsburg, and Jackson so relished it that he stored it away in a trunk for safekeeping until the appropriate moment (the Battle of Fredericksburg), not because he felt uncomfortable wearing it.[12]

Common sense also initially guided Jackson's intellectual pursuits as a struggling cadet at the military academy, where he found it necessary to focus all his mental energies on simply passing the required courses. By the time he graduated in 1846, however, the future general had not only raised his academic rank to the top third of the class but also discovered he actually enjoyed learning. He carried this newfound passion into Mexico and nourished it generously, especially after the fall of Mexico City. In the spring of 1848, while barracked at the sumptuous National Palace, he embarked on a crash course in Spanish, ethics, social etiquette, religion, literature, and history, with some books proverbially killing two birds with one stone, such as a Spanish translation of Alexander von Humboldt's social-historical treatise on Mexico. During this extraordinary period of cognitive growth, Tom's letters to Laura were filled with references to the contents of various tomes and subjects he was studying, reflecting his heartfelt enthusiasm and personal interest. On March 23, 1848, he exclaimed, "the book which I am studying is Lord Chesterfield's letters to his son translated into Spanish so that whilst I am obtaining his thoughts I am also acquiring a knowledge of the Spanish tongue." But thoroughness would not be sacrificed on the altar of pragmatic efficiency. "I have also purchased the work in English," he continued, "and after having read it in Spanish I then purpose on reading it in English." If that was not challenging enough, Jackson added, "subsequent to this I shall study Shakespeare's works which I purchased a few days since." This feverish, intense period of self-education continued all the way to the lieutenant's departure from Mexico in early July, a span of almost five months, and then apparently recommenced after his posting at Fort Hamilton. The obsession with New York City bookstores during that tenure was doubtless fueled by the intellectual awakening Jackson experienced in the Mexican capital.[13]

Despite his popular image as a grim Calvinist automaton that arose after the Civil War, Stonewall continued his love of learning and self-education during his career as a Rebel commander. Certainly, he was severely limited in the time he could devote to books during these last two years of life, but the demands of leadership did not altogether obviate intellectual pursuits. In 1861 his personal library in Lexington counted 122 volumes covering subjects as diverse as the campaigns of Caesar, Washington, and Napoleon; *Plutarch's Lives* and other classical texts; science and mathematics; and novels such as John Bunyan's *Pilgrim's Progress*. How many of these and other books accompanied him in the field is unknown, but visitors from England sought him out on several occasions and left accounts of lively scholarly and philosophical discussions with the general, especially about British cathedrals, historical bishoprics, and military history. During both the pause in operations after Sharpsburg, when Jackson's Corps was encamped near Winchester, and later at Moss Neck Manor (south of Fredericksburg) during the winter of 1862–63, Stonewall entertained two particular parties of Englishmen, who remarked on his command of these subjects as well as his congeniality. One Colonel Leslie later claimed Jackson was the "best-informed military man he had met in America," and Colonel Garnet Wolseley, future field marshal and commander of the British Army, wrote: "he put you at ease at once, listening with marked courtesy and attention to whatever you might say. . . . [H]e was a most interesting companion." While at Moss Neck, Jackson also had the opportunity to take the occasional book in hand again, a luxury he relished. His headquarters was the plantation owner's office, a small frame structure that stood in front of the main house, and it contained a modest library. Chambers contends that the general perused the owner's books there with noticeable interest as well as those in the formal library inside the manor house itself. Writing Mary Anna during this period, Stonewall asserted that a copy of Henry Hunter's *Moses* he had purloined was especially edifying and that he felt "more improved in reading it" than any other recent religious text. By the time of his fateful ride in the dark woods west of Chancellorsville in May 1863, Jackson was a highly educated as well as celebrated Confederate general, one whose intellectual blossoming began in Mexico. How much his long-term self-education program enhanced his military decision making in the Civil War is impossible to tell, but Wolseley, in his introduction to Henderson's biography of the general, was convinced it made him a superior commander.[14]

The specific effects of Jackson's Mexican War battlefield experience on his future generalship are likewise difficult to pinpoint, but certain episodes during 1846–48, documented in his own letters to his sister as well as commentary by observers, provide some clues. To begin with, a keen sense of duty and obedience to higher ranks distinguished both his United States and Confederate service. His sister-in-law Margaret Junkin Preston remembered him explaining that "duty was the paramount feeling of his nature, and even at [the Mexican War] he would have died rather than violate it." Just outside Mexico City, in the bitter fighting surrounding the fall of the San Cosme Gate, the young artillery lieutenant was ordered to hold a vital causeway against a determined attack of the enemy. When Preston asked later if he had had any concerns that his cannons' rounds might enter the city and harm civilians, he quickly answered, "none whatever. . . . My duty was to obey orders." This reflexive adherence to superiors' commands was even more evident thirteen years later. His own reservations notwithstanding, at Harpers Ferry in 1861 and up to the advent of the Valley Campaign, he complied with difficult orders from Richmond and his theater commander, General Joseph E. Johnston, including one that demanded he evacuate the town. Countless examples also exist of his deference to General Lee after he brought his Valley Army east and blended it with the newly christened Army of Northern Virginia. Despite fervent pleas expressed through his personal emissary and staff officer Alexander Boteler—Jackson requested to be unleashed in mid-June 1862 to invade Maryland and Pennsylvania—when Lee declined in favor of defending the capital, Old Jack quickly and uncomplainingly prepared to head to the Peninsula. Similarly, when Lee sent a dispatch during the winter encampment near Fredericksburg asking Stonewall to join him for a conference, the corps commander immediately departed the warmth and comfort of his own headquarters and rode twelve miles in a heavy snowstorm to the commanding general's tent. Astonished, Lee asked why he had come in such bad weather. Jackson simply replied, "I received your note, General Lee."[15]

His fervent Christian faith fortified Stonewall's courage under fire during the Civil War, a fact well substantiated in the literature. From the earlier fights against Robert H. Milroy, Nathaniel Banks, and John C. Frémont in the Valley, to the episode at Cedar Mountain where he rallied fleeing troops by raising his rusted sword in its scabbard, to his many near-misses on the first day at Chancellorsville, Jackson displayed a remarkable coolness during battle that never failed to impress observers. Resigned to accept the Lord's providential will in all things, the general stared danger squarely in its face and never flinched when Federal shells exploded around him or minié balls whistled past his face. "In the commander of an army at the critical hour," he wrote Mary Anna, an abiding faith "calms his perplexities, moderates his anxieties, steadies the scales of judgment, and thus preserves him from exaggerated and rash conclusions." Never fearing death but embracing it as the path to enter heaven, the Presbyterian general threw caution to the winds one too many times on May 2, 1863, when he insisted on personally reconnoitering the Federal lines near Chancellorsville after his flank attack stalled in the darkness. At that point his fearlessness permanently deprived both his army and his country of his irreplaceable services.[16]

That remarkable bravery bordering on recklessness, however, was first tested in Mexico. Prior to the Siege of Vera Cruz, Jackson was extremely concerned about his emotional and physical ability to withstand the pressures of combat. "I really envy you men who have been in action," he told future brother-in-law Daniel Harvey Hill, a fellow artillerist. Worried he might not ever get the chance to prove his valor, he added, "I want to be in one battle." The lieutenant got a lot more than that. By the time he was comfortably ensconced in the National Palace in the capital, he had participated in nearly every one of Scott's major battles and more than distinguished himself as a junior officer willing to risk his life to achieve the mission. He was "as calm in the midst of a hurricane of bullets as though he was on Dress Parade at West Point," claimed an academy classmate who witnessed him in action at Vera Cruz. At Contreras, his first major pitched battle, Captain Magruder officially reported that his subordinate's performance was "conspicuous throughout the whole day. I cannot too highly commend him to the Major Genl's [Twiggs's] consideration." Jackson received both a regular and brevet promotion for his courage in this prelude to the assault on Mexico City, but it was in front of Chapultepec on September 14, 1847, that he earned the respect of nearly all in Scott's army. After his return to the United States, the young officer recalled: "I was ordered to advance with a section of my battery upon a road swept by the fire of six or eight pieces of Mexican artillery at very short range. It was ticklish work, but there was nothing to be done but to obey orders. So I went on. As soon as [we] debouched into the main road, the Mexicans opened fire, and at the first discharge, killed or disabled every one of the twelve horses of my two guns. We unlimbered, however, and returned their fire."[17] But within minutes, the enemy fire became so accurate and heavy that all his gunners fled the roadway and took cover in ditches or behind rocks and bushes. Jackson suddenly found himself standing alone next to one functional 6-pounder cannon. Pacing back and forth beside the piece, he shouted to his men: "There is no danger! See? I am not hit!" After a cannonball literally passed between his legs, to the incredulity of all who witnessed it, an inspired sergeant decided his section chief might be right and jumped up to help him. With Mexican bullets and shot flying all around them, the two men carefully sighted the lone gun and fired it. Another of his artillerists now joined them, and Jackson sent him running to the rear with a message that he needed reinforcements if he was to carry the enemy position. The messenger flew past Major General William J. Worth, who was watching the action closely through his glass, and, impressed with what he saw, had already decided to send a brigade to relieve the beleaguered artillery lieutenant and press the advantage his valor had earned. Before that happened, though, Magruder rode forward to assist his subaltern, and together the two junior officers rehabilitated the disabled gun and joined its fire to its twin. Worth sent an order for Jackson to retire, but he replied that it would be more dangerous to do that than to stay where he was. Only after Worth's infantry had pushed beyond their position and carried the enemy redoubt did Jackson and Magruder obey the general's order. Their rest was short lived; within minutes, Jackson was racing ahead of the main army toward the San Cosme Gate, where he again exemplified himself in a courageous stand against the odds.[18]

For his actions at Chapultepec and the San Cosme Gate, Jackson was breveted to major and received official commendations in the reports of Magruder, Worth, Pillow, and Scott. Perhaps the crowning moment of his experience in Mexico, and final confirmation of his professional bravery, came at an official reception Scott held directly after the fall of Mexico City. Waiting in line to be presented to his commanding general, the young artillerist was awash in anticipation. When his name was called and he finally stood in front of Scott, Jackson was initially confused by the general's pretended sternness. "I don't know that I shall shake hands with Mr. Jackson," he blurted for all to hear. "If you can forgive yourself for the way in which you slaughtered those poor Mexicans with your guns, I am not sure that I can." Scott's extended hand and friendly smile immediately after this pronouncement must have been at once relieving and highly gratifying. Henderson, who first related the incident from the letter of an eyewitness, writes that no higher honor could have been bestowed on the young lieutenant, even though "none of his West Point comrades made so great a stride in rank" during the war. For Jackson the junior officer, recognition of his behavior under fire was most important and had been most assuredly achieved.[19]

While the future Stonewall relished the fact he had stood the test of combat and publicly demonstrated his courage, in Mexico the young subaltern also wrote of his observations about the nature of war, its political purpose, and victorious generalship. These snippets, sometimes blown out of proportion from their original context by later chroniclers, nonetheless portray a junior officer stretching his cognitive muscles in a manner that foreshadowed his thinking as the Valley Army commander and Lee's right hand in the Army of Northern Virginia. They reveal a mind that, even at junior rank, ranged well beyond the tactical level of war into the strategic, a skill that was well honed by May 1863.

Regarding the capitulation of Vera Cruz in March 1847, Tom wrote Laura that "the stronghold of this republic" was now safely in American hands and ranked as a great victory, but he could not approve of "allowing the enemy to retire." Like the future victor of Front Royal, Winchester, Harpers Ferry, and Chancellorsville would ably demonstrate, Lieutenant Jackson believed in a vigorous pursuit of or complete entrapment of a defeated enemy. "We had them secure and could have taken them prisoners of war unconditionally," he exclaimed. Although one should not read too much into this oft-cited statement, it does indicate he was grappling with the Jominian precept of clinching decisive operational or even strategic victory through full exploitation of battlefield success. From 1861 onward, Stonewall repeatedly yearned to crown tactical triumph with something greater. After First Manassas he urged superiors to pursue the routed Unionists into Washington, DC, and capture the Federal capital. After Winchester and again after Cross Keys and Port Republic, he requested Richmond to reinforce him so he could build on his limited victories by invading the North. And after the frustration of the purely defensive win at Fredericksburg, he and Lee jointly planned to do just that, much as they had following Second Manassas.[20]

War was not just about destroying the enemy and capitalizing upon it militarily, however. For both the younger and older Jackson, it appears that a hint of the future thought of the British military theorist B. H. Liddell Hart was at play: the object of war was to obtain a better peace than that which existed before hostilities commenced. To Laura in February 1848, he expressed a hope that the Mexican War "may soon terminate" because "it may be better for the United States & it may give me an opportunity of again entering your hospitable house." A long, protracted war, he believed, would not be in America's best interests, and like soldiers of all times and places, he wished to come home. He lamented the reality that some in the Mexican legislature wanted to fight to the bitter end and that the peace treaty contained an "article in reference to the Texan lands [that] will not be admitted by the United States." By early April, however, he was more buoyant, writing "the treaty has arrived from Washington with its amendments. Many think that it will receive the ratification of this government. . . . For my part I hope it will." He continued by listing some specifics necessary for the Mexican government to ratify the document, evincing a strong awareness of the political situation and the civilian role in overseeing the policy of war- and peacemaking. These were not the words of a simpleminded tactician, but rather the first realizations of a military brain reckoning with the realities of modern war, diplomacy, and civil-military relations. The Jackson of the Civil War displayed this understanding frequently, from his suggestion to implement a national Confederate draft; to his fervent desire of invading the North and inaugurating a "hard war," thereby shortening the conflict; to his dutiful if reluctant acceptance of the supremacy of the Richmond government and its officials. To his staff one cold day in the early winter of 1863, Stonewall declared, "we must do more than defeat their armies; we must destroy them." But half a year earlier, he had confided in his brother-in-law: "I have myself cordially accepted the policy of our leaders. They are great and good men." The general realized his preferences in war had to be tempered, as Clausewitz famously asserted, by political realities.[21]

A letter Lieutenant Jackson wrote to Laura preserved in the Library of Congress also portrays a mind thinking at levels much higher than that which his rank indicated. It is significant both for its frank critiques of the two principal American commanders in Mexico and what it discloses about the kernels of strategic thinking that germinated in him there. Once again, a presage of the Rebel general emerges. Scott, in comparison to Zachary Taylor, "is by far the most talented and scientific," Jackson claimed, "and at the same time the most vain and conceited. His comprehensive mind embraces not only different objects and ends but their general and combined bearings with regard to the ultimate objects." These sentences clearly extolled Scott's virtues and vices, but they also paralleled modern strategic theory with its triad of ends, ways, and means. The young officer literally used the term "ends" in the current U.S. military connotation of the term and appeared to comprehend that ends, or "objects," at lower levels of war nest within greater, theater-strategic goals. Taylor, on the other hand, "wants comprehensive views of means to an end," although he "is brave as a lion, and I believe . . . by his own personal bravery saved the battle of Buena Vista." Yet in that battle "his army was again slaughtered and he [was] unable to follow up Santa Anna." Scott, in contrast, "took Vera Cruz, a place stronger than Monterey, with but a slight loss," and, he continued, defeated the enemy easily at Cerro Gordo with an outnumbered army. In sum, although Jackson seemed to personally like Taylor better, he much preferred the generalship of Scott: Taylor "can not look beyond the gaining of a battle," but "Old Fuss and Feathers" wisely concentrated on "following up retreat" to convert tactical victory into operational and strategic triumph. Taken together, these startling sentences analyzing American generalship in the first half of the Mexican War prefigured one of Stonewall's most famous and oft-cited quotes from the Civil War:

Always mystify, mislead, and surprise the enemy, if possible; and when you strike and overcome him, never let up in the pursuit so long as your men have strength to follow; for an army routed, if hotly pursued, becomes panic-stricken, and can then be destroyed by half their number. The other rule is, never fight against heavy odds, if by any possible maneuvering you can hurl your own force on only a part, and that the weakest part, of your enemy and crush it. Such tactics will win every time, and a small army may thus destroy a large one in detail, and repeated victory will make it invincible.[22]

The war with Mexico affected Thomas Jonathan Jackson in ways we will never be able to discern with complete assurance, but the influences on his character and acumen as revealed by his own words and those of close observers were undeniable. More specifically, the parallels between his thoughts and actions of 1847–48 and those of 1861–63 are more than coincidental and point strongly toward the earlier war as a training ground for the later one. Yet the young Jackson was not "trained" in Mexico in a literal sense; rather, he experienced growth, realization, and awakening of personal, intellectual, physical, and professional traits, preferences, and skills that matured before and during the Civil War. In this he resembled many of his future comrades and foes of the blue and gray, yet those experiences were uniquely his own and, in comparison to nearly all his peers, proved remarkable, even when lined up against the likes of Ulysses S. Grant, Robert E. Lee, and James Longstreet, all of whom also won fame and recognition. In the end, Jackson's Mexican War was, much like his Confederate service, a testimony to his precept that one may become whatever one resolves to be.

NOTES

1. Lenoir Chambers, *Stonewall Jackson*, 2 vols. (New York: William Morrow, 1959), 1:98–100; Jackson to Laura Arnold [sister], Apr. 22, 1847, in Thomas Jackson Arnold, *Early Life and Letters of General Thomas J. Jackson* (New York: Fleming H. Revell, 1916), 87–89; Winfield Scott, *Memoirs of Lieut.-General Winfield Scott, LL.D.*, 2 vols. (New York: Sheldon, 1864), 1:467.

2. Jackson to Laura Arnold, Mar. 30, 1847, Stonewall Jackson Papers, MS0102, Virginia Military Institute Archives, Lexington, VA (hereafter cited as VMI); Chambers, *Stonewall Jackson*, 1:90, 119; A. Wilson Greene, *Whatever You Resolve to Be: Essays on Stonewall Jackson* (Knoxville: University of Tennessee Press, 2005), 5.

3. John Esten Cooke, *Stonewall Jackson: A Military Biography* (1864; repr., New York: D. Appleton, 1866); Robert L. Dabney, *Life and Campaigns of Lieut.-Gen. Thomas J. Jackson* (New York: Blelock, 1866); G. F. R. Henderson, *Stonewall Jackson and the American Civil War* (1898; repr., New York: Grosset and Dunlap, 1936); Chambers, *Stonewall Jackson, vol. 1*; Frank E. Vandiver, *Mighty Stonewall* (New York: McGraw-Hill, 1957); Greene, *Whatever You Resolve to Be*; Arnold, *Early Life and Letters of . . . Jackson*; James I. Robertson, *Stonewall Jackson: The Man, the Soldier, the Legend* (New York: Macmillan, 1997); S. C. Gwynne, *Rebel Yell: The Violence, Passion, and Redemption of Stonewall Jackson* (New York: Simon and Schuster, 2014). Of all these authors, Chambers and Robertson offer the most in-depth analysis of Jackson's time in Mexico.

4. Kevin Dougherty, in *Civil War Leadership and Mexican War Experience* (Jackson: University Press of Mississippi, 2007), makes a brief and unconvincing case for Mexican War roots regarding Jackson's supposed reliance on artillery during the Civil War. He offers the example of the artillery barrage at White Oak Swamp on the Peninsula that, Stonewall hoped, would drive away Major General William B. Franklin's Union defenders. There may be a correlation between Lieutenant Jackson's experiences in Mexico and General Jackson's Civil War tactic at the swamp, but Dougherty offers no other examples in Jackson's famous Confederate career to support his argument. A close examination of the general's many battles indicates, if anything, Jackson's deeper reliance on rapid maneuver, infantry assaults, and good cavalry screening to achieve success. Thus, it seems a stretch to correlate a preferred branch in the Civil War to his Mexican War background.

5. W. F. Bynum, *Science and the Practice of Medicine in the Nineteenth Century* (New York: Cambridge University Press, 1994); Drew Gilpin Faust, *This Republic of Suffering: Death and the American Civil War* (New York: Vintage Books, 2008); K. Jack Bauer, *The Mexican War, 1846–1848* (New York: Macmillan, 1974), 107, 205, 246–47; Jackson to Laura Arnold, Sept. 26, 1846, cited in Robertson, *Stonewall Jackson*, 49; Jackson to Laura Arnold, Apr. 10, 1848, Jackson Papers, VMI; Jackson to Laura Arnold, Oct. 26, 1847, Feb. 28, 1848, in Arnold, *Early Life and Letters of General Thomas J. Jackson*, 129, 131.

6. Robertson and Gwynne both spill considerable ink on the truths and misconceptions surrounding the stories of Jackson's health-related quirks during the Civil War, such as holding one arm high above his head to increase blood flow and sucking on lemons. Earlier chroniclers found these stories entertaining and used them, among other characteristics, to build a mythology around the man. Wallace Hettle perceptively engages this mythology in *Inventing Stonewall Jackson: A Civil War Hero in History and Memory* (Baton Rouge: Louisiana State University Press, 2011). For the argument that Jackson's preoccupation with health emerged at West Point and Maury's observation, see Robertson, *Stonewall Jackson*, 43–44.

7. Henderson, *Stonewall Jackson*, 39–40; Robertson, *Stonewall Jackson*, 73–74; Greene, *Whatever You Resolve to Be*, 5–6; Margaret J. Preston, "Personal Reminiscences of Stonewall Jackson," *Century Magazine* 32 (1886): 930; Jackson to Laura Arnold, May 25, 1847, Feb. 28, 1848, Jackson Papers, VMI.

8. Chambers, *Stonewall Jackson*, 1:135–36; Robertson, *Stonewall Jackson*, 73–74; Mary Anna Jackson, *Life and Letters of General Thomas J. Jackson (Stonewall Jackson)* (New York: Harper and Brothers, 1892), 48–49; Vandiver, *Mighty Stonewall*, 51–52.

9. Henderson, *Stonewall Jackson*, viii; Dabney, *Life and Campaigns of Lieut.-Gen. Thomas J. Jackson*, 96–112; Christian B. Keller, *The Great Partnership: Robert E. Lee, Stonewall Jackson, and the Fate of the Confederacy* (New York: Pegasus Book, 2019), 110–18, 198–200.

10. Jackson to Laura Arnold, Mar. 30, May 25, 1847, Jackson Papers, VMI; Jackson to Alexander R. Boteler, Dec. 31, 1862, in *I Rode with Stonewall*, by Henry K. Douglas (1940; repr., St. Simons Island, GA: Mockingbird Books, 1983), 40–41. Evidence of Longstreet's and McClellan's personal ambition is copious in both the primary- and secondary-source literature and requires no further elaboration here.

11. Robertson, *Stonewall Jackson*, 28–31; Jackson to Laura Arnold, Mar. 30, 1847, Feb. 28, 1848, Jackson Papers, VMI.

12. Vandiver, *Mighty Stonewall*, 52–53; Jackson to Laura Arnold, Mar. 8, 1850, in Arnold, *Early Life and Letters of General Thomas J. Jackson*, 158–59; Dabney, *Life and Campaigns of Lieut.-Gen. Thomas J. Jackson*, 584–87, 589–90; Chambers, *Stonewall Jackson*, 2:243; Keller, *Great Partnership*, 283.

13. Chambers, *Stonewall Jackson*, 1:60–64, 69; Vandiver, *Mighty Stonewall*, 43; Jackson to Laura Arnold, Mar. 23, Apr. 10, 1848, Jackson Papers, VMI. Vandiver and Robertson both conjecture that romantic interest in one or more señoritas may have been another motivation for Jackson's study of the Spanish language and Mexican history and culture. The historical record is conspicuously silent in this regard, although Jackson made it clear that "the formation of my manners and the rules of society and a more thorough knowledge of human nature" were major reasons behind his studies. See Jackson to Arnold, Mar. 23, 1848.

14. Robertson, *Stonewall Jackson*, 190; Chambers, *Stonewall Jackson*, 1:245–46, 311, 337, 338 (including Wolseley citation); *London Times*, June 11, 1863; Mary Anna Jackson, *Life and Letters of General Thomas J. Jackson*, 415; Henderson, *Stonewall Jackson*, viii.

15. Preston, "Personal Reminiscences of Stonewall Jackson," 929; Henderson, *Stonewall Jackson*, 94–95; Jackson to Lee, June 13, 1862, and Lee to Jackson, June 16, 1862, in *The Wartime Papers of R. E. Lee*, ed. Clifford Dowdey and Louis H. Manarin (Boston: Little, Brown, 1961), 156–57; Christian B. Keller, "Robert E. Lee, Stonewall Jackson, and Strategic Contingencies in the 1862 Valley Campaign," in *Southern Strategies: Why the Confederacy Failed*, ed. Christian B. Keller (Lawrence: University Press of Kansas, 2021), 35; Rev. J. P. Smith, "Stonewall Jackson in Winter Quarters at Moss Neck," address delivered in Winchester, VA, Jan. 19, 1898, Fredericksburg-Spotsylvania National Military Park Archives, typescript, 5.

16. Keller, *Great Partnership*, 111–12; Jackson quoted in Mary Anna Jackson, *The Memoirs of Stonewall Jackson* (Louisville, KY: Prentice, 1895), 394.

17. Chambers, *Stonewall Jackson*, 1:113–14; Robertson, *Stonewall Jackson*, 52, 54, 64, 66 (including Jackson quotations).

18. Mary Anna Jackson, *Memoirs of Stonewall Jackson*, 42; Vandiver, *Mighty Stonewall*, 37–39; Arnold, *Early Life and Letters of General Thomas J. Jackson*, 118–19; Jackson to Laura Arnold, Oct. 26, 1847, Jackson Papers, VMI.

19. Arnold, *Early Life and Letters of General Thomas J. Jackson*, 119; Henderson, *Stonewall Jackson*, 35.

20. Jackson to Laura Arnold, Mar. 30, 1847, Jackson Papers, VMI; Baron Antoine-Henri de Jomini, *The Art of War* (Philadelphia: Lippincott, 1862), 231–45; Keller, *Great Partnership*, 11–14, 59–62, 118–21.

21. Basil H. Liddell Hart, "Fundamentals of Strategy and Grand Strategy," in *Strategy*, 2nd ed. (1954; repr. New York: Penguin, 1991), 357–58; Jackson to Laura Arnold, Feb. 28, 1848, Jackson Papers, VMI; Jackson to Laura Arnold, Mar. 21, Apr. 10, 1848, in Arnold, *Early Life and Letters of General Thomas J. Jackson*, 135–37; Jackson to William Porcher Miles, Dec. 28, 1861, Mar. 15, 1862, Folder 47, Box 4, William Porcher Miles Papers, Southern Historical Collection, Wilson Library, University of North Carolina, Chapel Hill; Douglas Southall Freeman, *Lee's Lieutenants: A Study in Command*, 3 vols. (New York: Charles Scribner's Sons, 1942), 2:519; Mary Anna Jackson, *Life and Letters of General Thomas J. Jackson*, 310–11; Carl von Clausewitz, *On War*, ed. and trans. Michael Howard and Peter Paret (Princeton, NJ: Princeton University Press, 1989), 87–89, 91, 607–8.

22. Jackson to Laura Arnold, May 1, 1847, Thomas J. Jackson Papers, Library of Congress, Washington, DC; U.S. Department of Defense, *Joint Doctrine Note 2-19: Strategy* (Washington, DC: Joint Staff, Dec. 10, 2019); John D. Imboden, "Stonewall Jackson in the Shenandoah," in *Battles and Leaders of the Civil War*, ed. Robert Underwood Johnson and Clarence Clough Buel, vol. 2 (New York: Century, 1887), 297. Historians have questioned the authenticity of the precise verbiage in the Jackson quote, but its intent and major points are generally accepted.

MY FAIR FAME AS A SOLDIER AND A MAN

Joseph E. Johnston in the Mexican-American War

CRAIG L. SYMONDS

Joseph Eggleston Johnston was—and remains—an enigma. His champions insist that the strategy he embraced during the Civil War was exactly what was necessary to achieve southern independence. They argue that his preference for the defensive—forcing the enemy to attack him and trading space for time if necessary—was a strategy designed to conserve Confederate manpower and to force the enemy to squander his resources while undermining northern public support for the war. His difficulty, these defenders assert, was that this commonsensical strategic blueprint ran counter to the belligerent culture of the South and led (disastrously, in their view) to his dismissal. Johnston's critics, who are far more numerous, insist that his tendency to give ground in front of Federal armies, both on the Virginia Peninsula in 1862 and in Georgia in 1864, demonstrated that he was unwilling to fight at all except under ideal circumstances, which, because of southern numerical inferiority, never existed. They note, too, that he was more confrontational in dealing with the Confederate government (and in particular with President Jefferson Davis) than he was with the enemy. Joe Johnston, then, was either the martyred proponent of a winning strategy or a timid and argumentative commander who should never have been entrusted with command in the first place.[1]

There is evidence for both of these views in Johnston's experience during the war with Mexico. The one jarring difference between the Joe Johnston of 1847 and the Joe Johnston of 1862–64 is that during the Mexican War, he was positively eager, even frantic, to come to grips with the enemy, to throw caution to the winds and take the lead in bold attacks against difficult obstacles and daunting odds. There is nothing of the timid commander in the Joe Johnston of 1847. There is, however, tantalizing evidence of a tendency to quarrel with authority, or at least with bureaucracy, especially over questions of rank and status, though that trait did not fully emerge until after the fighting in Mexico was over.

Graduating from West Point in 1829, Johnston ranked thirteenth in a class of forty-six. His friend and fellow Virginian Robert E. Lee graduated second in that class. Though Johnston joined the artillery branch upon graduation, he spent most of his early years in the army as a de facto infantryman engaged in small-scale Indian wars on the American frontier. The largest of these was the Seminole War of 1836–37, during which he served on the staff of the army commander, Winfield Scott, who would also command the American army in Mexico a decade later. Pleased as Johnston was to be at the center of things, his experience in that conflict was disappointing. After a frustrating campaign pursuing elusive hostiles in Florida's challenging terrain, in 1837 a disillusioned Lieutenant Johnston submitted his resignation from the army.

Johnston then took a job as a civilian surveyor on a navy expedition to map the Florida coast. Ironically, it was as a civilian that he fought his first battle. When the surveying party encountered a Seminole campsite on the Florida coast near Jupiter Inlet, the commander of the expedition, U.S. Navy lieutenant Levin Powell, decided to attack. As a civilian, Johnston was under no obligation to participate, but he did. When the Seminoles turned and counterattacked, many of the young recruits in the expedition fled; only a few dozen veterans remained to confront the Seminoles. It was Johnston who took charge of this group and organized a fighting retreat back to the boats, for five hours directing a staged withdrawal. Bullets flew all around him, and he later claimed to have found thirty bullet holes in his clothing, including two in his cap. This rear guard made it back to the landing site, with Johnston himself the last to embark in the boats. In his official report of the event, Powell credited him with saving the expedition, and Johnston was publicly lauded by name in the semiofficial *Army and Navy Journal.*[2]

Critics may see in this episode not a cool response to a difficult situation but early evidence that Johnston's particular skill was conducting a retreat. In any case, the experience convinced him that his proper place was in the army after all. So after only a single year as a civilian, he sought a commission in the brand new Corps of Topographical Engineers, created in July 1838 to survey, map, and design fortifications and other defensive works. Johnston's brief hiatus from the army, however, had cost him seniority among his peers. One officer in the "topogs" who had graduated with him (and Lee) in the class of 1829 made captain on the same day that Johnston became a first lieutenant. It would take Johnston another decade to catch up.[3]

Johnston's concern about his rank was not unusual in the nineteenth-century U.S. Army; virtually every young officer sought professional advancement. Yet he feared that he had already made two mistakes that were likely to hold him back. First, he had chosen the artillery upon graduation, a branch of service in which promotions came more slowly than in the infantry. When his nephew Preston Johnston graduated from West Point some years later, Joe Johnston advised him to choose the infantry. Second, being out of the army for a year had cost him nearly a decade of seniority. And when he rejoined the army in 1838, he found that promotion in the Topographical Corps was also slow. All this encouraged him to look for ways to catch up with his peers.[4]

In 1846, as President James K. Polk maneuvered the nation into war with Mexico, Johnston was in Washington working at a desk on the coastal survey. Now thirty-nine years old, he felt like he was falling further behind and that his opportunity for advancement was slipping away. What he wanted, what he longed for, was the chance to lead troops in battle; he wanted, he told his nephew Preston, "the chance of one hostile shot." Thus, when Congress declared war on Mexico in May 1846, Johnston saw it as his great opportunity.[5]

Initially, he feared that he might miss out again. That winter and spring, while he remained in Washington studying coastal charts, Brigadier General Zachary Taylor moved to and then crossed the Rio Grande, winning widely celebrated victories at Palo Alto, Resaca de la Palma, and Monterrey. None of those victories brought the Mexicans to the negotiating table, however, and Polk approved a proposal from Major General Scott to open a second front by landing an army at Vera Cruz on the Gulf coast and marching to Mexico City itself. The Democrat Polk was initially reluctant to name Scott to the command, for the general was a Whig and a potential political rival. In the end, however, the president appreciated that he had no realistic alternative, so Scott began preparing for the expedition. One of his first decisions was to choose a staff, and among those chosen were Johnston's West Point classmate Lee and, as his topographical engineer, Johnston himself.

Though it was not a combat position, Johnston hoped and expected that once the army arrived in Mexico, he would have a chance to lead troops in combat—which as it proved, he did.

For the trip to Mexico, Johnston and Lee shared a cabin on the army steamer *Massachusetts*. Johnston did not enjoy the trip, for he was prone to seasickness. The fact that Lee seemed impervious to *mal de mer* only made his own sufferings worse. After a short stop, during which Scott sought, unsuccessfully, to meet with Taylor, the *Massachusetts* and the rest of the command flotilla arrived off Vera Cruz on February 27, 1847.[6]

The anchorage off Vera Cruz was positively crowded with American shipping: navy warships, army transports, and even a few old ships of the line from the Age of Sail. It was, in fact, the largest overseas expedition of American arms in the nation's history. When Scott decided to survey the area from the small navy steamer *Petrita* accompanied by the navy commander, Commodore David Connor, both Johnston and Lee went with them. The *Petrita* reconnoitered the city and the citadel of San Juan de Ulúa, a massive sixteenth-century fortress built on an offshore shoal. Johnston thought it was irresponsible to steam so close to enemy batteries with both the army and navy commanders on board. The Mexicans sent a dozen cannon balls in their direction, though without effect. After that the *Petrita* headed south to investigate possible landing beaches for the army.[7]

On March 9, 1847, U.S. soldiers landed on the Mexican coast south of Vera Cruz. Johnston watched from the *Massachusetts* as the troops climbed down into whaleboats and were rowed shoreward by navy sailors. After splashing ashore, the soldiers ran up a slight rise and planted a U.S. flag on the dunes. There was no resistance. The next day Scott and his staff, including Johnston, joined them.

The troops were safely landed, but the walled city of Vera Cruz, three miles to the north, remained in Mexican hands, as did San Juan de Ulúa. Many of Scott's eager young staff members—very likely including Johnston—urged an immediate assault. The general opted instead for a siege. The army established siege lines around the city, and according to the etiquette of siege warfare, Scott offered the defenders an opportunity to capitulate before he began a bombardment. Of course, that same code obliged the Mexicans to refuse the demand, at least until some blood had been shed. In conformity with this ancient protocol, Scott penned a note to the city's governor, Juan Morales, expressing his hope that it would be possible "to spare the beautiful city of Vera Cruz" from a bombardment and destruction. To deliver it, he sent an officer under a white flag to the city gates. The officer he sent was Captain Johnston.[8]

At two o'clock in the afternoon on March 22, Johnston, bearing a white flag and accompanied only by a bugler, rode up to the Puerta de la Merced, the southern gate to Vera Cruz, and announced that he had a communication for the governor. The Mexicans greeted him courteously and asked him to wait while Morales composed a reply. With the politely worded rejection of Scott's entreaty in hand, the captain rode back to the American lines. Even though the entire pantomime was largely a charade, it appealed to Johnston's notion of chivalry.

Later that day the American batteries opened fire. Four days later, the obligation of making a defense now fulfilled, the city's defenders hung out a white flag. During the ensuing negotiations, the Mexicans agreed to surrender not only Vera Cruz but also San Juan de Ulúa. That last was critical, since logistical support for the subsequent inland campaign would have been difficult as long as the fortress remained in Mexican hands. In his official report on the capture of the city, Scott mentioned Johnston favorably along with many others. Such official notice was gratifying to Johnston, though so far he had not yet had an opportunity to engage in combat.[9]

Two weeks later the American army began its march inland toward Mexico City. As a member of Scott's staff, Johnston was in the vanguard, tasked with assessing the terrain and gathering information. Vera Cruz was connected to the capital city by what was called the National Road, so it was not necessary for Johnston to use his topographer's eye to assess the army's route. He did, however, use his halting Spanish to interview civilians he met along the way to gather information about enemy dispositions. From them he learned that the General Antonio López de Santa Anna had established a strong defensive position at Cerro Gordo, thirty-five miles inland and where the National Road passed through a narrow defile in the Sierra Madre.

After reporting the news to Scott, the commanding general ordered Johnston and another officer, Zealous Tower, to reconnoiter the position. Creeping up to the enemy lines on foot, they were spotted, and Mexican artillery opened fire with grapeshot. Johnston was severely wounded and had to be carried back to friendly lines.[10]

He spent the next two weeks in a makeshift hospital in Plan del Rio. During that time, his friend Lee found a path around the flank of the Mexican army that allowed the Americans to circumvent Santa Anna's defenses and win a decisive victory in the Battle of Cerro Gordo (April 18, 1847). Though Johnston had missed the battle, Scott nevertheless acknowledged his role in the campaign. Perhaps to compensate him for his wounds, the general breveted him to the rank of lieutenant colonel. It was, in effect, a double promotion, for Johnston was still a statutory captain; a brevet to lieutenant colonel thus passed over the rank of major altogether. That double promotion would provoke thorny problems after the war, but for the moment it was extremely gratifying.[11]

After victory at Cerro Gordo, the American army continued westward to Jalapa, higher up in the Sierra Madre. Johnston went as well, and the cooler air at the higher elevation speeded his recovery. There, too, reinforcements reached Scott from the States, enlarging his army to about 12,000 effectives leading him to reorganize his command. Most of the new arrivals were volunteers, not regulars, and Scott incorporated one group of them into a unit of "Voltigeurs"—a French term initially intended to describe infantry that could be quickly transported by cavalry but that, by 1847, had come to mean simply light infantry. He assigned Colonel Timothy P. Andrews, formerly the army's paymaster, to command the Voltigeurs and named Brevet Lieutenant Colonel Johnston, now fully recovered, as its second in command. Brigaded together with two infantry regiments under Brigadier General George Cadwalader, Johnston and the Voltigeurs marched westward from Jalapa toward the city of Puebla, arriving on August 8.[12]

There, Scott decided to abandon his long supply line to the coast and head for Mexico City without a logistical umbilical cord. In his subsequent report he declared rather colorfully that he threw away the scabbard and went forward with the naked blade.[13]

Mexico City was (and is) surrounded by rugged hills and large lakes, and those natural barriers funneled any approaching army into easily defensible positions. Mexican president Santa Anna, leading his army in person, took advantage of the geography by placing his army south of the city in a position that was well protected on both flanks. Lake Xochimilco guarded its left, while a vast dried lava bed called the Pedregal covered its right. Scott's only option seemed to be a frontal assault. Once again, however, Johnston's friend Lee found a way around, discovering a narrow but usable path through the Pedregal. This allowed several regiments under Brigadier General Persifor F. Smith to thread their way through the lava bed to outflank the Mexican defenses near the small village of Padierna, often misidentified as Contreras. The Voltigeurs were among the units to make that march.

The commander of the Mexican defenders at Padierna was General Gabriel Valencia, a former interim president of the Mexican Republic and a bitter rival of Santa Anna. He did not think it was possible for an enemy army to cross the Pedregal and therefore discredited reports of the threat to his flank. Santa Anna ordered him to withdraw from his position to cover the road north to San Angel, but Valencia liked his position at Padierna and declined to comply.[14]

The flank march by Smith's command, including the Voltigeurs, effectively isolated Valencia's troops from Santa Anna's main body, yet it also separated Smith's force from the main body of Scott's army. Valencia had good reason to like his defensive position, which was bolstered by twenty-two artillery pieces on high ground. Despite that, a confident Smith was determined to attack as soon as possible. After initiating an uneven artillery duel with Valencia's gunners, he sent the much-traveled Lee back to tell Scott of his plan and to ask him to cooperate.[15]

At dawn the next day, Johnston and the Voltigeurs began another march, this time around Valencia's left flank though the village of San Gerónimo to attack Valencia from the rear. Soon afterward, Scott attacked from the other direction. In what has been called the Battle of Contreras (August 20, 1847), the Mexicans held for only about a quarter of an hour before they broke. The Americans swarmed over their lines and captured all twenty-two of Valencia's cannon. As Johnston stood amid the captured enemy position, he was delighted to see Lee approaching from the other side. They met in the middle of the abandoned Mexican defenses and shook hands.

For a brief moment, it was the peak of Johnston's professional career. An assault that included troops under his command had routed the Mexican army. Yet as he shook hands with his friend, Johnston's expression quickly changed from exaltation to anguish when Lee told him that the night before, during the cannonade between the armies, Johnston's nephew Preston had been killed.

Preston had long been Johnston's particular favorite. When Preston had been orphaned at age twelve, the unmarried Joe Johnston had offered himself as a surrogate father. He told the boy to "regard me not as a formal old uncle, but as a brother." He had followed Preston's career closely and took great pride in his achievements. "Nothing in my own professional prospects even gave me such satisfaction," he wrote Preston, "as I derive from your position." And he told his brother Beverly that no one "has a nobler, purer heart" than young Preston. The news of his death turned the victory at Contreras into ashes, and that night he wrote Beverly, "I have never before known the full bitterness of grief."[16]

But Johnston had no time to indulge his grief. The American army, including the Voltigeurs, pursued the fleeing Mexicans northward. The principal obstacle to a further advance was the looming citadel of Chapultepec, home of the Mexican military academy. At its western end, and about 1,000 yards from the citadel itself, was a group of stone buildings called the Molino del Rey. Rumor had it that the Mexicans there were melting down the church bells to turn them into cannon, though that subsequently proved to be a myth. Nevertheless, Scott concluded that before Chapultepec itself could be assaulted, Molino del Rey had to be neutralized. Major General William Worth, whose troops would make the attack, disagreed. Scott overruled him.

The attack took place on September 8, 1847. Worth initially kept the Voltigeurs in reserve. As he had feared, the initial attack was repulsed with heavy casualties, and the Mexican cavalry counterattacked. To halt this onrushing threat, Worth committed the Voltigeurs. They successfully checked the Mexican horsemen, and afterward Worth sent them, plus the 11th Infantry Regiment, to assault the Molino itself. Johnston led his troops up to the walls, where they used a battering ram to break down the gate, then fought room to room to drive the Mexicans from the buildings. Though ultimately victorious, the battle was costly and yielded no particular advantage; nor was there any evidence of church bells being turned into cannon. Worth never forgave Scott for what he considered a blunder, and their feud would outlast the war. For Johnston and the Voltigeurs, however, it had been a bracing victory; they felt they had proved their mettle.[17]

Johnston had embarked on the campaign hoping for an opportunity to lead troops in combat, to behave well in front of the enemy, to earn recognition, and perhaps even to gain promotion. He had fulfilled all of those ambitions. He had been wounded, mentioned in dispatches, promoted—twice—and successfully led troops in fierce combat. His greatest moment in the war, however, was still in front of him: the assault on the Mexican citadel of Chapultepec.

Chapultepec was a daunting obstacle. Set on a high plateau 150–200 feet above the plain that surrounded it, its masonry walls rose another

15–20 feet above that. Around the base of the plateau, another 15-foot wall enclosed the grounds. There was only one entrance—a gate on the southern face. Among the several units assigned to the assault, Major General Gideon J. Pillow included the Voltigeurs, which he divided into two groups: one under Colonel Andrews, and four companies under Johnston. It was his first independent command.[18]

In preparation for the attack, Johnston put his four companies to work building scaling ladders. Once past the outer wall, they were to use them to assail the walls of the fortress itself. A preliminary bombardment would soften up the defenders, with a lull in the bombardment being the signal to attack.

In the predawn darkness of September 13, Johnston deployed his command outside the lower walls as American artillery pounded the target. At 7:30 a.m. the bombardment ceased, and Johnston led his battalion over an outlying redan, broke through the outer wall, and charged up the slope to the main defenses. There, his troops overwhelmed the guard at the gate and forced their way through. Linking up with Andrews's men and others, they took cover at the base of the plateau and began sniping away at the defenders above them and inside the citadel while waiting for the ladders to be brought forward. Unwilling to be left out of the action, another of Scott's staff officers, Captain Pierre G. T. Beauregard, had attached himself to Johnston's battalion for the assault. He recalled later that "the gallant Colonel Johnston" encouraged his men forward "against as terrible a fire as I had yet seen." Though the men were volunteers, Beauregard claimed they behaved like regulars.[19]

Steady they may have been, but they were also effectively pinned down. At least Mexican marksmanship was execrable; not wishing to expose themselves, the defenders simply held their muskets up over the wall and blindly pulled the triggers. Still, the volume of fire was daunting. To steady the troops, Beauregard and Johnston engaged in some lighthearted public banter. Beauregard called out to Johnston to suggest a wager. He was willing to bet that he could hit his man, and if he did, Johnston would have to buy drinks in Mexico City. Joining in the spirit of the challenge, Johnston called back his agreement, and Beauregard fired. Whatever the outcome of that shot, he claimed to have hit his mark, so Johnston would have to buy the drinks. Johnston replied that he would do so cheerfully.[20]

By then, the storming party with the ladders had arrived at the foot of the hill, and the Voltigeurs began to ascend. They climbed to the parapet and fought the defenders hand to hand. An officer in Johnston's battalion, Captain Moses Barnard, first surmounted the wall, and others quickly followed. Soon the blue flag of the Voltigeur Regiment, riddled with bullet holes, flew from the parapet. Johnston, too, clambered over the wall, from which he could see the whole Valley of Mexico laid out before him: the mountains in the distance, the glittering lakes, and less than two miles away, Mexico City itself. It was both literally and metaphorically the peak of his military career. He had led a charge of his own command in the decisive engagement of the war. In recognition of that, Scott subsequently rewarded him with another brevet promotion, from lieutenant colonel to full colonel.[21]

Or so Johnston thought.

Brevet promotions were not permanent. They were awarded in the field to recognize excellent service or to fill an immediate need. The officers who received them knew that with the coming of peace, they would revert to their statutory rank. This time, however, the American victories around Mexico City, followed by a swift and completely satisfactory end to the war, put Congress in an expansive mood, and it voted to make permanent all brevet promotions made during the war. This was tremendously good news for Johnston, who had entered the war as a captain and emerged from it barely a year later as a full colonel. Soon, however, that assumption morphed into a dispute that sowed seeds of resentment that would bear bitter fruit for decades.

The War Department acknowledged that Johnston had received two brevets during the war—one after his wounding at Cerro Gordo, and one following his success at Chapultepec. Given that he had begun the war as a captain, two brevets should have made him a lieutenant colonel, and that is how he was listed when the *Register of Officers* was published after the war. Johnston protested that this was a mistake. He insisted that the first of his two brevets had elevated him to lieutenant colonel, and it was in that capacity that he served as second in command of the Voltigeur Regiment at Molino del Rey and Chapultepec. The second brevet, therefore, made him a full colonel.

Secretary of War William L. Marcy denied his claim, and the U.S. Senate confirmed that decision. Johnston refused to accept it. This was partly a measure of his ambition, but it also revealed a tendency to querulousness. He was convinced that he was right—he may have been—but a more pragmatic officer would have accepted the department's ruling and moved on. Johnston could not do that. He nursed his indignation and bided his time in the hope that a different secretary of war might reverse the decision. Six years later, in the summer of 1855, he appealed his case to the new war secretary, Jefferson Davis. Davis was from the West Point class of 1828, one year ahead of himself and Lee, and Johnston may have hoped that the connection would make the Mississippian more sympathetic to his argument.[22]

It did not. Davis declined to reopen the case, arguing that it had been decided years before and that no additional evidence had emerged since to justify revisiting it. Davis should have left it at that, but like Johnston, he felt a compulsion to win the argument. He went on to assert that the first brevet after Cerro Gordo had made Johnston a major and that he had been a major during the battles for Molino del Rey and Chapultepec. It was a foolish argument to make since Johnston had not only held the rank of lieutenant colonel in both of those battles—all of the orders and even the *Official Register* listed him as a lieutenant colonel prior to Chapultepec— after which he had received another brevet. Johnston was angered as well as disappointed and chalked Davis's ruling up to personal animus. It was a view he never completely relinquished.[23]

Johnston did not give up. Even as he served as second in command of the 1st U.S. Cavalry in "Bleeding Kansas" during the 1850s, he continued to believe that he should rightfully be holding the next higher rank. He saw another opportunity when newly elected president James Buchanan named John B. Floyd as his secretary of war. Johnston had close ties to Floyd, who was the brother-in-law of John Warfield Johnston, Joe's oldest brother. Whether it was due to that connection or simply a new set of eyes on the documents, Floyd overturned the previous decisions by Marcy and Davis and ruled that Johnston had, in fact, been breveted to the rank of colonel back in 1847. The decisions by his predecessors, he ruled, had been "simply a mistake."[24]

Johnston believed that he had at last been vindicated. His victory, however, came at a high price. Much of the army saw his persistent pursuit of rank as unseemly and grasping. And the army's officer corps raised its collective eyebrow again only a few months later when Floyd named Johnston as the army's new quartermaster general, a job that came with an automatic promotion to brigadier general. At last Johnston had not only caught up with his peers, but he had surpassed them, becoming the first member of the class of 1829 to pin on a general's star. This time even Lee, who had stoutly defended Johnston against critics, concluded that his elevation to a general's rank was a product of favoritism. "I think it must be evident to him," Lee wrote his brother Custis, "that it never was the intention of Congress to advance him to the position assigned him by the Sec'y."[25]

Johnston's elevation to brigadier general was another brevet promotion since it was contingent on his holding that job. Still, it was significant because, only a few years later, it triggered another controversy.

Johnston's predilection to quarrel with authority, especially over issues of rank—or, indeed, any issue that he believed touched his personal honor—manifested itself again during the Civil War. Because he was a brevet brigadier general in the U.S. Army when that war began, he was the highest-ranking U.S. Army officer to resign his commission and go south. Soon afterward, the Confederate Congress passed a law stating that officers would hold the same relative rank in the new Confederate army that they had held in what was already being called the "old army." Johnston thus assumed, not unreasonably, that he would be the highest-ranking general in the Confederate army. When, soon afterward, President Davis announced the five men who would hold four-star rank in that army, Johnston was astonished to learn that instead of being ranked first, he was ranked fourth behind Samuel Cooper, Albert Sidney Johnston, and his own West Point classmate, Robert E. Lee.

As he had done in the 1850s, Johnston protested. And he did this through a self-indulgent and intemperate letter to the president, characterizing Davis's ranking of him as a direct assault on his character, including what he called his "fair fame as a soldier and a man." Davis was infuriated. The letter thus ignited a feud between the two men that was never resolved. It colored Davis's opinion of Johnston during the Vicksburg Campaign in 1863 when he decided that the general failed to do all he could to rescue the city; it affected Davis's decision to sack Johnston as commander of the Army of Tennessee in 1864 and replace him (disastrously, as it proved) with John Bell Hood; and it colored Davis's reluctance to return Johnston to command in the waning days of the war in 1865.[26]

Johnston's service in Mexico was a critical turning point in his career. His experience there established his personal bravery and his ability to in-

CRAIG L. SYMONDS

spire and lead troops. At the same time, however, it also exposed a querulous tendency to bicker over issues of rank and in particular a stubborn unwillingness to let go of an issue when he was convinced he was in the right. Those tendencies continued into the Civil War years and defined both his service as a Confederate general and his relationship with Jefferson Davis. Whatever Johnston's merits as a tactician or as a leader of men, his inability to swallow what he considered to be a personal slight—a tendency first revealed in the aftermath of the Mexican War—undermined his effectiveness in command and did much to destabilize the Confederate high command.

NOTES

1. For a full discussion of Johnston during the Civil War, see Craig L. Symonds, *Joseph E. Johnston: A Civil War Biography* (New York: W. W. Norton, 1992), from which much of this essay is drawn.

2. Powell's report, Jan. 17, 1838, *Army Navy Chronicle* (1838), 7:125.

3. Symonds, *Joseph E. Johnston*, 43.

4. Johnston to Preston Johnston, May 25, 1843, Folder 3, Box 1, Joseph E. Johnston Collection, Earl Greg Swem Library, William & Mary (hereafter cited as W&M).

5. Johnston to Preston Johnston Apr. 4, 1843, ibid.

6. Symonds, *Joseph E. Johnston*, 55–56.

7. Douglas Southall Freeman, *R. E. Lee: A Biography*, 4 vols. (New York: Charles Scribner's Sons, 1934–35), 1:221; William H. Parker, *Recollections of a Naval Officer* (New York: Charles Scribner's Sons, 1883), 92–93.

8. Alfred Hoyt Bill, *Rehearsal for Conflict: The War with Mexico, 1846–1848* (New York: Alfred A. Knopf, 1947), 13; Robert W. Johannsen, *To the Halls of the Montezumas: The Mexican War in the American Imagination* (New York: Oxford University Press, 1985), 101; Scott to Juan Morales, Mar. 22, 1847, and Scott to Marcy, Mar. 23, 1847, in *Mexican War Correspondence*, H. Exec. Doc. 1, 30th Cong., 1st sess., 115–16, 224.

9. General Orders No. 80, Mar. 30, 1847, in *Mexican War Correspondence*, 240.

10. Twiggs to Scott, Apr. 19, 1847, ibid., 277.

11. Symonds, *Joseph E. Johnston*, 61.

12. Ibid., 62–63.

13. Bill, *Rehearsal for Conflict*, 265.

14. E. Kirby Smith, *To Mexico with Scott: Letters of E. Kirby Smith to His Wife* (Cambridge, MA: Harvard University Press, 1917). 192.

15. P. G. T. Beauregard, *With Beauregard in Mexico: The Mexican War Reminiscences of P. G. T. Beauregard*, ed. T. Harry Williams (Baton Rouge: Louisiana State University Press, 1956), 52.

16. Johnston to Preston Johnston, Mar. 23, 1839, July 12, 1840; Johnston to Beverly Johnston, Mar. 11, 1840, Aug. 25, 1847; and Johnston to Eliza Johnston, Jan 12, 1848, Folders 2, 4, Box 1, Johnston Collection, W&M.

17. K. Jack Bauer, *The Mexican War, 1846–1848* (New York: Macmillan, 1974), 310–11.

18. Symonds, *Joseph E. Johnston*, 67–68.

19. Beauregard, *With Beauregard in Mexico*, 79–80.

20. Ibid., 81.

21. John R. Kenly, *Memoirs of a Maryland Volunteer* (Philadelphia: J. B. Lippincott, 1873), 458–59; Bauer, *Mexican War*, 316–19.

22. "Report on the Claim, April 15, 1858, Colonel Johnston, 1st Cavalry, to the rank of Brevet Colonel," Folder 3, Box 1, Johnston Collection, W&M.

23. Ibid.

24. Floyd to Adjutant General, Mar. 6, 1860, Folder 3, Box 1, Johnston Collection, W&M.

25. Lee to Custis Lee, Apr. 16, 1860, in Freeman, *R. E. Lee*, 1:411.

26. Johnston to Davis, Sept. 12, 1861, *The War of the Rebellion: A Compilation of the Official Records of the Union and Confederate Armies*, 70 vols. in 128 pts. (Washington, DC: Government Printing Office, 1894–1922), ser. 4, 1:605.

MAKING THE ASSAULT WITH THE DETERMINATION TO SUCCEED

James Longstreet's Attack on Fort Sanders

ALEXANDER MENDOZA

On the morning of November 29, 1863, Lieutenant General James Long-street, commander of the First Corps, Army of Northern Virginia, accompanied Major General Bushrod Johnson and his two brigades as they advanced toward the Union-held Fort Sanders (previously named Fort Loudon) in Knoxville, Tennessee. The morning was bitter cold. A freezing rain and snow flurries had made the night of the twenty-eighth a torturous one for the Rebel soldiers. Though the rain had stopped well before dawn, the plummeting temperatures merely led to frost and frozen patches of earth on the field of battle. Adding to the gloomy ambience was a heavy fog that rolled into the environs of the city. A bitter north wind cut through Long-street and his party as they made their way across the tracks of the East Tennessee and Georgia Railroad and toward the Federal lines. Longstreet never wrote what he thought about that morning as they waited for the first rays of dawn to mark the winter sky, but it is likely he tried to remain resolute in trying circumstances. Just two months earlier he had been proclaimed the "Bull of the Woods" after he and his men contributed to the Confederate victory at the Battle of Chickamauga. In the weeks since, however, he had quarreled with his commanding officer and lost a string of engagements leading up to the assault on Fort Sanders. Now, facing formidable odds, the general waited to see if his planned charge would succeed.[1]

Longstreet had arrived in East Tennessee via a circuitous path through the U.S. Military Academy at West Point, service in the war with Mexico, and by the fall of 1863, a prominent place in the Confederate high command as General Robert E. Lee's right hand. Born in the Edgefield District of South Carolina on January 8, 1821, to James and Mary Anne Longstreet, the couple's fifth child, young James spent only a few weeks in South Carolina before his family moved to Gainesville, Georgia. He spent his formative years in the heavily wooded frontier region of northwestern Georgia, being called "Peter" or "Pete" to distinguish him from his father. Though he only devoted a mere three pages in his memoirs to his childhood, Longstreet conceded that he preferred a military career as opposed to the life of a planter. To that end, the elder Longstreet recognized that he would likely be unable to finance his son's education with his livelihood. Thus, the pursuit of an appointment to the U.S. Military Academy became a focus for the family. "From my early boyhood he conceived that he would send me to West Point for army service," Longstreet later wrote about his father.[2] To ensure his son would meet the school's rigid entrance requirements, the elder Longstreet sent his son to live with his brother, Augustus Baldwin Longstreet, and attend the Richmond County Academy in Augusta, Georgia, at the age of nine. For the next seven years, young James met his school's tough curriculum and strict discipline requirements. Through his uncle's political connections, he received and accepted a commission to the U.S. Military Academy in March 1838, thus beginning his military career.[3]

Longstreet entered the academy as a plebe, one of eighty members of the class of 1842. In its fourth decade of existence, West Point served as the principle institution for the preparation of the nation's professional soldiers. Yet cadets had opportunities to pursue careers not only in the military but also in railroad engineering, fort construction, exploration, and academics. Longstreet, however, had no illusions of a career outside the army. In his later years he confessed that he had more interest in the "school of the soldier" than the academic courses at West Point. He clearly gravitated more toward the academy's rigorous physical demands, which included many hours of drilling and long marches. At the age of seventeen, Longstreet stood six feet two inches tall, with broad shoulders and a strong soldierly bearing. He acknowledged that he preferred the outdoors to schoolwork, which showed in his academic record, as he ranked near the bottom of each class during his four years at West Point. His lackluster classroom performance hurt his career upon graduation, for the sum of all academic scores determined a cadet's final class standing and earned the academic board's recommendations for a particular branch of service. In 1842, at age twenty-one, Longstreet graduated fifty-fourth out of fifty-six cadets and received a commission as a brevet second lieutenant in the U.S. Infantry.[4]

Soon after graduation, army officials assigned Longstreet to the 4th Infantry Regiment at Jefferson Barracks, Missouri, just outside of St. Louis. Under the command of Lieutenant Colonel John Garland, the garrison offered all the monotony of a peacetime army. As he did at West Point, Longstreet quickly adjusted to his new life and different routine. In May 1844 he received orders to report to Brigadier General Zachary Taylor's Army of Observation, assembling in Louisiana for the possibility of war with Mexico over the annexation of Texas. Tensions with Mexico escalated quickly, and by 1845, Longstreet received a promotion to second lieutenant and a transfer to the 8th Infantry Regiment, with orders to depart for Texas. By September, he reported to Taylor's camp near Corpus Christi. The young lieutenant and the other soldiers in Taylor's army had a short time to adjust before receiving orders to move south toward the Rio Grande. As 1845 ended, the American force camped on the northern bank of the Rio Grande, in sight of Mexican troops on the opposite side of the river. For the next several months, the two sides sparred in minor skirmishes until April 25, 1846, when a Mexican cavalry force attacked an American patrol. Taylor's report on the initial attack took two weeks to reach Washington. Meanwhile, on May 8 and 9, his forces engaged the Mexicans at the Battles of Palo Alto and Resaca de la Palma, a few miles northwest of their camp. On May 11 President James K. Polk addressed Congress and asked for a declaration of war against Mexico, which he received two days later.[5]

The American victories at Palo Alto and Resaca de la Palma marked Longstreet's first experience in combat. Unfortunately for the historian, Longstreet left no record of his observations in any surviving correspondence. Even his memoirs, written more than half a century after the war with Mexico, make no mention of his first impressions of battle. The two engagements near the Rio Grande did give him the opportunity to fight as the soldier he had long striven to become. Late in life Longstreet visited Mexico, planning to write a history of the Mexican-American War, which he never published. His second wife, Helen Dortch Longstreet, ultimately used his manuscript in her book to devote a chapter to Longstreet's exploits during the war with Mexican. Neither account examines how that conflict shaped Longstreet's views on strategy and tactics, however, nor do they discuss his impressions on witnessing the carnage of battle. Instead, Longstreet writes about the more memorable personal events dealing with his fellow soldiers. In fact, he devotes most of his writing about the war to his fallen comrades, even though he himself was wounded in combat. His analysis of Generals Taylor and Winfield Scott indicates a great admiration for the two leading figures of the war. His wife writes that Longstreet believed Taylor and Scott overcame great adversities in advancing against the Mexican army. She argues that Longstreet, despite his Lost Cause reputation for fighting on the defensive during the Civil War, admired the risks that both generals overcame to achieve victory on the battlefield.[6]

Soon after Congress declared war, Taylor's army prepared to advance to Monterrey, in northern Mexico. Officials assigned Longstreet to command Company A, 8th Infantry in the First Brigade of Brigadier General William Worth's Second Division. After a delay of several months to gather volunteers and supplies, the American troops, 6,000 strong, reached the outskirts of the city on September 17. Taylor's army faced General Pedro de Ampudia's 7,000 Mexican soldiers situated in a formidable defense system of barricaded streets and defended with artillery pieces strategically placed throughout the city. Taylor divided his outnumbered army, a risky move, and sent the 8th Infantry to attack the city's western defenses while other units advanced against the northern and eastern sides of Monterrey. On September 22 Longstreet led the approach of Worth's division toward the Saltillo Road, which entered the city from the west and isolated the rest of the Mexicans defenders from their supplies and line of communications. The army's two wings then closed in on the remaining Mexican positions within the city; General Ampudia surrendered on September 24. Taylor held Longstreet's regiment in reserve, but the young lieutenant led his company in the house-to-house fighting that finally secured Monterrey. For his actions, Longstreet earned a promotion to first lieutenant and adjutant of his regiment. In this new assignment he assumed responsibility for the unit's routine orders, daily returns, and all noncombat correspondence.[7]

After several weeks in Monterrey, Taylor's army ultimately advanced to Saltillo, sixty-eight miles southwest, where it remained until the end of the year, establishing a strong defensive line. Thereafter, General in Chief Winfield Scott ordered Taylor to evacuate Saltillo, establish a defensive perimeter at Monterrey, and secure northeastern Mexico. The authorities in Washington had decided to relieve Taylor of troops to reinforce Scott's invasion of the Mexican heartland via the Gulf coast city of Vera Cruz. On January 10, 1847, officials ordered the 8th Infantry to Brazos Santiago, on the Mexican coast, to join Scott's newly formed Army of Invasion. Longstreet, detained by a previous assignment, did not reach his regiment until February 5. He landed at Vera Cruz on March 9 along with Scott's 9,000 men. By April, the army advanced inland. After defeating the Mexicans at the Battle of Cerro Gordo and securing control of the city of Jalapa, approximately fifty-five miles from Vera Cruz, General Scott ordered his troops toward Mexico City.[8]

Abandoning his line of communications at Puebla in a risky venture designed to force the Mexicans to sue for peace, Scott's army marched inland toward the enemy capital. The Americans reached the southern edges of the Pedregal, a large dried-lava field south of Mexico City, on August 17. The next day Scott sent Worth's division around the eastern edge of the Pedregal on a direct path toward the capital while an additional force advanced across the southern edge of the lava field, seeking a viable route toward the western side. On the nineteenth the Americans successfully pushed Mexican forces back, then defeated them in the Battle of Contreras on August 20. This quick victory allowed Scott's army to advance on both sides of the Pedregal, thus overwhelming the Mexican defenders and causing them to hastily retreat to the town of Churubusco, near the Rio Churubusco. The fighting would continue as the Mexican army also retreated from Contreras.

On the southern side of the Churubusco, the Mexicans constructed a *tête de pont*, a semirectangular earthwork protected by a water-filled ditch and defended by more than 7,000 soldiers. Additional troops defended the San Mateo Convent about 500 yards away. The two strongholds stood as the main defensive points to the bridge at Churubusco. Scott ordered an immediate attack on the two bastions.[9] As the Americans advanced toward Churubusco, enemy gunfire decimated Worth's men as they struggled in the surrounding irrigation ditches during their assault. The general sent the 5th and 8th Infantry to attack the *tête de pont*'s eastern flank, while the 6th Infantry attacked it head on. The 8th Infantry, the only force to reach the earthworks, stalled in the bastion's surrounding moat. Carrying the regimental flag, Longstreet led his comrades as they came under heavy fire from the Mexicans. They then jumped into the ditch, where they received heavy musketry from the enemy troops within the enclosure. The Americans struggled to scale the fort's slippery walls with their bare hands until they cooperated by standing on each other's shoulders. Once on top of the wall, they engaged the Mexicans in fierce hand-to-hand fighting. Scott's army won the day, however, and the Mexicans, recognizing that the enemy had pierced their defenses, retreated toward Mexico City's defenses three miles north. The Americans, having suffered approximately 1,000 casualties, could not immediately pursue the disheartened enemy.[10]

Longstreet received a promotion to brevet captain for his actions at the Battle of Churubusco, in which his superiors described him as displaying "gallant and meritorious conduct" on the field of battle. The accomplishments of the 8th Infantry against such formidable odds also left General Worth "filled with wonder." On September 8, after a two-week truce, the Americans advanced on the defenses of Mexico City. Three main fortifications—Chapultepec, Molino del Rey, and Casa Mata—protected the city's southern entrance. Two days later, after scouting the enemy's positions, Scott ordered Longstreet's regiment to create a diversionary attack on Casa Mata, the westernmost of the three strongholds, while the main force assaulted Molino del Rey, the central bastion of the Mexican forces. In a tough battle the defenders inflicted heavy casualties on the American troops, including the 8th Infantry, which lost 27 killed and 132 wounded in the diversionary attack. Longstreet had fought admirably and received General Worth's commendation and a further promotion to brevet major for his actions. After the Americans took Molino del Rey, the Mexicans at Casa Mata retreated to Chapultepec, the country's military academy and the key to the capital. Scott's army attacked the hillside fortress on September 13. Longstreet, once again carrying the regimental flag and leading the 8th Infantry's assault, received a bullet wound to his right thigh during the charge. He entrusted the regimental flag to Lieutenant George E. Pickett, who then led the 8th Infantry in its final charge. Despite tough resistance, the Americans overran the Chapultepec stronghold and subsequently entered Mexico City.[11]

Longstreet recovered from his wound in an army field hospital and, later, at the home of a Mexican family, the Escandóns, who cared for wounded American soldiers. Longstreet remained with the family until December 1847 due to his slow-healing wound. In the interim he probably reflected on his experiences in Mexico. Although he left no written record of his reflections during this time, it is likely that the young officer ruminated on what he had witnessed. Certainly, he observed how Scott repeatedly utilized flanking movements against the Mexican forces and learned to appreciate the value of a maneuver in lieu of a frontal assault. Significantly, too, he had witnessed the success of the strategic offensive, as Taylor and Scott defied logic and pursued numerically stronger foes into the country's interior while foraging for the army's food and supplies from the Mexican countryside. Longstreet had been an active participant in a spirited charge against a formidably defended bastion at Chapultepec and observed how troops, if properly motivated, could also overcome great odds and overtake a strongly fortified position. Considering Longstreet's lackluster performance at West Point, his experiences in Mexico rather than the lessons in the classroom influenced his thinking. This was not a unique phenomenon, for the war with Mexico served as a training ground for scores of officers who commanded on both sides in the American Civil War.[12]

After his service in Mexico, Longstreet resumed his duties with the 8th Infantry, now stationed in Texas. He remained in active field duty on the frontier for the next ten years until transferred to New Mexico in 1859. It was there that he witnessed the sectional tensions wrought by the election of Republican Abraham Lincoln to the presidency. As the nation moved toward secession and war, Longstreet supported the South. In December 1860 he wrote to Alabama officials to offer his services if the state seceded, then on May 9, 1861, resigned from the U.S. Army and left Albuquerque bound for the Confederate capital. A month later Longstreet accepted a brigadier-general rank in the Confederate army. From that point, he rose quickly through the Confederate command ranks, serving in the key battles of the Rebel army in northern Virginia. Accordingly, he received promotions to major general and lieutenant general in October 1861 and October 1862 respectively. By the spring of 1863, Longstreet remained one of General Robert E. Lee's most trusted generals, along with Lieutenant General Thomas J. "Stonewall" Jackson, leading the First Corps in the Army of Northern Virginia.

Longstreet and his supporters used their influence to obtain a transfer of the First Corps to the West and the Army of Tennessee, commanded by General Braxton Bragg, in the autumn of 1863 in the hopes of stopping the northern advance into the Confederate heartland. Integral to the Tennessee army's victory that September in the Battle of Chickamauga, Longstreet later became part of a cabal who criticized Bragg and urged Richmond authorities to remove him from command in October. Bragg survived the generals' attempt to oust him, but it created an untenable situation with Longstreet as the Confederates besieged the U.S. Army of the Cumberland in Chattanooga. After continued tensions and a failed assignment to protect the Rebel left flank on the siege line, culminating with a loss at the Battle of Wauhatchie on October 28–29, Longstreet's reputation was on the wane. President Jefferson Davis suggested to Bragg that he transfer Longstreet and his corps to East Tennessee, and the Army of Tennessee commander readily jumped at the chance to rid his army of one of its leading malcontents.[13] By early November, Longstreet received orders to advance to Knoxville, about 110 miles to the northeast, to clear out the Federal presence in the region, then return to Bragg's army to operate against the enemy at Chattanooga by maneuvering toward the enemy's left or rear.[14]

Bragg's decision to detach Longstreet's corps in the face of a numerically superior enemy in Chattanooga remains one of the most controversial decisions of the campaign. Historians have generally criticized him for dividing his smaller army. Most scholars maintain that Bragg was motivated to rid his army of a rebellious lieutenant and not rational thought or sound strategic judgment. In the wake of the round-robin meeting with President Davis and the cadre of senior officers who wanted to oust him, the embattled general managed to demote or transfer most of his critics. Since Longstreet had voiced his displeasure at serving under Bragg, he certainly recognized his precarious position in the eyes of the authorities in Richmond.[15]

When Longstreet and his First Corps arrived in Tyner's Station, eight miles east of Chattanooga, on November 5, they were elated with their new mission, probably believing that the move toward East Tennessee would bring them better rations and place them closer to returning to the Army of Northern Virginia. Optimism soon gave way to the hardships of active campaigning: rain, cold weather, long delays, and a lack of provisions. Within a week, Bragg wrote to Longstreet complaining about his failure to move quickly on Knoxville. In his memoirs Longstreet suggested that Bragg assigned him the task of moving into East Tennessee with the hopes of seeing him fail. While that cannot be proven, it certainly provides a glimpse into the general's mindset as he marched toward Knoxville. Adding to the difficulties of logistics and his embittered superior, Longstreet also had to deal with internal strife in his own command in the form of a rivalry between Brigadier Generals Micah Jenkins and Evander Law, each vying to assume command of Hood's Division in the wake of Major General John Bell Hood being wounded at Chickamauga. The acrimony and jealousy impaired their ability to collaborate around Chattanooga and continued during the march to Knoxville. Moreover, Longstreet struggled with another subordinate. In October he ordered Brigadier General Jerome Robertson, commander of the Texas Brigade, removed from command due to his disorderly retreat at Wauhatchie on the twenty-ninth. Bragg simply restored Robertson to active command on November 8 and instructed him to accompany Longstreet into East Tennessee. To make matters worse, Longstreet also had to deal with Major General Lafayette McLaws, his other division commander, who resented his transfer to the West and had viewed his corps commander with disdain since the Gettysburg Campaign. Accordingly, the external pressures to quickly destroy the Union presence in East Tennessee coupled with the internal strife in Longstreet's Corps portended ill for the campaign.[16]

The advance to Knoxville may have started poorly, with harsh weather and long delays, but about a week after leaving Bragg's army, on November 14 and 16, the First Corps engaged the Federal troops, under the overall command of Major General Ambrose Burnside, in skirmishes at Loudon and Campbell's Station, about twenty miles southeast of Knoxville. In both instances Longstreet's force failed to defeat Burnside's men due to poor tactics and a general lack of cooperation among the division commanders. Longstreet, too, did not fare well in his strategic decisions, ordering his cavalry away on a raid, thus depriving his army of their reconnaissance and screening abilities, and making other poor choices that surrendered the initiative to Union forces. Unbeknown to the Rebel general, Burnside had received orders from Major General Ulysses S. Grant to delay the First Corps's advance and buy time for the Federals in Chattanooga before withdrawing his forces toward Knoxville. As such, his maneuvers in East Tennessee allowed for the besieged Federals in Chattanooga to receive reinforcements that were already in route. Burnside had approximately 14,000 men to oppose Longstreet's two divisions of approximately 10,000 men. Yet he only used a fraction of his force in this task while the bulk of his army strengthened the defenses around Knoxville. By November 17, Burnside had skillfully eluded Longstreet's Corps and retreated to the city, just as he intended. By nightfall that same day, the Confederates had posted their defenses on a line stretching along the city's western edges.[17]

As Longstreet's men extended their positions through the northern edge of Knoxville, the general's instructions to rid East Tennessee of enemy troops and return to Bragg's army as quickly as possible became far more challenging. The city lay north of the Tennessee River, sitting on a square-mile plateau rising about 150 feet above the river. From east to west, First, Second, and Third Creeks flowed in a southerly direction into the Tennessee. Burnside's defenses, prepared by Captain Orlando M. Poe, the general's chief engineer, ran in a semicircular arc, with the flanks anchored on the river. Fort Sanders stood as the salient point of the U.S. defenses, on the northwest edge of a line of entrenchments and perched atop a large hill north of the river, between Second and Third Creeks, and south of the East Tennessee and Georgia Railroad line. Originally built by the Confederates when they held the city months earlier, Fort Sanders was shaped like a half-star, with salients on the northwest and the southwest corners, while the eastern side was kept open to ferry troops into and out of the compound. The other three sides of the Federal bastion had twelve-foot-high earthen walls topped with rawhide-wrapped cotton bales along the parapet, extending the height to nearly fifteen feet. A water-filled ditch, about ten feet wide and six to eight feet deep, surrounded the fort and reached to the edge of its walls. Poe wrapped telegraph wire around tree stumps encircling the citadel to present an even more formidable impediment to the attackers. By November 18, Longstreet and his men lay siege to the Federals in Knoxville.[18]

In addition to the physical challenges of attacking a well-fortified enemy position, Longstreet also had to deal with the question of morale. Two problems that plagued the First Corps remained the general's lack of self-confidence and a want of harmony between his senior officers. The events of the previous month caused Longstreet to doubt his ability as a commander. When Bragg failed to heed his messages about poor transportation, lack of sustenance, and the need for reinforcements, Longstreet probably imagined the worst. He worried that the mission seemed destined to fail—most likely at his expense—and thus advanced cautiously toward Burnside's forces, frequently complaining to army headquarters and thereby increasingly incurring his commander's resentment. The pressure on Longstreet not only came from Bragg and the authorities in Richmond, but it also came from his men. The Army of Northern Virginia veterans who had joined Bragg's army brimming with confidence now grumbled over lost opportunities, and they blamed Longstreet. After Chickamauga the Confederate troops had given him the moniker the Bull of the Woods. They now had a new nickname for their commander: "Peter the Slow."[19]

After his troops arrived at Knoxville, Longstreet probed Burnside's defenses for weaknesses for a few days. He immediately notified Bragg that he needed reinforcements. In response, Bragg complained about him to the authorities in Richmond and, instead of reinforcements, dispatched his senior engineer, Brigadier General Danville Leadbetter, to assess the situation. Meanwhile, Longstreet's desperation grew. Operating in a hostile Unionist region in East Tennessee and noticing a want of coherence in his command, he explored all his options, including a night assault and an artillery barrage on Burnside. Leadbetter arrived on November 25 and, after a brief inspection, urged Longstreet to attack the Federals quickly and return to Bragg's army. A West Point graduate from Maine, Leadbetter had supervised the construction of Fort Sanders months earlier, when the Confederates held the city. He implored the need for alacrity in Knoxville. He and Longstreet reconnoitered the Federal defenses on the twenty-sixth. A second reconnaissance the next day, this time accompanied by Longstreet's leading lieutenants, suggested that Fort Sanders was vulnerable to a direct assault. While examining the northern bastion, Longstreet noticed a Federal soldier walking across a ditch that was previously reported to have been four to five feet deep and filled with water. Determined they were previously led by poor intelligence, Longstreet reasoned that they had an opportunity to strike immediately. Unknown to him, however, was that the Union soldiers had been using wooden planks mounted just below the water's surface to walk across the deep ditch surrounding the fort.

On November 27 Longstreet ordered McLaws and Jenkins to launch a frontal assault on Fort Sanders at dawn the next day, the tenth day of the siege. Once more, as they had experienced the entire campaign, the weather failed to cooperate as a heavy rain and thick fog rolled in, preventing the Confederate artillery from supporting the infantry advance. At first Longstreet simply ordered a slight delay so the attack could be launched in the afternoon. The brigade commanders, not enthused with the prospect of a midafternoon assault, especially amid circulating rumors that the Yankees had ousted Bragg from his siege position at Chattanooga, petitioned their commander to delay the offensive until the following morning so they could at least have the element of surprise. Longstreet acquiesced and postponed the assault one more day.[20]

From his position overlooking the Federal lines across the East Tennessee and Georgia Railroad, Longstreet figuratively stood at a crossroads.

Civil War commanders had limited choices when facing an enemy force. Of course, they could launch a flanking maneuver and try to cut off their opponent's line of communications or entrap him in a pincer movement. Yet Burnside demonstrated no propensity to cooperate with Longstreet and leave his fortified position. Commanders could also fight on the defensive, a strategy Longstreet seemed to have preferred up to this point in the war. As another option, they could launch a frontal assault across a broad front. But at Knoxville the U.S. defensive perimeter along the Tennessee River deterred such tactics. Finally, they could probe the enemy's defenses, find a weak spot, and attack with the hopes they could break through. It was the last strategy that Longstreet chose.[21]

At about 4:00 a.m. on the morning of November 29, Rebel guns fired three successive shots to signal the assault on Fort Sanders. The brigades of Generals Benjamin Humphreys, Goode Bryan, and William Wofford advanced toward the fort. Within minutes, men in the front lines began tripping over the telegraph wire, causing the supporting troops to falter as well. Recovering from this first obstacle, hundreds of Rebel troops plunged into the ditch and struggled to scale the fort's walls. The rain of the previous days had coated these with a sheet of ice, making them nearly impossible to climb. Despite this, the Confederate soldiers tried to boost each other over the top on their backs and shoulders while Federal troops tossed lighted artillery shells over the parapet and into the masses floundering in the water below. A few Confederate color bearers somehow managed to scale the Federal bastion only to be shot down or captured by the defenders. Without the means to cross the ditch or climb the walls, the attackers faced certain failure. After thirty minutes of carnage, the Rebel soldiers began to withdraw. Confederate artillery provided McLaws's troops with cover as they climbed out of the ditch and made their way back to the rifle pits, all the while under Federal fire.[22] Once it became obvious that the fort could not be taken, Longstreet's tenacious veterans reluctantly withdrew. In less than thirty-minutes, the First Corps suffered more than 800 casualties, while the Federals lost only about a dozen men.[23] One Union soldier observed that the Confederate dead "presented the most horrible sight that I ever witnessed."[24] Later that afternoon Longstreet learned that Bragg had been routed at Chattanooga and that no reinforcements would come to his aid. The First Corps was on its own.[25]

The decision to launch the attack on Fort Sanders proved to be Longstreet's worst as a commander. Without learning much from his West Point instruction—as his low class-standing indicates—and without extensive reading about military history and the art of war in his years since, he probably relied on some of the lessons learned in the war with Mexico. Longstreet, like many of his contemporaries, did not record his thoughts about lessons he learned while serving under Taylor and Scott. Yet he did travel to Mexico late in life to do research and write about his experiences there, drafting a manuscript he ultimately never published. What historians can glean from his service in the Mexican-American War is that it probably affected him in more ways than he cared to admit in his memoirs. Though the war with Mexico was seventeen years prior to the Civil War, there were lessons learned that carried through over time. From his service with Taylor, Longstreet likely realized that delays and stagnation did not lead to promotions or to the ability to hold on to a command. As Taylor learned after capturing Monterrey in 1846, President Polk disapproved the armistice the general negotiated and the inaction that followed, ultimately shifting troops from his army to Scott's organizing command at the onset of the new year.[26] Significantly, Longstreet faced a formidable bastion in Fort Sanders. Frustrated and lacking the self-confidence that marked his tenure under Lee's command, Longstreet likely reverted to his lessons with Scott and his experience facing similar odds against a numerically superior foe entrenched in a strong bastion. Longstreet's insistence to launch the assault on Fort Sanders by urging his men forward likely harkened back to his service in the Mexican-American War. At Churubusco his regiment faced a similar obstacle in the Mexican *tête de pont*. The successful attack on an apparently impregnable stronghold had profoundly impressed Longstreet. Years later and facing the Federal stronghold at Knoxville, he desperately sought a victory that would triumphantly conclude the campaign. Unlike Scott, Longstreet failed to properly reconnoiter and call off the assault when it no longer suited the purposes of helping Bragg's effort at Chattanooga.

The dichotomy of Longstreet's East Tennessee Campaign, from the rapid movements and engagements at its onset to the lethargy, indecision, and siege of Knoxville at the end of November, are notable. Following the assault on Fort Sanders, Longstreet continued to flounder around East Tennessee until April 1864, when he returned to Lee's army in Virginia. In the meantime, he suggested to the War Department that he could retake Knoxville if given additional men or might even invade Kentucky that spring. Meanwhile, following another example from Scott's army in Mexico, he continued to pursue charges against his subordinates during those months, arresting troublesome lieutenants Robertson, Law, and McLaws in the weeks following the Fort Sanders debacle. By the winter of 1863–64, Longstreet appeared bitter and a shell of his former self. Scholars generally attribute his failures to his ambitions to rise through the ranks of Confederate generals and the fact that he could not function outside of Lee's guidance. He was, in the assessment of historian Steven E. Woodworth, a poor general.[27]

Longstreet's failures in East Tennessee can generally be attributed to weak leadership. Those months marked the worst period in his professional career, to be sure. After the Civil War, General William T. Sherman posited that successful West Point graduates, those who finished near the top of their respective classes, often became poor leaders of men. "They are good scholars," he maintained, "but . . . begin to look down upon the rest of the army."[28] Longstreet was certainly no scholar. At the onset of the war, his headquarters was often praised for the wholesome and boisterous atmosphere that reflected the commander's gregarious nature. Yet by 1863–64, Longstreet failed to retain that same spirit of merriment. Instead, he demonstrated an outward appearance of stoicism probably designed to project calm and confidence with his troops. In fact, all evidence suggests that Longstreet had lost confidence and was afraid. He feared the failure of his first true endeavor with an independent command. He feared demotion or removal, something foreshadowed by the episode with Bragg in October. In addition, he feared losing the confidence and support of his men. Longstreet probably tried to mask those fears and demonstrate a calm demeanor to his troops by convincing himself and others that spirit and élan could lead to victory.[29] To deal with an unfamiliar and hostile situation, he likely remembered his time with Taylor and Scott in Mexico, particularly the drive to Mexico City, and how those generals dealt with the similar challenges he now faced.

If Longstreet reverted to some of his experiences during the war with Mexico, it is because there were some parallels. Longstreet served in the 8th Infantry when it joined Scott prior to his army's landing at Vera Cruz. He witnessed how that general had to deal with dissension and rivalries among his subordinates, particularly after the Battle of Cerro Gordo in May 1847. At that time, some of Scott's subordinates urged immediate action, while others supported their commander and his cautious approach as he dealt with the challenges of logistics and a hostile civilian population. The 8th Infantry's division commander, General Worth, proved to be a harsh critic of Scott, something Longstreet echoed in his unpublished manuscript on the war. Scott, for his part, proved able in dealing with the dynamics of bickering personalities among his lieutenants and in making prudent decisions on the battlefield. Later in the campaign, Scott agonized over the decision to launch assaults on fortified positions. Longstreet may not have been privy to the general's thinking, but he certainly could draw inspiration from how a commander could lead men and win battles by inspiring them through sheer will. At Chapultepec, in fact, Longstreet was wounded while carrying the colors for the 8th Infantry. Curiously, he never wrote about that incident in his 1896 memoirs, although his widow did in her 1904 book.[30]

During the first few years of his service to the Confederacy, Longstreet favored flanking maneuvers and avoiding the pitfalls of frontal assaults. Yet by the Knoxville Campaign, Longstreet felt vulnerable with the authorities in Richmond and with Bragg. He could blame himself for this. The general had campaigned for a transfer to the West by aligning himself with some of President Davis's political foes within the Confederate high command, he led the cabal that formally petitioned to remove Bragg following the Battle of Chickamauga, and he further alienated the Confederate president when he demonstrated no confidence in Bragg when Davis visited the Army of Tennessee in early October 1863. Longstreet sealed his own fate. Thus, in late November Longstreet faced immense pressure to perform well at Knoxville. He lost confidence in his decision making and faith in the decisions that had marked his successful campaigns in Lee's army. He failed to face the pressure and sought a way out of his predicament. Longstreet launched an ill-fated frontal assault hoping that it would turn the tide of disappointments he had experienced since the victory at Chickamauga. If his lieutenants doubted his plans, then, he countered, they must be wrong, ironically missing the similarities between himself and Bragg. On the eve of the Fort Sanders assault, Longstreet had to convince McLaws to demonstrate more support. "Please urge your officers the importance of making the assault with a determination to succeed," Longstreet pleaded. "If the assault is made in that spirit, I shall feel no doubt of its success."[31] The appeal to McLaws was reiterated later that evening when the division commander still seemed despondent about the planned attack.[32] It was as if Longstreet was trying to convince himself that the frontal assault would succeed.

Longstreet's reliance on flanking maneuvers and implementation of the strategic offensive for most of his service in the Civil War probably derived from an aversion to the costly results of attacking fortified positions he had witnessed or participated in during the Mexican-American War.[33] The fact that he was wounded scaling the walls of the Chapultepec and did not mention such a significant event in his memoirs suggests that it caused him a great deal of the trauma. Yet Longstreet did not completely ignore launching an assault against an enemy force. His experiences at Gettysburg, Chickamauga, and the Battle of the Wilderness (May 1864) attest to this fact. While he preferred employing the defensive, if practicable, he did not eschew launching an assault when called upon or necessary. Certainly, after the first few campaigns, Longstreet recognized the brutality of the war and the ability of modern weaponry to kill or maim. At Knoxville he relied on another element of his service in Mexico, wrongly believing that men, if properly motivated, could overcome great obstacles. He had witnessed that firsthand at the gates of Mexico City. But the Civil War was not the same as the war in Mexico. And in less than thirty minutes on a cold day in East Tennessee, Longstreet's failed assault against Fort Sanders would forever tarnish his reputation as a commander.

NOTES

1. Earl J. Hess, *The Knoxville Campaign: Burnside and Longstreet in East Tennessee* (Knoxville: University of Tennessee Press, 2012), 151–74; James Longstreet, *From Manassas to Appomattox: Memoirs of the Civil War in America* (1895; repr., New York: Konecky and Konecky, 1992), 497–98, 505–7.

2. Longstreet, *From Manassas to Appomattox*, 15.

3. Alex Mendoza, *Struggle for Command: General James Longstreet and the First Corps in the West* (College Station: Texas A&M University Press, 2008), 2–3.

4. Jeffry Wert, *General James Longstreet: The Confederacy's Most Controversial Soldier—A Biography* (New York: Simon and Schuster, 1993), 27–32.

5. Longstreet, *From Manassas to Appomattox*, 20; Wert, *General James Longstreet*, 36. For a detailed study of the events of the Mexican-American War, see John S. D. Eisenhower, *So Far from God: The U.S. War with Mexico, 1846–1848* (New York: Random House, 1988).

6. Helen Dortch Longstreet, *Lee and Longstreet at High Tide: Gettysburg in Light of the Official Records* (Wilmington, NC: Broadfoot, 1989), 127–61. Dortch Longstreet writes: "Several years ago General Longstreet hastily prepared in the rough quite an elaborate history of the Mexican War, the publication of which was forestalled by the book of a brother officer in that war of which he had no hint. The incidents and historical data of this short story are from that unpublished history, with the addition of General Longstreet's comments

on the official personnel of the armies of Taylor and Scott and their subsequent careers in the Union and Confederate armies." Ibid., 127.

7. Wert, *General James Longstreet*, 40–41; William Garrett Piston, "Lee's Tarnished Lieutenant: James Longstreet and His Image in American Society" (Ph.D. diss., University of South Carolina, 1982), 62–64.

8. Eisenhower, *So Far from God*, 262–63; Wert, *General James Longstreet*, 40–43; Piston, "Lee's Tarnished Lieutenant," 66–67.

9. Timothy D. Johnson, *Winfield Scott: The Quest for Military Glory* (Lawrence: University Press of Kansas, 1998), 196–200; Allan Peskin, *Winfield Scott and the Profession of Arms* (Kent, OH: Kent State University Press, 2003), 176–83.

10. Quoted in H. D. Longstreet, *Lee and Longstreet*, 214.

11. Johnson, *Winfield Scott*, 201–5. A brevet rank was an honorary promotion given for gallant or meritorious action during time of war. Although it had no real significance, it was temporarily recognized in courts-martial and assignments to different regiments or companies. Ibid., 201; Peskin, *Winfield Scott and Profession of Arms*, 181.

12. Wert, *General James Longstreet*, 45–46. See also "James Longstreet and the Changed Mind?," in *Civil War Leadership and the Mexican War Experience*, by Kevin Dougherty (Jackson: University Press of Mississippi, 2007), 158–63.

13. Mendoza, *Struggle for Command*, 104–8; Steven E. Woodworth, *Davis and Lee at War* (Lawrence: University Press of Kansas, 1995), 248.

14. *The War of the Rebellion: A Compilation of the Official Records of Union and Confederate Armies*, 128 vols. (Washington, DC: U.S. Government Printing Office, 1880–91), ser. 1, 31(1):455 (hereafter cited as *OR*, all references to ser. 1 unless otherwise stated); James Longstreet to Simon B. Buckner, Nov. 5, 1863, Civil War Papers—Army of Tennessee, Tulane University, New Orleans; Longstreet, *From Manassas to Appomattox*, 480–81.

15. Wert, *General James Longstreet*, 339; Peter Cozzens, *This Terrible Sound: The Battle of Chickamauga* (Urbana: University of Illinois Press, 1993), 33, 34, 48, 57–59; Steven E. Woodworth, *Six Armies in Tennessee: The Chickamauga and Chattanooga Campaigns* (Lincoln: University of Nebraska Press, 1998), 19–46; Thomas Connelly, *Autumn of Glory: The Army of Tennessee, 1862-1865* (Baton Rouge: Louisiana State University Press, 1973), 172–73. Biographer Judith Lee Hallock argues that Bragg "probably did not injure his chances" at Chattanooga by sending away the First Corps. See Hallock, *Braxton Bragg and Confederate Defeat*, vol. 2 (Tuscaloosa: University of Alabama Press, 1989), 126. Jeffry Wert points to Longstreet's insecurity after the Knoxville Campaign. See Wert, *General James Longstreet*, 359.

16. Mendoza, *Struggle for Command*, 110–14; McLaws to Wife, July 7, Oct. 14, 1863, Southern Historical Collection, University of North Carolina, Chapel Hill.

17. Hess, *Knoxville Campaign*, 111–15.

18. Mendoza, *Struggle for Command*, 124–25; Terry A. Johnston, "Failure before Knoxville: Longstreet's Attack on Fort Sanders, November 29, 1863," *North and South* 2, no. 7 (September 1999): 61–62; E. Porter Alexander, "Longstreet at Knoxville," in *Battles and Leaders of the Civil War*, ed. Robert Underwood Johnson and Clarence Clough Buel, vol. 3

(New York: Century, 1887), 749–50. See also Orlando M. Poe, "The Defense of Knoxville," ibid., 734–36.

19. Woodworth, *Six Armies in Tennessee,* 206; Mendoza, *Struggle for Command,* 125–26.

20. *OR,* 31(1):479, 486.

21. Albert Castel, "Mars and the Reverend Longstreet: Or, Attacking and Dying in the Civil War," in Albert Castel, *Winning and Losing in the Civil War: Essays and Stories* (Columbia: University of South Carolina Press, 1996), 126–30.

22. The best secondary accounts on the assault are found in Hess, *Knoxville Campaign,* 155–64; Krick, "Longstreet Versus McLaws," 96–102; and Johnston, "Failure before Knoxville," 69–73.

23. *OR,* 31(1):290–92; Benjamin J. Humphreys, "History of the Sunflower Guards," J. F. H. Claiborne Papers, Southern Historical Collection, University of North Carolina at Chapel Hill; Johnston, "Failure before Knoxville," 74.

24. Terry A. Johnston, ed., "A Fort Sanders Survivor's Story," *Columbiad* 4, no. 1 (Spring 2000): 61.

25. Hess, *Knoxville Campaign,* 171.

26. Felice Flanery Lewis, *Trailing Clouds of Glory: Zachary Taylor's Mexican War Campaign and His Emerging Civil War Leaders* (Tuscaloosa: University of Alabama Press, 2010), 158, 192–93.

27. Steven E. Woodworth, *Lee and Davis at War* (Lawrence: University Press of Kansas, 1995), 268; Woodworth, *Jefferson Davis and His Generals: The Failure of Confederate Command in the West* (Lawrence: University Press of Kansas, 1990), 246.

28. Christopher H. Hamner, *Enduring Battle: American Soldiers in Three Wars, 1776–1945* (Lawrence: University Press of Kansas, 2011), 144–45.

29. Ibid., 123.

30. Johnson, *Winfield Scott,* 186–87, 204; H. D. Longstreet, *Lee and Longstreet,* 158–59. Kevin Dougherty suggests that Longstreet "fully experienced the offensive" in the Mexican-American War and perhaps that influenced his defensive-minded approach during the Civil War. See Dougherty, *Civil War Leadership,* 159.

31. *OR,* 31(3):755.

32. James Longstreet to McLaws, Nov. 28, 1863, McLaws Papers, Southern Historical Collection, University of North Carolina at Chapel Hill. A version of Longstreet's letter to McLaws appears in *OR,* 31(1):494.

33. Dougherty, *Civil War Leadership,* 159.

CONTRIBUTORS

Sean Michael Chick currently works in New Orleans, leading historic tours of his hometown. He is the author of *The Battle of Petersburg, June 15–18, 1864* (2015) and *Dreams of Victory: P. G. T. Beauregard in the Civil War* (2023). He is working on a multivolume study of the Battle of Shiloh.

Thomas W. Cutrer is professor emeritus of history and American studies at Arizona State University. He is the editor of *The Mexican War Diary and Correspondence of George B. McClellan* (2009) and author of *Ben McCulloch and the Frontier Military Tradition* (1993) and *Theater of a Separate War: The Civil War West of the Mississippi River, 1861–1865* (2017).

Stephen D. Engle is professor of history and associate provost for faculty affairs at Florida Atlantic University. He is the author of *Don Carlos Buell: Most Promising of All* (1999), *Gathering to Save a Nation: Lincoln and the Union's War Governors* (2016), and *In Pursuit of Justice: The Life of John Albion Andrew* (2023).

Gary W. Gallagher is the John L. Nau III Professor of History Emeritus at the University of Virginia. He has published widely on the Civil War era, including *The Enduring Civil War: Reflections on the Great American Crisis* (2020) and *The American War: A History of the Civil War Era* (coauthored with Joan Waugh; 3rd ed., 2023).

Joseph T. Glatthaar is the Stephenson Distinguished Professor of History at the University of North Carolina–Chapel Hill. He has authored numerous books on the Civil War and military history, including *General Lee's Army: From Victory to Collapse* (2008), *Soldiering in the Army of Northern Vir-*

ginia: A Statistical Portrait of the Troops Who Served under Robert E. Lee (2011), and *American Military History: A Very Short Introduction* (2020). He is also the recipient of the Samuel Eliot Morison Prize for lifetime achievement from the Society for Military History.

Timothy D. Johnson is the Elizabeth Gentry Brown Professor of History at Lipscomb University in Nashville, Tennessee. His previous books include *Winfield Scott: The Quest for Military Glory* (1998), *A Gallant Little Army: The Mexico City Campaign* (2007), and *For Duty and Honor: Tennessee's Mexican War Experience* (2018).

Christian B. Keller is professor of history and director of the Military History Program at the U.S. Army War College in Carlisle, Pennsylvania, where he teaches courses on military theory, national security policy, and the American Civil War. He is the author, coauthor, or editor of seven books, including the award-winning *The Great Partnership: Robert E. Lee, Stonewall Jackson, and the Fate of the Confederacy* (2019) and *Southern Strategies: Why the Confederacy Failed* (2021).

Alexander Mendoza is associate professor of history at the University of North Texas. He is the author of *Confederate Struggle for Command: General James Longstreet and the First Corps in the West* (2008) and *Chickamauga, 1863: Rebel Breakthrough* (2013) and is coeditor of *Texans at War: A New Military History of the Lone Star State* (2012).

Jennifer M. Murray is a teaching associate professor with a specialization in the Civil War at Oklahoma State University. She is the author of *On a Great Battlefield: The Making, Management, and Memory of Gettysburg National Military Park, 1933–2013* (2nd ed., 2023). Murray is also the coeditor of the forthcoming *Civil War Memories in a Polarized America* and is currently writing a biography of George G. Meade.

Ethan S. Rafuse is professor of military history at the U.S. Army Command and General Staff College at Fort Leavenworth, Kansas. His publications include *McClellan's War: The Failure of Moderation in the Struggle for the Union* (2005), *Corps Commanders in Blue: Union Major Generals in the Civil War* (2014), *From the Mountains to the Bay: The War in Virginia, January–*

May 1862 (2022), and guides to the Manassas, Antietam, and Richmond-Petersburg battlefields. In 2018–19 he was the Charles Boal Ewing Distinguished Visiting Professor at the U.S. Military Academy.

Timothy B. Smith is a veteran of the National Park Service and currently teaches history at the University of Tennessee at Martin. He is the author or editor of more than twenty books, including *Shiloh: Conquer or Perish* (2014), *Grant Invades Tennessee: The 1862 Battles for Forts Henry and Donelson* (2016), *The Iron Dice of Battle: Albert Sidney Johnston and the Civil War in the West* (2023), and a five-volume study of the Vicksburg Campaign.

Craig L. Symonds is professor emeritus of history at the U.S. Naval Academy and a former Ernest J. King Distinguished Professor of Maritime History at the U.S. Naval War College. He is the award-winning author or editor of more than two dozen books, including *Joseph E. Johnston: A Civil War Biography* (1992), *Decision at Sea: Five Naval Battles That Shaped American History* (2006), and *Lincoln and His Admirals* (2010).

Brian Steel Wills is the director of the Center for the Study of the Civil War Era and professor of history at Kennesaw State University. He is the award-winning author of numerous works on the American Civil War, including biographies of Confederate generals Nathan Bedford Forrest and William Dorsey Pender and U.S. general George Henry Thomas.

Cecily N. Zander is assistant professor of history at Texas Woman's University in Denton. She was previously a postdoctoral fellow at the Center for Presidential History at SMU, where she completed work on her book, *The Army under Fire: Antimilitarism in the Civil War Era* (2024).

INDEX

With Beauregard in Mexico (Williams), 151–52

Wolseley, Garnet, 191, 192

Woodworth, Steven E., 229

Wool, John, 117, 118, 121–22, 129n59, 134, 177

Worth, William James, 18, 31, 34, 37, 38, 39, 43, 54, 55, 101, 113, 115, 137, 138, 209, 230; actions at the Battle of Chapultepec, 194–95; actions at the Battle of Churubusco, 220; actions during the Monterrey Campaign, 219

Yorktown, 65, 79, 82–83, 142

Zacatepec, 58

Zander, Cecily N., 11, 237